Shades of Eternity ❦ Book III

CRIMSON SKIES

Also by Lisa Samson

Indigo Waters

Fields of Gold

Shades of Eternity ❦ Book III

CRIMSON SKIES

❖ LISA SAMSON ❖

ZondervanPublishingHouse
Grand Rapids, Michigan

A Division of HarperCollinsPublishers

We want to hear from you. Please send your comments about this book to us in care of the address below. Thank you.

ZondervanPublishingHouse
Grand Rapids, Michigan 49530
http://www.zondervan.com

Requests for information should be addressed to:

ZondervanPublishingHouse
Grand Rapids, Michigan 49530

Library of Congress Cataloging-in-Publication Data

Samson, Lisa, 1964-
    Crimson Skies / Lisa Samson.
        p. cm. -- (Shades of eternity ; bk. 3)
    ISBN: 0-310-22370-9
    1. Youngblood, David (Fictitious character)--Fiction. 2. Nobility--Fiction. 3. Great Britain--Fiction. I. Title.

PS3569.A46673 C75 2000
813'.54--dc21   00-039267
                                                                    CIP

Interior design by Sherri Hoffman

Printed in the United States of America

---

00 01 02 03 04 05 /❖ DC/ 10 9 8 7 6 5 4 3 2 1

❖

To the girls of Carrington Road
Of which I am a thankful part
Jennifer McLeod Hagerty,
Heather Born Gillott,
and Chris Parton Burkett
Here's to the years ahead
I love you guys

LISA EBAUER SAMSON

Acknowledgments

Any book is truly a collaborative effort. And so I'd like to thank the people who were so helpful to me. From my Zondervan family: Lori VandenBosch, Dave Lambert, Amy Peterman, Joyce Ondersma, and Sue Brower. Genevieve Crabe, whose Web site, Lebonmot.com, gave me invaluable French phrases. Wish I'd had that resource for the first book in this series! Angela Townsend of the House of Lords Information Office Education Unit. And family and friends, Joy Ebauer, Lori Chesser, Jennifer and Michael Hagerty, Dawn Huth, Chris Burkett, and Heather Gillott. I'd also like to thank those who make it all worthwhile: Will, Tyler, Jake, and Gwynneth—love, love, love.

Jesus is Lord of all.

ACKNOWLEDGMENTS

BOOK ONE

But to be really loved by a courtesan: that is a victory of infinitely greater difficulty. With them, the body has worn out the soul, the senses have burned up the heart, dissipation has blunted the feelings.

ALEXANDRE DUMAS *FILS, CAMILLE*

CHAPTER ❖ ONE

The steam from the great black locomotive engine had dissipated. The shrill echo of the whistle had faded down to reveal the shouts of porters and those seeking their assistance. There was a finality to the picture before David Youngblood, and he wasn't sure whether to laugh or cry. His hand covered his mouth briefly, the mangled, harelipped mouth given him at birth.

"Ready, then, Camille?" He asked a question that meant more than simply, "Would you like to leave the station and go back to the house?"

In all actuality, now that the train was carrying Miranda Wallace and Tobin Youngblood back to Scotland, now that Claude Mirreault was counting roaches in the Bastille, the question meant, "Are you ready to begin the next five years of separation? Will you wait for me while I serve my sentence on Devil's Island?"

"We have three days left, *chéri*," the famed Paris courtesan said, slipping her arm inside of his coat and curving it around his waist. "I say we make the most of it. And Paris is just the city for that."

His abdomen constricted involuntarily at her touch, so assured yet soft. And the way she rested it just below his rib cage, settling it there in a quiet possessiveness, made the thought of his soon coming exile even more cruel. "You're right, Camille. Let's not make a funeral of the next three days. Let's celebrate life a little."

That's what they did, passing the time in small, dimly lit cafes, strolling in the quiet of the Louvre, fingers mingled and smooth, voices much the same. They tried not to speak of what lay around the corner. Instead, they talked about all the things they never knew about one another, sharing from their childhoods, laughing, crying.

Falling in love.

Each night David fell into bed accompanied by exhaustion. Each night he remembered her lovely gowns, her scent, the way she laughed. He drowned to sleep in the memory of her green eyes, eyes that held an expression of such love, he found himself responding in kind. He loved her. And prayed for the strength to tell her.

But he couldn't. The words expanded in his throat, stuck down deep, and refused to be released. The final days of freedom sped by and the time to part confronted them.

The day, not rainy or icy as such a situation might rightfully demand, bloomed like a crocus in the snow. David Youngblood, earl of Cannock, sat in Camille's parlor. Aching to caress the smooth skin of the ivory arms, he regretted how he had failed to return the love she had given him without cost or commitment. Camille, whom he had sullied and used, now told him things he couldn't believe, things that would probably save his life.

In two hours the penal department of France would receive him into its custody. The time to pay for the murders of Armand and Collette de Courcey had arrived. Devil's Island awaited. The thought astonished him. He remembered when Evariste Lyell, France's minister of justice, handed him down his sentence in secret. Someday he would rejoin society as someone who merely "disappeared" for five years. After regaining his title, he would marry Camille. The minister, a man who loved Camille as a daughter, handed that stipulation to him. Not that he minded! In fact, if he could be spirited away from here and into the closest church, if he could kiss her mouth and slide his ring onto her finger, nothing would please him more. When compared to the guillotine he deserved, he knew that nothing but thankfulness was appropriate.

The rosy hues of the room heightened Camille's soft pink skin and tinted the blond of her heavy, wavy hair to strawberry. It also accented the red rims of her moss-colored eyes. David suspected she had cried away the dark hours.

She handed him a small metal tube, a screw-on cap at one end, both ends rounded, "For easy insertion," she said, eyes thickened by a shining dome of tears.

"For easy in . . ." The acidic shock of the dawning coated his tongue, the taste of his own mouth metallic and sharp. "You can't possibly mean . . ."

"I do, my lord. I'm sorry, but I do."

David shook his head, his innards tightened in a stinging, nauseous grip. "No. I won't stick anything up there, Camille. That's too much to ask of anyone."

"Then you will be one of the only men there who won't, my lord. I assure you. Please. Evariste told me about these things. And he wouldn't have if there wasn't a good reason. You *must* have money. You must bribe guards and officials for better food, better work assignments." She pulled a small velvet sack out of her pocket, reclaimed the tube, and unscrewed the cap. "Here." Cut diamonds tumbled from the mouth of the sack into the container. "These will keep you protected for quite some time."

He lit a cigarette, his hands shaking, willing an inner calm but finding it could only be pretended. "Where did you get them?"

"You know how we courtesans adore our jewels. I had two of my necklaces disassembled."

Indeed, a sacrifice on her part.

She reached into a drawer on the ornamental table beside the couch. A roll of currency emerged. He hadn't realized one could roll up so many bills into such a compact cylinder. She tucked that inside, screwed the cap back on, and presented it with downcast eyes. "It is the best I can do for you, my lord."

If he didn't have so much to live for, he might have shot himself on the spot. But he took the cylinder. Men like David always took the cylinder. "Why are you doing this? How can you afford to do this?"

Camille lit a cigarette as well, inhaled deeply, and blew out a thin flume of blue smoke. "I knew of Claude Mirreault's treasure trove at the chateau. I convinced Didier by my usual means to let me in the day he was arrested, before you trapped him with Sylvie de Courcey's baby."

Didier had wanted Camille for years.

David grinned and shook his head, remembering the night they had taken Claude Mirreault, the infamous criminal money-lender who employed them both. That night he had literally exchanged the guillotine for Claude Mirreault. Camille's revelation came as no surprise.

Camille.

Four years ago she arrived fresh from the country looking for honest work. Finding no woman in any house prone to hire such a beautiful girl and risk tempting the man of the house, Camille found instead David Youngblood, Claude Mirreault, and a life of selling her wares to the upper classes.

Resigned now, he set the capsule down beside him. "So you will be all right?"

She shrugged. He loved her shrug, so fluid, a ripple of movement running from her neck to her shoulders to her arms. "Of course. I'm a resourceful sort."

"What will you do for the next five years?" He ground out the cigarette in a silver ashtray on the table in front of them.

"I'm leaving Paris for good, I believe."

This surprised him, and then no, it didn't. "Going back home?"

She shook her head and laughed with curled-down lips. "I'd be a fool to try and fit in there. I never did before. No, I'm going to travel for a while, see all the cities you've told me about, my lord. I may take up residence in Tuscany for a couple of years, then go to a Greek island and live there. It's hard to say what I'll do." She grinned. "I remember, a couple of years ago, you told me one night as we smoked out in the garden, 'Always go where the food is good.'"

He didn't remember the conversation. "Where will we meet then? In five years when I am free?"

"You tell me where you would like me to be."

"I have estates in Cornwall, you know. My sister Adele lives there."

Camille stubbed out her cigarette as well and leaned back into the upholstery of the settee. "But will she welcome me? She doesn't know me."

David took her hand. "No, she doesn't." He thought a minute, conjuring up a way for Camille to convince his sister Adele that she spoke the truth. "Tell her Cookie sent you."

The corners of Camille's mouth quivered. "Cookie?"

"An old childhood nickname, mind you. Hasn't been used in decades by anyone."

"Cookie?"

About to explain some more, he knew his words would never reach her ears. Camille doubled over in laughter, hooting, "Ohh! Cookie Youngblood, the earl of Cannock, brigand, outlaw, libertine!"

Finally, she came up to breathe.

"Are we quite finished guffawing, Camille?" he asked with a drawl, lighting up another cigarette.

She snorted back another round of laughter, looking fetchingly merry considering that they both stood at a precipice, knowing not what lay at the bottom or if they'd even live to see it.

"On second thought," he said, "just get me a piece of your stationery and I'll write a letter."

She gracefully arose and pulled out a sheet of the engraved paper. Her name flowed up at the top, one of the few words she could read. "Here." She handed him a lap desk complete with inkwell and pen.

"What will you do without me around to make your life interesting?" he asked as he wrote.

Camille's mood, as unpredictable as the weather surrounding David's Scottish estates, clouded. "I don't know, my lord. Perhaps I will find myself turning to drink, or religion. Although I suppose the drink will be a little more forgiving."

"Hardly." David thought of God's grace, just recently measured out in a Saul-of-Tarsus-sized portion onto his eternal plate. "We've been down those roads, Camille. It makes for an amusing evening but a horrible morning."

"Religion never did a thing for me."

"I wasn't talking about religion, Camille. I was talking about God."

"You speak in riddles, my lord."

He took her smooth hand and kissed its back. "No, Camille. I only speak the truth."

He left it there. And he left Camille's soul in the hands of the One who made it.

They took one last walk along the Champs Elysees, and he bought her a small ring for her pinkie. Simple and elegant, the emerald ring slid easily onto her finger. He kissed the column of flesh, the precious stone cold against his chin. "Don't take this off, Camille. Please."

She pulled him close, her lips finding his mangled mouth with ease. So many times she'd kissed him, so many times she'd told him of her love, and she did so once more as they stood before the building that housed the Ministry of Justice. He wanted to return the words so desperately, but before he realized it, she had bid him good-bye, and was running up the street.

He walked in alone, saying his prayers, resigned to his fate. Without wait, he was shown into the office of Evariste Lyell.

"I've come," he told the minister of justice.

"I will escort you myself," Lyell said, pulling on his coat. "You will have no favors, my lord. You will be treated as every other prisoner."

"I expected no less, sir."

"Then shall we?" He swept a hand toward the door.

"I place myself in your hands."

They walked quietly together down the wide corridor, the high ceiling and marble floors bouncing their words back to them. "You'll inquire about the welfare of my daughter, Elspeth?" David asked.

"Yes. Lord Tobin and Lady Miranda will be taking care of her?"

"That is what has been arranged."

Lyell nodded. "She is in good hands, then."

"Still, it would ease my mind. And if something should happen to her ..."

"I will send you word, my lord."

Oh, Elspeth. Oh, Bethie. His heart ached for the child who shared his malformation and owned his heart. God be with her.

～

David Youngblood possessed a shame far more dense than he needed for simple rehabilitation. An inner shame had coated his conscience, reminding him that he deserved everything he was getting. In a way, it freed him. He had nothing left to prove.

He stood naked in the Paris square with the rest of the prisoners sentenced to rot away in South America. A man in uniform, voice deep, impersonal, and droning, banished them from the country David had called home for many years. Banished for the murders of the parents of the woman he had loved, Sylvie de Courcey. Yes, of both shame and humiliation he was learning a great deal in a very short amount of time.

The sun, bright and warm, stung his eyes.

"We are as good as dead to this country," a man next to him said, an Englishman like himself.

"As well as our homeland," David muttered from the side of his mouth, not daring to look to the side. "It could be worse, I suppose. At least we're at the northern part of the continent."

"What's so good about that?"

David didn't know, but it seemed like something for which to be thankful, and at that moment he was ready to grab at anything to keep from openly weeping.

A new voice, a barking voice, ordered them to dress in clothing provided for the long ocean journey. And they obeyed. Rough woolen trousers, homespun shirts, and thin wool pea coats lay in piles at their white, bony feet. And ridiculous little felt hats sat on their heads like terra cotta pots. Hopefully they'd prove worthwhile on the cruise through the driving rain of the Atlantic and the fierce, saline sun as they sailed to the tropics of South America.

The young man stayed close to David as carts hauled them like livestock toward a train bound for Le Havre. The two men talked softly to one another, trying desperately to stay out of the fights that erupted. Becket Door, baron of Dividen, had a face belonging to an archangel. His bright blond hair spoke of heavenly places as well. Normally, these were qualities for which to be thankful. But on Devil's Island . . . comeliness was another matter altogether. David was almost thankful for his deformity.

Herded aboard the hulking steamer, they stumbled below deck and down into the gloomy hull. Slowly, they inched along together, the iron surrounding their ankles biting into the delicate skin stretched around their bones.

The Englishmen were bound by more than their crimes, although Becket Door protested his innocence on more than one occasion on the journey to French Guiana. Such protestations failed to bother David as they did some of the other men who chucked stale bread in Door's direction more than once during one of his earnest homilies. David just picked up the bread and stored it in his hat for later. He knew he deserved his own fate, and whether Becket lied or not didn't change that fact.

On the third night of their journey, as they hung in their hammocks in the belly of the ship, the body odors of the prisoners rose so strong David prayed for a congested nose.

Becket shifted to a more comfortable position. "Forty percent of the convicts in French Guiana die the first year. Malaria and sorts are the culprits, I'd wager."

David said nothing. He believed the statistic, he just refused to doom himself to such a fate. He would survive. He must. Elspeth waited for him. Camille waited for him. There was so much to live for.

They found themselves on deck at mealtimes. Broth and bread, sogged down by rain a good bit of the time, became the swill du jour each and every jour. Otherwise, they rotted in the stinking hold of the ship. Three servings of nothing became everything. David knew no other freedom.

Just five years, he prayed each night as the ship divided the waves that rocked their hammocks. But he knew that in the end his justice would be meted out by God himself. Would he live? Would he die? Devil's Island had broken stronger men than David Youngblood. God be the judge.

CHAPTER ❖ TWO

French Guiana, South America

The brutal streets of St. Laurent simmered as hot and hard as the convicts who filed through the penitentiary gates. The scrape of feet, loud and abrasive, annoyed David Youngblood. The once earl of Cannock followed humbly along, forsaking the station of his birth, endeavoring not to solicit any further attention than he did already with his blistered, harelipped mouth and scorched auburn hair.

And now they stood in the stark prison courtyard, the humid heat pressing against every square inch of smelly skin. Naked once again, he quickly shoved his legs into the new garments, these striped and of a lighter fabric. Pajamas really. "Too bad Claude Mirreault isn't here with me!" he joked inwardly regarding the perennially pajamaed man who had masterminded the foul plot leading to the deaths of four people—two of them at the hand of Youngblood himself. Camille, soldered onto Mirreault's machine by David himself, had played her role in the destruction, to be sure. But strangely enough, it bound him to her. She knew him better than anyone else. Better than Sylvie de

Courcey, the woman he had loved insanely. But this love with Camille would endure. Had she not promised to wait for him? Had he not promised to love her? God himself bore witness to this promise worth keeping.

Five years. One can endure anything for five years, can they not? Five years. It became his hymn, his unending prayer.

The blistering present surrounded him once more, the weave of the new uniform brushing against his skin as he filed into the examination room to be checked over by the prison doctor. They'd be allowed some food soon, then to bed. Tomorrow would decide who stayed in St. Laurent and who crossed to Devil's Island. There was no escape from Devil's Island. Life on the mainland was a holiday compared to existence on Devil's Island. But many other capsules had been removed from their dubious hiding places. Money had exchanged hands. The strong currents of the channels that ran between the three islands off of French Guiana's coast would not jostle those with the right amount. But David already knew his fate. Everything Camille had given him remained safe and as yet replete, though still terribly uncomfortable.

The meal was much the same as on the boat, only less of it. Broth, bread, nothing more. Five years of broth and bread and water. He breathed in the scent of the guards' cigarette smoke and thought of all the cigarettes he had stubbed out halfway through, all the glasses of water and cups of tea he had refused, all of the muffins, the breads, river trout, the lamb chops he'd shaken his head over, all the second helpings of treacle pudding he had waved a hand regarding. He thought of Mrs. Wooten's buns, a hunk of Gruyère, and a large bunch of grapes from the de Courcey vineyards. It bordered on torture—another tightening of the thumbscrews on Devil's Island.

New iron shackles were fitted around his ankles. The barracks awaited. Long wooden platforms ran down each side. Some bed! He wondered how sleep could possibly descend amid the heat and the stench, the cramped quarters and the hardness of the boards beneath him.

But he did sleep. His dreams flashed a garbled spectacle of vivid, almost painful color, clear sound, and comforting aroma. He dreamed of the people so dear to him, the people who had prayed for him when he had cursed God for making him so deformed on one hand, and so smart, so intuitive on the other. They were blessedly alive, almost touchable in the mosquito night. He dreamed of his daughter, Elspeth. He dreamed of Miranda Wallace, port-wine stain eclipsing her beautiful features, who had shown him the Lord. He dreamed of his uncle, Tobin Youngblood, now the earl of Cannock in his stead, and married to Miranda. He thought of Matthew Wallace, who had shared the way of God many times during their days together at Oxford, Matthew Wallace who had married Sylvie de Courcey. All of their faces, all of their voices, the love they had for him, the kindness they had shown resonated in the deep tropical darkness, a coolness in his brain.

He dreamed of Camille. One day when he rejoined society and retrieved his title, he would return her to the realms of decent women. She deserved that. Although he couldn't quite imagine her sitting in the park with other young mothers gossiping about the vicar! One could accuse Camille of a boatload of sins, but gossip wasn't one of her favored transgressions.

Whistles blew. Guards awakened the prisoners. David fought to stay asleep to hold onto these dreams.

"Wake up!" Becket Door hissed in his ear. "Quickly, before the guards—"

"What is this?" another voice yelled.

Youngblood opened his eyes and sat up immediately only to feel a rod slam down across his lower back. The pain blasted through him, wide at its point of origin, honing down to a violent point just left of his spine. He ground his teeth against the blow.

A guard towered at the edge of the sleeping platform. "And what have we here? Malbouche, eh? Sleeping in this morning?"

"I'm sorry, sir," he said in French, finding that these days he was starting to think in the language, something he'd never done despite his years in France. He swore he would slit his own throat if he found himself laughing like a Frenchman though, that "haugh, haugh, haugh, haaauugh" guffaw he'd come to utterly despise on the voyage to South America.

"Get going, Malbouche. Today is the day you meet the devil himself and on his own island."

Malbouche. Yes, they had christened him that on the boat because of his harelip. Malbouche. "Bad Mouth." No one would ever know his true identity. No one, of course, except for Becket Door.

Good, then.

"Do you think I will be sent to Devil's Island?" the young baron asked as they ate a breakfast only a stoic might deem worthy of the title. "I've heard the death rates are even higher there."

David took a good look at Becket Door. The man's features bore nature's equivalent of a Christopher Wren facade, a Bach prelude. "You'd better hope so, Door. For I will not be around to protect you here." David had made more threats to men of the unnatural persuasion regarding Becket Door than he would care to count. How he managed to become the young man's sole protector, he didn't know. God's will be done.

By nightfall David Youngblood sat next to Becket Door on the transport to Devil's Island. The island swelled before them, more daunting than David could have imagined as it stood staunch in the belligerent current.

Hell had only just begun for the Englishmen.

Chapter ❖ Three

A month later

After a brief period of adjustment, life took on a normal quality. An appalling sort of normal, but a normal they'd come to expect. The leg irons still abraded their ankles, each man chained to another as they cleared jungle for an unnecessary road across the island. Sometimes a man's death early in the day forced his partner to drag the dead body around for hours. If it occurred before the noontime meal, those sitting nearby split the rations. A macabre order to life existed on Devil's Island.

Fortunately, or maybe not, Camille had been right. He needed the contents of the small capsule. It had garnered him the position of croc shooter, enabling him to protect the other prisoners from the scaly beasts that terrorized the marshes. He now thanked God for his lonely boyhood days in Scotland when shooting in solitude at small game and birds had been a favorite pastime. He had a good eye. Not a well-known fact in England or on the continent. David had always settled his fights before guns could be drawn.

"I still can't believe they let you carry a gun," Becket Door said one night as they lay in hammocks in the barracks. The stifling night air seemed to spin in microscopic swirls of disease and death. David realized, having already seen so many fall dead in just the first month, that Becket Door's statistics weren't just an exaggeration of an already jumpy sort of fellow.

"They cut me a deal," David whispered. "A good deal."

"But aren't they worried you'll shoot the guards and try to escape?"

David shook his head, staring up at the dark ceiling. "First of all, Door, you know the currents between Ile de Royale, this island, and the mainland are horrific. I'm not that strong a swimmer. They'd only push me right back here and I'd land myself hog-tied in solitary confinement. That is not how I plan to survive this junket. Secondly, they give me only one bullet at a time, and I'm not going to shoot just one guard and expect to get away when there are always more of them. Last of all, the day I use that gun in a manner other than shooting a croc, you go into the custody of the first lieutenant's son."

Becket Door's winsome brown eyes closed at the mention of Phineas La Roche, a cruel, effete homosexual who had his way with anyone who had decent teeth and no gut. He was in charge of the supplies. His supplies for your supplies. Not many people found themselves immune to the large man's venom.

Becket Door reached out and grabbed David's arm. "So they know about your stash? They know how much you have?"

"Of course not."

"How can you guarantee La Roche won't cut you open during the night? How can you be certain he won't kill you?"

David knew Becket Door's questions were built upon a foundation of bedrock. But why did the man always have to be so frantic about everything? "I can't be. Any more than any other man here."

"And that doesn't frighten you?"

David had to think about that. The thought should have frightened him. It should have scared him into a stupor. But it didn't. Strange. "No."

Becket Door sucked in a breath. "I don't see how it cannot."

David thought some more. Questions like this had become somewhat of a hardship to him these days when all he wanted to do was survive. "My life is not my own," he finally said.

Door shifted in his hammock. "You're one of those religious men, aren't you?"

"You could say that."

"I've seen you bow your head in prayer, and I've seen the way you control your temper when they taunt you by your nickname and take it further. And yet you are here on Devil's Island. It makes no sense to me." Becket Door began warming up for one of his speeches. "I've heard that fifteen percent of all convictions are unjust. So, are you innocent, as I am? You say nothing regarding what you've done. So different from the rest."

"It is all behind me now, Door. I am a new man in Christ."

Becket Door sighed. "So you are religious." Disappointment lowered his tone to half mast.

"I am a Christian if that's what you mean, yes."

"And that is what makes you unafraid."

David shifted onto his side. "I deserved the guillotine."

"According to France, I did as well, but those who framed me couldn't have quite that amount of guilt on their conscience."

"But I committed the crimes. I was sent here instead." His voice thinned to the barest of whispers. "So justice will prevail. If God wishes me to be with your forty percent who die the first year, so be it. If God wishes me to survive, I will."

Becket Door whispered a derisive laugh. "You are a fatalist."

"No, I am a realist. God's will be done, whether you or I like it or not. It's best to like it."

"I'm not too fond of his ways, right now," Becket Door muttered, turning his back on David. "But if it is he who gives you the strength to protect me, I'm not going to be unthankful. Perhaps he hasn't completely forgotten us, Malbouche."

David lay in the damp night, his uniform clinging to his person like cheesecloth on a buttered fish. The equatorial sun continued to burn his fair skin, and bleached his hair yet further to a carrot shade. It was probably only a matter of time before malaria slithered into his veins. But God had not forgotten him. David hadn't come to Devil's Island alone. God evidenced himself all around David. In the sudden rushes of cool air out of nowhere, God lived. In an inexplicably lovely taste in the broth, God lived. In the sudden laughter of a well-told joke at slop time, God lived. God was more real than ever, for he was all that David possessed.

Sometimes he hummed William Blake's hymn, the words of *New Jerusalem* soothing his tired, lonely mind. "'Bring me my bow of burning gold! Bring me my arrows of desire! Bring me my spear! O clouds, unfold! Bring me my chariot of fire! I will not cease from mental fight, nor shall my sword sleep in my hand, till we have built Jerusalem in England's green and pleasant land.'"

He prayed long each night, wide eyes watching as the jungle moon sailed from bar to bar of barrack window. David prayed for Becket Door, and that God would use David's blistered, tired hands as his own.

Life didn't change after that. David shot crocs and, when necessary, paid a diamond for extra rations for himself and Becket Door. The English nobleman turned out to be a pleasant enough companion, well versed in literature and politics. His cynical nature housed a sense of humor that kept David from strangling him when he started spouting statistics.

Unfortunately for David, no one had told Becket Door about the need for money on Devil's Island. David knew he was being tested by the Almighty. Helping Becket Door had become not only a matter of charity, but of faith.

David learned a great deal about the young English baron and about his wife, Lady Charlotte, a beautiful, exotic woman raised in India, who waited for him back home. Exotic not by her features, which were purely English, or so Door claimed, but by her eccentric dress and haughty ways. He felt sorry about the severe, frightening childhood she had endured in India, how she had vowed never to see her parents again. He learned about the murder of Becket Door's parents by his younger brother, Cyprian Door, who'd coveted the title ever since he was old enough to realize it would never be his.

"It was a neat plot," Becket said one night as they walked from supper back to the barracks. "Cyprian murdered them while we were all in Paris for a wedding. Poisoned with a castor bean. He framed me for the crime and is now the baron of Dividen. I never even got my chance to enter the House of Lords."

"Three people out of the way for the price of two," David remarked dryly when Becket Door finally divulged the entire tale. It had surprisingly taken David a while to pick open the story from beneath a scab of betrayal so deep and painful it would never be healed.

"That's one way of looking at it." Becket refused to look him in the eye just then. A moment later he looked up, his expression frank. "You're the best friend I have ever had, Malbouche. Do you know that?"

David nodded, but didn't quite know how to respond to such overt affection.

"I don't know what I would do without you."

David slapped a hand on Becket's shoulder as they entered the long room and made for their hammocks. "You may have well been in that forty percent who die the first year!" He laughed. "Shame we didn't meet in England."

Becket shook his head. "We would have hated each other in England!"

"That, my friend, is the truth." He felt as if his own sanity rested on the slight shoulders of Becket Door. But he'd never tell that to Becket. The man couldn't bear the weight. "I never had a brother," he said, not knowing why.

"I did. They're not all they're cracked up to be."

David chuckled as they swung into their hammocks. "Good night, Becket."

"Same to you, Malbouche." His voice was infused with an irrevocable sadness. He turned back around. "Pray for me, my friend."

Surprised at the request, David kept his voice even as he said, "I do, Becket."

After several minutes, Door asked, "Did you ever have a pet, Malbouche?"

"No. What about you?"

"No. Animals make me sneeze. I can't even ride a horse without tearing up. Why didn't you have a pet?"

"I barely had parents, let alone a pet, Door."

"Oh, it was that way at your home, was it?"

"Yes."

"Not with me. Mother and Father were lovely, really. She probably wore the pants more than she ought to have, but she protected my father from a lot of the small problems."

"He was well respected in the Lords, if I remember correctly."

"Yes, absolutely."

"I'm sorry you didn't get your chance there."

Becket sighed. "It looks like neither of us will get our chance to serve our country."

"It's never been all that important to me."

"Really? Why?"

"Politics, at least for the past three generations, had little to do with the Youngbloods. They always enjoyed the antics of the royal court, but . . ."

"My parents hated it at court."

"Country gentleman?"

"Oh, yes. Mother too. A very good woman. Their funeral at our home in Sussex must have been attended by five hundred people from the area. Not that I was there, mind."

David stared up above him at the black ceiling. "I wonder what it would be like to be loved so well by so many? How did they manage that?"

"That was the easy part, Malbouche. They loved their people and served them well. They respected them."

"Do you really think it's that easy?"

"I do."

It must have been nice to have been raised in such a home, David thought. And yet, despite the differences in their upbringings, here they were together, rotting in the same room, on the same island, halfway around the world.

"That's the hardest part of the scandal," Becket said. "The Door name has been sullied forever. And everyone believes I am responsible."

"We must pray that you live out your sentence."

"I'm never going home, Malbouche."

"Come, now. We'll both get off this island someday. Get back to England."

"Not me."

"How can you say that for sure?"

Becket sighed. "Some things a man just knows."

After three years of accompanying David everywhere, spouting more statistics and asking more questions about God than David knew existed, Becket lay dying. Taken to the infirmary in St. Laurent, he gratefully allowed David to pay the rest of his diamonds to be transported back to the mainland with him. Only two years remained to David's sentence, and the francs remained untouched. It should buy him another good job after Becket needed him no longer. His good behavior was paying off. God bless Camille.

The thought of life in French Guiana without Becket frightened him. Being in it together, another Englishman along for the ride, had made life bearable. But when the loneliness began, when he found himself surrounded by annoying Frenchmen, then the real trials would begin, for then, he realized, he would finally be completely imprisoned.

He was allowed to visit his friend in the infirmary when his duties in the fields were finished for the day. It was the best job he could buy. But with only two years left to serve, he wouldn't waste his money for such luxury. The work clawed at his back, and he knew the remnant of such strain would plague him for the rest of his life. Sometimes he thought of the pain as God's little reminder of the price a willful life of sin will exact.

It wasn't easy to think of God in a positive light every minute of every day these days. But David knew God could take it.

On a rainy, spring night Becket Door, having once again returned to speaking terms with his Creator, exacted a promise from David. A rampant fever pushed sweat through Becket's pores, a fever that fed the infection that had filled his lungs.

"Sing, Malbouche. Sing of England. Sing of God."

David's heart broke. But he tried to sing, his voice breaking on each word. "'O clouds, unfold! Bring me my chariot of fire! I will not cease from mental fight, nor shall my sword sleep in my hand, till we have built Jerusalem in England's green and pleasant land.'"

"That's good, Malbouche. Jerusalem awaits me. The chariot is coming to get me."

"To take you home, Becket. You're finally going home."

Becket Door gasped a request. "Clear my name." His voice sunk to a breath rasp and David lowered his ear to his friend's mouth. "Clear my name . . . David Youngblood."

It was the first time David had heard his name in three years. It was the last thing Becket Door ever said. He died five hours later.

David wept more for himself than he did for his friend. Becket's soul rejoiced in heaven. Becket Door was free. But David remained a prisoner. Only Malbouche.

Solitude claimed him.

CHAPTER ❖ FOUR

Three years later

The sun skirted the treetops, dancing with the occasional cloud as it rose upward into the sky. Camille watched as Adele Youngblood Smythe conquered the lush lawn at Blackthorne, the crumbling Youngblood estate in Cornwall.

Adele had absolutely nothing in common with her brother David, except for her propensity to laugh at a good joke and be one with the couch on which she sat. No sitting up straight and ladylike with Adele. Comfort was the key. With thick hair the shade of a strong Pekoe tea leaf, she was quite plump, well, fat really, yet utterly unapologetic for that fact. While her older brother dressed himself in an understated, elegant manner, Adele's garb had never left the nursery. Layers of lace and ruffles lent her an impossibly confectionery appearance at times. Light on her surprisingly delicate feet, she was always blowing air from her inability to walk fifteen feet without becoming winded. Camille had never met a more genial, sunny woman.

But right now, Adele's expression spoke to the contrary. "I finally received word from France."

Camille, sunning herself on a blanket, took Adele's hand and climbed to her feet. Dread coiled in her throat. "He's not dead, is he?"

In one simultaneous quake of emotion, Adele shrugged, shook her head, and began to cry. "They have no record of a David Youngblood."

"You're certain?"

"Yes. As certain as I can be without going there myself and finding out. He's a year late and no one knows a thing about it." She blew her nose. "He's dead. I know it."

"He can't be." Camille scooped up the blanket and gathered it into a sloppy heap, hardly believing her time with David's family was coming to a close. And without warning. "Where are you going?" Adele called from behind her, unable to catch up.

"I'm going to Paris!"

They traveled to Dover as quickly as British rail would allow. Camille's daughter, six-year-old Lily, sat in wide-eyed silence beside her, knitting furiously, a pastime learned from Adele. Camille stroked the child's blond hair, formulating a plan of action.

"Of course they wouldn't have record of you on Devil's Island!" she quipped to herself, wondering why she had been foolish enough to allow Adele to make formal inquiry. "You were imprisoned in secret!"

"What, *Maman*?" Lily asked, looking up from her work.

"Nothing, my love. It's just your crazy old *maman* muttering as usual." She'd found herself fully ensconced in that habit soon after David's exile had begun. Following a brief renewal of her affair with Evariste Lyell, the minister of justice, and the subsequent pregnancy, David entered her mind almost constantly, and so to David she spoke.

She had betrayed him. Had been unable to say no to the lonely man who had granted her many favors. A man who'd had a little too much to drink on a night when she could say exactly the same. Dear Evariste.

Her arm tightened around her daughter. Her pregnancy had saved her life. Lily's birth had jolted her from her life of prostitution. After Lily's weaning, Camille had traveled with her to Tuscany, then to Greece. She had even gone to Rome for a while and tried to renew her faith in the church. But she kept feeling like Mary Magdalene without the forgiveness, and the paintings and statues in the Sistine Chapel only mocked her, God's finger not giving life to Adam, but pointing in accusation at her.

Sinner!

Well, that was hardly news! *Ciel!* But to even stand before such a holy God? Hah! She'd *never* make it out of purgatory!

So much for Rome. So much for the holy church.

By then, the time arrived to go to Cornwall. Just as she and David had arranged. At first she was worried about meeting Adele and her brood of children. But when she said, "Cookie sent me," Adele threw out her arms, pulled Camille into an embrace, and told her they'd set another place for her at the dinner which they were just sitting down to eat.

That evening they showed her to a room upstairs on the second floor. It was decorated in white and blue, looking as though someone had taken a Wedgewood box and expanded it into a bedchamber. It was a peaceful haven. Camille immediately felt as if perhaps God wasn't so far away after all. Adele pulled an extra quilt out of the armoire and said with a wink, "You should have come much sooner, dear. And we can always use an extra child around here!" Never once had she questioned Lily's presence, or inquired as to her obviously checkered conception.

And so Camille waited, surrounded by the Smythes, with the occasional visit from the interim Lord and Lady Youngblood, Tobin and Miranda. Christmas, New Year's Day, and Easter were celebrated without much verve, for they keenly felt David's absence. Camille felt his suffering.

And now summer had arrived. And she was on her way to Paris. With a mission.

Lily enjoyed the boat ride across the channel. Truly she was the world's child, having grown up in many countries. She chatted with the deck hands, played cards with the older travelers, and proudly displayed her knitting to anyone who stopped to comment. Camille watched in awe as she sat with an ancient woman with puckered eyelids and deflated cheeks. The woman, teaching her a more complicated stitch, spoke in patient tones, and Lily sat motionless, her small hand resting comfortably on the lady's arm as she demonstrated.

Lily brought sparkle to the world. She had given Camille back her life. Because of this Camille knew, way down beneath her skin, past the layers of reason and logic and even experience, that God truly cared.

Calais materialized out of the morning fog. After boarding a train for Paris, she would have to get to work! Figure out a plan. If David Youngblood still lived, she would find him.

They entered the foyer of Camille's old Paris town house late on a Sunday night in August. A stiff breeze swirled the fragile sheers by the windows into a slanted shadowed dance of flips and flutters, arcs and spirals. The house smelled newly picked. Like flowers, lemon wax, and fresh paint. Summer in the darkness, echoes of times past. The memories briefly whisked her away until she remembered her reasons for coming.

Camille helped Lily off with her hat.

"How long will we be here, *Maman*?" she asked, eyes scanning the dim room and coming to rest on a colorful dome of flowers placed on a gleaming ebony table beneath a gilt-framed mirror at the far end of the hall. "It's very pretty, *Maman*. Even in the dark."

The only remaining servant was the old Chinese woman who'd never left Camille's employ. Camille didn't have the heart to let her go. And, to be honest, Mai-Ling knew too much. Though all stood at the ready, Camille knew Mai-Ling would be asleep in her small chamber off the kitchen.

Camille looked to her right, into the parlor. Dustcovers safe-guarded the precious antique furnishings of the crimson-hued room. To her left, the emerald dining room appeared much the same. Oh, the parties they had in those two rooms so long ago! David, quite the host then, spent his ill-gotten gains as quickly as he had pocketed them. Yet now, all these years later, when she pictured herself so wild and immodest, a creature of the night, she felt ashamed. But the memories of David, eyeing her hungrily from the other side of the room, made her tingle with excitement. Six years from her sight, and he still had the power to drive her mad with desire. What would happen to them when he returned?

Lily tugged on her mother's coat. "I'm hungry, *Maman*."

Camille had to admit the same. She'd gained at least twenty-five pounds in Cornwall, thirty to be honest. Being around Adele all the time made the weight understandable. Still, it had left her with more of an appetite than she'd ever had before. "We'll go down to the kitchen after the driver brings in our bags and I'll make us a nice soup. I'm sure Mai-Ling has the kitchen well-stocked."

They followed the driver up the steps, Camille directing him from behind.

"Here we are," she announced. "This suite here with the connecting door."

He dropped off the baggage, waited while Camille paid him, then left with a hefty tip in one hand, the other tipping his hat. "*Bon soir, madame*," he said.

"*Bon soir, monsieur*."

Camille looked around her, hands on hips. "They'll do nicely for just you and me, Lily. I remember when I had them decorated."

Lily ran into her room. "Look, *Maman*. A doll is on my bed. May I play with it?"

Camille rushed over and picked up the doll. She hugged it before handing it to Lily. "Do you like her? Poor dear has been waiting for me all these years." In her haste to leave Paris, she'd forgotten to take her on her travels, something she regretted. "Her name is Fifi."

Lily hugged it too. "Isn't that a doggy name?"

Camille took her hand and knelt down next to her, looking the child in the eye. "My mother wouldn't let us have a dog, so I renamed my dolly Fifi in protest. Her real name is Iris."

"A flower! Like me!"

Camille held the doll's head up to her mouth. She spoke in a high, squeaky voice, as if the doll addressed the child. "Would you take care of me while you're here, Mademoiselle Lily? Your *maman* will be so busy, I'm afraid she'll forget to bring me my food."

Lily laughed and shook the doll's hand. "I'd be glad to, Fifi. Come on, *Maman*!" Lily hollered, her skinny legs beginning a jig. "Let's go have supper."

Camille knew the last thing she needed to do was eat. What would David think of her when he saw her so plump and busty? With a sigh, she followed Lily out of the room. She'd better find David soon or she'd end up as fat as Adele!

The next afternoon Camille set out alone. Lily, already old friends with Mai-Ling, was busy in the kitchen learning how to make dumplings. Camille had whiled away the morning eating croissants, drinking coffee, and catching up on all that had taken place since she had left.

The Monday sky shone bright, a harbinger of good fortune. Monday was always a fine day to begin anything. You didn't have the previous week's failures bogging you down, and five entire days stood before you begging you to do something right, perhaps even up the score a bit.

Only one place to start. The minister of justice. Poor Evariste Lyell could no longer be of help. He died in a fire before Lily's birth, only months after David's exile had begun. Six years later her heart still stung when she recalled the kind, gentle man who had loved her in his inimitable, yet tender manner.

His replacement would be more than happy to help her, she realized upon hearing his name. But would Peter Metery recognize her twenty-five pounds overweight and wearing clothing? She'd never get on with it entertaining such thoughts! Camille would be running into old clients no matter which direction she turned. Best to keep her head high and let them know she meant business. A different breed of business now.

Maybe she'd trade in her fashionable blue day gown with a slightly daring décolleté for something serviceable and brown, something like Miranda Wallace used to drag around before she started writing librettos and giving birth to lots of adorable children.

Ushered into the minister of justice's office without delay or fanfare, Camille breathed a prayer. He recognized her, but was gentleman enough not to mention their shared experiences. She quickly explained the situation, growing increasingly uncomfortable as the life she had fought so hard to suppress rose to float on the surface of the calm pool she had created for herself.

"Six years on Devil's Island, you say?" Peter Metery sat back in his chair and drummed his fingers on the polished surface of his desk. He had grown hard since taking office. The deep creases around his delicate mouth, the flat quality to his hazel eyes, the cold edges of a voice once full of mischief jolted Camille's hopes. Power etched its indelible mark. "The earl of Cannock. Interesting."

She sat forward in her chair. "Why do you say that?"

"When I moved into this office, I was looking through the desk and I found a document. It was mysterious at the time, but I kept it around. It was signed by the emperor himself. I assumed it was one of Lyell's deals and that somehow the meaning of this would come to light and its purpose would be revealed. But it never did. In fact, I'd forgotten about it for several years."

"Was David Youngblood's name on it?"

Peter's eyes rounded with incredulity. "You still love him that much, Camille? After all that scoundrel did to you?"

Camille's stomach muscles tightened as she focused on the paneled wall behind him. The wainscoting blurred before her eyes. "I didn't come to talk about me, *monsieur*."

He laughed harshly. "Women like you never change, Camille. Not really."

"What about the document?" she insisted. She'd heard the term "women like you" so many times, it had ceased to sting.

"It's filed away. Come back next week. No . . . two weeks. My clerk should have had time to locate it by then."

Camille bravado deflated. "Two weeks?"

"Unless, of course, you wish to speed things up a bit . . ." His smile brimmed with a meaning Camille knew only too well.

She stood to her feet. "Two weeks, then."

David would just have to wait some more, she decided. Camille had enough about which to feel guilty when they were finally reunited. She didn't care to add Peter Metery's name yet again to her extensive list of moral failures.

CHAPTER ❖ FIVE

For the next six months, Peter Metery managed to drag the matter down to its stumps. But Camille refused to budge, standing firm on the virtues of motherhood and memory. Sooner or later that document would be hers. She could only hope David still breathed when she arrived in French Guiana.

One day in February, 1869, after having Lily fitted for a spring wardrobe, they walked along the Champs Elysees. The biting wind chilled them both to brittle, and they stopped in a small restaurant for something warm. Coffee for Camille and a chocolate for Lily.

An old woman cocooned in heavy furs and sweet perfume sat quietly alone at a table next to theirs. Camille recognized her immediately, watching the heavily ringed fingers rest against the sunken cheek. It had been many years since she had cast an eye on Dowager Countess Racine de Boyce, the mother of the late Count Rene de Boyce. And back then, all viewings had been from afar. Everyone in Paris thought the young nobleman's demise at the hand of Claude Mirreault's henchman was hastened by his mother's refusal to acknowledge his faults. His debts had accumulated, his opium addiction had grown, and finally, all the sins his mother had overlooked, all the sins he had successfully hidden from the world, finally shot through him. A mortal wound. And then he was gone. Not a quick hot light burning itself to bits. No. Rene had never quite got his fire truly burning.

Camille had slept with this boy-man for several years, had been responsible, in part, for his downfall as well, feeding him opium to ease a damaged leg, pinching his fortune by means of jewels, trips, furs, parties. All in Claude Mirreault's employ, mind you. Not that such an excuse really meant anything at the end of the day. Not anymore.

However, the Dowager Countess Racine de Boyce knew nothing of Camille's existence. Rene had been a good son in that regard. Even if someone had tried to tell her that her precious son had kept a woman, she wouldn't have believed it.

Camille looked her way. The countess caught her eye and smiled, lighting up her very lonely, sheer blue eyes. Lily thought the smile was for her and waved a hand. The child itched about in her chair. "We've just been shopping!"

Racine de Boyce smiled more broadly, her teeth now yellowed with age. "One of my favorite pastimes. And what did you buy?"

Camille had never heard the woman's voice before. Though much like her son's had been, it had that needy edge, that little eager tremolo that said, "Please keep talking to me. Thank you for paying me mind."

Lily had no trouble answering the question, followed by more. The child astounded Camille, day after day, by her vibrant personality, her interest in other people, the way she invited conversation and sustained it with an aptitude far beyond her years. Lily allowed people to feel special. Camille watched as the two chattered away about what kind of purple they liked the best, Lily declaring orchid the loveliest color ever and the countess saying she quite liked it too, but wasn't lavender a dilly as well?

When an uppity waiter plonked down the coffee, the countess invited them to sit with her, merely introducing herself as

Racine de Boyce. No title, no airs. "And you two lovely girls are?"

Lily jumped from foot to foot. "I'm Lily! And this is my mother Camille. My father's dead, you know. I never knew him at all. So it's just the two of us and it always has been, but we find all sorts of fun things to do, don't we, *Maman*?"

Camille nodded, laughed. "I suppose she's said it all."

The countess laid a vibrating old hand on the sleeve of Camille's gold gown as the pair sat down. "I'm sorry to hear that you've had to raise her by yourself. I have a granddaughter in much the same circumstance. Well, she has a stepfather, actually, but . . ." She let the sentence fade into a shrug.

Camille waved a hand. "It was many years ago now, Madame de Boyce. And Lily and I enjoy each day as it comes, don't we, my love?"

Lily smiled and took a sip of her chocolate. She came up with a thick foam mustache.

And everyone laughed as the check arrived.

"Let me," the countess said, reaching out and taking the slip of paper. When Camille protested she raised a hand. "No, no. You must humor this old woman, girls. I haven't had this much fun in years."

Lily jumped to her feet. "May we come and see you some-time, Madame de Boyce?"

"Lily!" Camille issued one of her few reprimands.

But the countess laughed and held out her arms. Lily rushed in to give the woman a hug. "I hope you shall. In fact, why don't you come and have lunch with me in three days time?"

Lily clapped, then suddenly knit her brows. "Will there be pork? Because I hate pork."

"Lily!" Now Camille's embarrassment grew riper than the bleu cheese the man at the next table consumed on a baguette.

But the countess took the child's hands in hers. "I promise, there will be no pork to be found."

Camille apologized. "You must excuse her. She's a little over-enthusiastic at times!"

"It's just what I've been needing. You know, I was praying this morning that God would bring a little sunshine into my life. Just a little."

Lily took the final sip of her chocolate. "Well, I'm little!"

The countess ran a tender hand over Lily's arm. "And so you are, my dear." She looked up at Camille, eyes earnest. "In three days then? Friday?"

"If you'd really like." Camille smiled. "I'm not sure you know what you're getting yourself into with this little imp."

The countess dug out a calling card from an embroidered handbag and offered it to Camille. "One o'clock. We'll be ready and waiting. With no pork!"

Camille took the card. "All right, then. We'll be there."

After bustling into their coats and scarves, Camille laid a hand on the countess's shoulder. "Shall we walk you home?"

"Ah, no. I'm going to sit here a while longer and watch the young lovers coming in to dine. One of the servants will be round to fetch me in an hour or so."

Lily hugged her once more; Camille bent down and kissed the soft cheek. And they left the restaurant.

Lily held tightly to her mother's hand. "Is she a sad lady?"

"I suppose so." Camille squeezed her daughter's hand in her own, thinking that nothing could comfort one so well as the hand of one's own child.

⁓

Lily looked at herself in the cheval mirror in her mother's bedchamber. She pulled her skirt out by the sides and dipped her knees. "I think I like it, *Maman*. But I'd say it isn't truly lavender. It's more of a periwinkle."

The child spoke the truth, of course. "Perhaps Madame de Boyce is a bit blind. She is quite old, don't you think?"

"*Maman!*"

Camille laughed and examined herself as well. The dresses, made of the same light purple brocade, glinted with an iridescent sheen. A different pattern had been employed for Lily's gown. *I do have my pride*, Camille thought.

She turned and gathered their gloves. "I'd say we are an acceptable pair."

Lily turned away from the mirror. "Why would we be anything else?"

"Exactly. Shall we go?"

Camille held out a hand and Lily slid hers inside. Bundled up warmly, they quickly navigated the two blocks that separated them from Maison de Fleur. Small gardens at the front of the house lay dormant. But it wouldn't be long before the clematis bloomed, bejeweling the latticework, or the bulb flowers pushed their shards of pulsating green up through the black spring soil. The gardens at Blackthorne had been stunning. Perhaps by the time the rose garden swam with happy bees, fat on nectar and flying in lazy, tipsy circles, they'd be home to enjoy them. And David would as well.

Maison de Fleur. Camille inhaled and sucked all the fresh air she could possibly hold into her lungs. Never had she ever thought to enter this house. Never did she entertain the thought that the dark green door might open in welcome to her.

She helped Lily up the few steps and allowed her to turn the key in the middle of the door, and a hollow thrummy ring emitted from the bell-like device on the other side. Half a minute later a manservant answered. A wide smile divided his face, and he motioned them in with a loud welcome. Then, "Madame de Boyce! They are here!"

Camille raised her brows, unprepared for such an informal atmosphere, but she rather liked it. The countess must have done some changing in the past eight years.

"In my salon, August!" came the reply, and Camille escorted Lily as they followed the jovial servant down a portrait-filled corridor to the back of the home. A distinct smell of orange and mint permeated the air. Refreshing, yet calming.

The countess rested in a comfortable chair cozied near the fireplace. Lily rushed over, jumped into her lap, and was rewarded with a hug.

Camille took stock of the feminine room. Shades of white, ivory, pink, and gold shone in the sunlight. Curious round tables glittered and sparkled with crystal, porcelain, and silver baubles, and fringed satin pillows embellished the ivory sofa. Truly a woman's room.

Camille smiled at her hostess. "Good afternoon, madame."

"And how are my lunch guests? We've been waiting for you. I was so busy making sure everything was going just so down in the kitchen this morning I fear I've exhausted myself."

Camille sat on a chair matching the countess's. "I hope you didn't go to too much trouble, madame."

Lily hugged her friend. "I do!"

The countess chuckled. "Of course I did. I haven't had such important guests come to Maison de Fleur in ages." Her gnarled, arthritic hand touched a ragged Bible on the side table nearby. "Now, I want to give you a choice, Lily. We can dine in luxury in the dining room, but the table is awfully large and we'd have to shout at each other. Or we can eat in the breakfast room with the sun coming in through my windows and talk in our normal voices."

She hopped to her feet. "I believe it would be fun to shout, please."

Countess de Boyce laughed out loud and winked at Camille. "As if that was really a choice. Let's go in, then. I figured a growing, smart girl like you would want to eat right away."

Camille helped her to her feet. "Here you go, Countess."

The old woman froze. "You know who I am?"

"Doesn't everyone?"

She relaxed. "I suppose so. I was hoping . . ."

Lily took her hand. "You were hoping what, madame?"

The countess squeezed Lily's hand. "That you would come just because you wanted to see me."

Lily laughed as if the funniest joke she'd ever heard had just been told. "Of course that's why we came!" She leaned forward. "Do you know, when we were in Rome, I met the pope once? He patted me on the head!"

The countess's laughter rang out. "Well, then, compared to the pope, I must be a simple cream cheese."

"It's my favorite kind!"

Camille's eyes met the countess's. "We even tried to wear your favorite color. Lily so wanted to please you, Countess."

"You must call me Racine. I feel that this is the start of a friendship I've needed for many years now." The countess pulled a shawl around her shoulders.

Camille felt guilty, vowing she would do her best to ensure this sweet old person would never know that the woman she had befriended had also destroyed her only son. "One cannot have too many friends."

"If they truly are friends," the countess replied, rising to her feet and tucking her hand in Camille's arm. She led them out of the room.

"I remember hearing you used to be quite a presence at the court," Camille said.

"Ah, yes. But that was long ago, and that was when I learned the difference between a true friend and someone who only wants a seat on the front row. So to speak. I'm glad to be away from that life now. It's for the young, I'd say. But it is times like these, times with children and the lovely young women who mother them, that make this old heart young again."

Lily cried out with delight at the sight of the dining room. All the candles had been lit, and flowers overflowed their vases onto the fine white table linen.

"I'm glad you approve, Mademoiselle Lily," the countess said with a tiny dip of her head.

Both Camille and Lily ate enough of the oyster barquettes to make an entire meal. But out came braised mutton cutlets, browned first in bacon and butter, then simmered in white wine and garnished with a golden sauce. Fresh broad beans mingled with savory glazed carrots and currants. They all clapped their approval when fancy bread in the shape of a rabbit was delivered to the sideboard.

Racine resembled a portrait of an aging madonna. Eating little, she smiled gently at her guests and made fascinating conversation. They all talked about their travels and agreed that Tuscany beat all others for a little relaxation, and wasn't that lifestyle good for the soul?

Racine laid her fork down without a clink. "I found God once again in Tuscany."

Camille remembered the talks she'd endured with David before he had left for Devil's Island. She'd forgotten the countess had been so religious, but once reminded, she thought of the conversations she and Rene had shared regarding his mother's Christian faith. "Really?"

"Ah, yes, it is so. I used to have a son, but he became more important to me than even God was. From the day he was born . . ." Her voice swelled with regret. "But he is dead now and there is nothing that stands between God's Son and me."

Lily swirled a rabbit ear shape of bread in her gravy. "That sounds like a nice place to be. God's Son is Jesus. Lady Miranda told me that when she visited."

Racine sat forward. "Lady Miranda?"

Camille waved a hand, dismissing Miranda as an unimportant Miranda. "Just an old friend of the family."

"Do I know her?"

"Oh, no! From the country." Camille wanted to change the subject, but something had happened in that short conversation. This was Racine de Boyce doing the talking! The enemy! Or at least that's what she had been when Camille was sleeping with her son. And now, here sat a weary old lady, sad yet peaceful, giving and wise.

Could David have spoken the truth? Could the power of Christ be so transforming that it could change a man, or a woman, so completely?

"I noticed that Bible you had in your salon, Countess."

"Oh, yes. That book has seen better days, I'm afraid. But I hate to get a new one and it's such a comfort to me now that it's becoming as ragged as I am! Why don't we have dessert in the salon?" She rang a bell and rose to her feet.

Lily jumped out of her chair and took her hand. "Do you mind if I call you *Grandmere*? I don't have a grandmother and I thought maybe you needed a granddaughter. Do you have any grandchildren?"

Racine laughed. "As a matter of fact I have five. But I'd never refuse another. My late son had a daughter before he died, and my daughter Cecile has four children now. And they all ride horses!"

The child jumped up and down. "I love horses. We used to ride in England, but since we've been in Paris I haven't gone out for even one ride."

"Well, then. That shall soon be rectified. My daughter Ceci would be delighted to help you out." The countess leaned forward and placed a hand on Lily's. "I quite suspect she's part horse herself. Now, let us have our dessert. It's my favorite part of the meal."

"Mine too!" Lily hollered.

Camille confessed that she had never been able to live without her sweets. So much for losing weight before David came home.

⁓

That night, when stillness hugged the house and everyone but Camille slept, she slid open the drawer of her nightstand. Inside lay only one item: a small, black Bible. David had entrusted it to her before his exile.

She turned up her lamp and flipped it open. If only she could read.

Down in the kitchen the next day, Mai-Ling read the inscription, her slanted eyes squinting as she held the book far down her arm. "'Presented to Miranda Wallace on Christmas Day, 1859, by your loving brother, M. Wallace.' And there is more," the old Chinese woman said, holding up a finger.

"'Read with an open heart. Read to find the God who is, not the God you wish for. "For those who seek me will find me if they seek me with all their heart." Given this day, August 26, 1861, to David Youngblood, earl of Cannock, by Miranda Wallace.'"

An open heart. *Well, that is something I've never had a problem with*, Camille thought. *In fact, I can love too easily.* Camille took the Bible from Mai-Ling and walked upstairs to find Lily in her bedchamber.

"Can you still remember what Aunt Adele taught you?" she asked, embarrassment quickly fading at the eagerness on Lily's face.

"You mean reading?"

"Yes."

Lily nodded.

"Well, then." Camille handed her the book. It seemed that Lily was always saving her life in one way or another.

CHAPTER ❖ SIX

Every Wednesday Peter Metery received Camille in his office, and every Wednesday he refused to hand over what she needed. Oh, he extended other offers to be sure, obviously still finding Camille alluring. She remembered the necklaces she had had disassembled for David's exile. How could she not miss those airy, sparkling works of art? Not to mention the fact that they might have come in very handy now. Why wouldn't the man just give her the document and be done with it? And would he be above a bribe? *Ciel.* It was a stupid thought to entertain. The jewels were gone and had hopefully been put to good use by the man she adored.

May had arrived. Almost three months had passed since Camille and Lily's first visit to Maison de Fleur. Visits had occurred every Tuesday since then, sometimes Fridays too. And something happened in Camille's heart.

Actually, *someone* happened *to* Camille's heart.

The seed of faith David planted so long ago had been rooting ever since, coupled with Mai-Ling's and Lily's daily Scripture reading. The countess reaped the harvest on a rainy March afternoon. Lily, listening to the conversations about faith and forgiveness and a Father willing to sacrifice his perfect Son, believed before Camille. Her daughter's simple conversion spoke to Camille's soul more than all the words she'd heard from the lips of Racine or David.

But sitting with the countess, doing not much more than gazing into the fire, it dawned on Camille. She believed. She had been changed. And she wondered if she had believed before that moment, and thought that, yes, perhaps she had. But the moment itself contained a defining quality. As if her mind had finally caught up to her heart and her soul. "You are my Lord," she mouthed silently. "And I love you."

Christ filled her heart, cleaning out much of the hate, the anger, the lack of respect she had always felt not only for herself but for others. He warmed her cold soul, refreshed her tired will. He was all things for all times for all the rest of her days. The lover of her soul. It was a phrase David had said, one she could readily understand, one she could easily accept. Now.

"You're a child of God now," the countess said when Camille shared the new truth of her heart several days after the reality of it struck.

"I thought it would feel different, somehow. Not that I don't, on many levels. But I thought I would feel as if I was suddenly clean and that my past transgressions would be forgotten."

"For some it is like that, I believe." The countess smiled. "But not for everyone. Our paths to Christ, even our feelings once we find him, are as unique as we are."

"I suppose." Camille took some comfort in that. And surely, her dark, copious sins would never be forgotten. But the blood of Christ's sacrifice covered them. How could she ask for more? In her brimming lifetime, there hadn't been many people who sacrificed themselves for her.

Yes, the lover of her soul.

And so, in the middle of the month of May, Camille finally decided her current tack with Peter Metery bore little resemblance to a successful plan. In David Youngblood's old terminology, she had played her cards too close to the vest.

The time to show her hand had come.

Peter Metery first appeared shocked, then angry, then sick as Camille talked. She'd taken great pains with herself that day. Mai-Ling had buttoned her up in a peacock blue silk gown with a pert little hat. Her hair, smoothed away from her face, fell in long ringlets down her back. Just a few cosmetics added the polish the already shining veneer needed to transition her appearance from lovely to staggering.

"... and don't forget about that evening at the Moulin Rouge. Remember afterwards, when you took me to that small apartment on the Rue de la—"

"Enough!" He held up his hand. "You've made your point, Camille." His mouth turned down as though a stale wind had wafted up his nose.

"If you'd have played the gentleman, Peter, it would not have come to this. I've waited nine months, very patiently, I might add, so as not to offend you in any way. But I see no other alternative."

Peter reached into a desk drawer and yanked out the document. "Here. Take it and get out."

Triumph. Victory at last. Camille's eyes quickly skimmed the paper, then she beamed her most bewitching smile. She snapped the document from his fingers and turned toward the door.

"It's a shame you've gotten so chubby, Camille. You used to be such a beautiful woman."

The words stung. Without turning she said loudly as she walked, "And you used to get anything you wanted." She put her hand on the doorknob and turned to face him. "Good-bye, Peter."

Mai-Ling was dusting in the foyer when Camille careened through the portal. "I got the paper!" Her cry was triumphant. "We leave tomorrow!"

She bowed. "Congratulations."

"Another journey, *Maman*?" came a voice from the top of the stairs.

Her daughter's voice covered her like a healing balm after Metery's comment. Camille ran up the stairs. "Yes, Lily. I'm going to drop you off in Cornwall first, and then I'm going to French Guiana."

A gasp sounded from the bottom of the stairs. Mai-Ling hurried up. "You going all the way to tropics by yourself? Isn't there other way?"

"No," Camille said. "He's waited long enough. David needs to come home. And he needs to come home with me."

It was the sort of moment Camille dreaded more than any other. A moment of confession. A moment of humility. A moment of honesty. But she knew that she might never make it back from French Guiana. Ships were lost at sea every day and nothing in life was truly certain. *Juste Ciel!* But she'd learned that lesson long ago!

Maison de Fleur flourished with color. Fuchsia hollyhocks, swaying in the breeze, guarded the lower growing columbine in the small gardens next to the steps. Large bushes of peonies in white and vibrant lavender waved their delicate, pinked petals toward the busy street.

Despite the home's gentle beauty, Camille felt sick to her stomach. Bringing Lily along would have helped, but she'd refused to hide behind her daughter. She had an apology to make. The countess deserved to know the truth.

Or did she?

Camille wrestled with the question even as she raised her hand to ring the bell. She'd been wrestling with it since she had seen the countess for the first time. Was ignorance indeed bliss here? Would such news upset the countess to illness?

She turned the bell and soon found herself in the countess's salon.

"What a wonderful surprise! And just as I was getting bored!" Racine de Boyce's eyes sparkled with delight. "What brings you here to see me, my dear?" She held out a hand.

Camille took it and sat down beside her on the ivory sofa. "I'm afraid I've come to say good-bye."

The watery eyes saddened. "Leaving Paris?"

"Yes. I'm going away for a while."

The old woman forced a smile on her puckered lips. "But that is wonderful! I shouldn't be so selfish. I loved my traveling days. Where are you going?"

Camille shook her head. "It doesn't matter. It's a long journey, though."

Concern grew on the countess's features. "And Lily?"

"Will be taken care of by a good friend."

"You could leave her here with me if you'd like."

"I'm not sure how long it will be before I get back to France. It would be better if I left her in England. That's where I'll be returning to after my journey."

"I see." Her lip quivered with disappointment.

"It's not that I don't think you would take good care of her!" Camille rushed to reassure her.

"Oh, I know, my dear! I'm just a silly old woman sometimes. I've always been a bit silly."

A servant delivered a pot of coffee, and Camille poured them each a cup. "There's something else I have to tell you, Countess, and I don't know where to begin."

The countess sipped delicately from her cup. "Just go ahead, dear. It's not bad news, is it?"

"Not exactly. Just old news."

"Proceed then, my dear."

Camille cleared her throat and prayed for guidance. "I knew your son, Countess."

"You did?" The pale eyes flared to greater life.

She dropped her gaze, twisting her fingers together painfully. "Yes. I was the woman who took him away all of those nights. It was me who kept him from his wife."

The countess set down her cup. "You were . . . his mistress?"

Camille nodded. "I couldn't pretend any longer."

Racine's eyes welled with tears. "Did he . . . love you?"

Camille shook her head. "No," she whispered. "He never did."

"Perhaps he should have. Perhaps he'd still be alive if he did. But you . . . loved him?"

"No." Camille's heart broke. "I've only loved one man."

"Who, my dear?"

This was the news she'd really dreaded. She didn't know it until that very second, however. "David Youngblood. It is he who I am going to find. I wanted to say I'm sorry about Rene's death. I'm sorry for anything I had to do with it."

The countess's hands curled around the arms of her chair and she called to her servant. "August! Come here!"

Camille sat, not daring to ask a question, not daring to say a word.

August arrived. "Yes, my lady?"

"Get Camille her wrap, please. It is time for her to go."

Camille said nothing more. When she turned to look at the countess one last time, the woman averted her gaze, tears spilling onto her parchment skin.

Have I done the wrong thing, she asked herself, and thought, yes, perhaps she had. But the path before her now was clear and it was clean. Her dear father only told her one good piece of advice that she could remember. "Make peace with the dying, Camille. But for heaven's sake, live for the living."

She would be with David soon.

CHAPTER ❖ SEVEN

Two months later

The people in Paris had obviously been more used to a beautiful woman than the people of St. Laurent were. But Camille held her head high and found herself standing at the wrought iron gate of the prison compound. Amid gawking stares, she asked to see the warden. Perhaps yellow had been the wrong color to wear for the occasion.

The guard on duty eyed her, something that Camille had accepted years ago. Her newfound faith hadn't dulled her well-honed power over men. Poor creatures. They didn't really have a chance. All those sexual needs driving them, not to mention that fragile part of them deep inside that needed constant bolstering and approval, that "manly" essence to their nature she did not possess—she somehow understood it all. No wonder she had been so good at her old profession.

She awarded him with a smile, and dumbed up her voice several notes. "I'm sure this is not your usual occurrence, however ..." Her eyes pleaded for help. No one could be as feminine, as vulnerable as Camille.

The guard bit the hook she offered, the barb going deep into his loins. Ah-hah! She laid a gentle, almost shaking hand on his arm. "Right this way, madame."

In much the same way she dealt with the warden, playing upon his sense of protectiveness. Finally, the next morning, after a night spent at an inn crawling with bugs she'd never known existed, she shoved her belongings into her carpetbag, hurried down to the dock, and waited for the love of her life.

"Keep tight hold of that satchel," the innkeeper had warned, and so she did, looking in the distance for the ferry.

"Should be here soon," one of the prison workers told her as he stacked some supply crates ready for a trip out to Devil's Island. "You meeting someone?"

"*Oui.* I've come to take someone home."

"Lucky man."

Camille grinned. "I should say. But somehow, I think a little bit more than luck is involved in this one, *monsieur.*"

The money was gone. He'd hurled the capsule into the jungle two years before, wondering what portion of God's mind had decided to grind him down to meal. Why he had been forgotten by the world, by France, by his relatives, by Camille?

Five years. Five years.

He no longer said those words.

Seven years and counting now. How many more leered at him, daring him to survive? His health had worsened considerably as the necessary funds to buy a better diet, better work orders, steadily dwindled to nothing. And escape?

Less than a dream now. In this weakened state, his emaciated body now shaved of a third of its weight by malnutrition and dysentery, he knew better than to attempt to swim that raucous expanse. Ile de Royal appeared to be so close, but the busy highway of current assured David Youngblood he would never cross to freedom.

"Five years or death" seemed an easy enough equation all those years ago. He hadn't foreseen another scenario. An indefinite life of cruel servitude, hunger, pain, disease, and humiliation had never been an option. Until recently.

Oh, God, will I die here?

He'd grown silent over the past year. Some still came to him for prayer. But David was weak. Death seemed like a good thing these days.

His body was bruised forever. His will lay in pieces. His spirit was dying. But still he clung to the Savior.

"Malbouche!"

The early morning call issued from the peeling lips of a surly, one-eared guard. David raised his head from the hammock. "Yes, sir?"

"Get up."

It took all his strength to obey. His back, wrenched and twisted from all the beatings he had endured, all the trees he had helped remove for the unnecessary road across the jungle, the many days in the fields, screamed in pain at the sudden movement. Wincing as he swung his legs over the side and rolled off, he landed on the floor on hands and knees.

"Off your knees, Malbouche. The lieutenant wishes to see you."

La Roche! The lieutenant's son had succeeded his father several years earlier.

Oh, dear God, not this! He prayed, gaining his feet by excruciating inches.

"Now, Malbouche," the guard said, voice box growling. "The man's insistent."

David shook. Bile burbled in his esophagus and blood pooled in his face. It felt hot. So hot.

The guard laughed without a smile. "I wouldn't worry if I were you, Malbouche. You've got no diamonds left, no money, and you're by far the ugliest, scrawniest man on the island. La Roche likes only pretty faces, good bodies."

True enough. He'd come to Devil's Island at thirty-seven years of age, and though he hadn't seen a mirror in years, he'd spotted his dim reflection in mud pools and rain puddles. He'd swiped white hairs as well as red now from his shoulders. He'd been able to count his ribs for the last five issues of new striped uniforms. Yet, he knew he couldn't count on La Roche to behave in any way normal or predictable.

David followed the guard out of the barracks, down the path toward the lieutenant's bungalow. La Roche met him on the steps. "Haugh, haugh, haugh, haugh," he laughed, and David cringed. "By the look of you now, I cannot believe you were so successful with the ladies. But when you first came to Devil's Island ... ah, I remember you well, Malbouche. Horrible mouth, yet you were a goodly specimen in your body then. Lucky for you your diamonds were even more beautiful to me. You have no diamonds now, though, do you?"

David froze, eyes glued to the large face of the man in front of him, a fresh ham studded with boorish features. La Roche's dressing gown reminded him so much of Claude Mirreault he tasted bile again. Swallowed.

"But now I *know* you were a ladies' man, indeed."

David didn't know whether he should respond or not. Moments like this confused him these days. He used to be so good at them.

La Roche crossed his flabby arms in front of his chest. "Aren't you at all curious as to why you've been called here?"

David could only nod.

"Malbouche." La Roche smiled. "It appears that God made your ugly face for a reason most beneficial to you, after all. Someone came to St. Laurent yesterday asking after a David Youngblood, earl of Cannock. I said, 'There is no David Youngblood on Devil's Island! And certainly no earl!' And she said, 'I have papers from the emperor himself granting his freedom.' And I said, 'I tell you, there's no David Youngblood here.' And then, Malbouche, then the woman described your gruesome face and I knew she could mean only one person!" He had that sort of queer triumphant tone David had come to despise over the years.

"She? Who? Where?"

"She's waiting for you on the mainland. Prettiest woman I've ever seen. Blonde and sophisticated. A little heavy, but still pleasing to the average fellow, I'd guess."

Quite a statement coming from La Roche. It could mean only one thing. Camille had come for him.

She'd come to take him home.

He hoped.

"You are scheduled to go to the mainland in ninety minutes. It's why we awakened you so early."

He wouldn't allow relief to wash away his doubts yet. "You speak the truth?"

"Would I be so nice to you if I didn't?"

David couldn't answer. A feeling of helplessness overwhelmed him, as though someone had suddenly turned on the light after years of darkness.

"It's not every day someone is freed by the emperor." La Roche held up a document, yellowed with age, scrawled at the bottom with Louis Napoleon's signature. "If I'd have known you were nobility, I'd have bartered with you for many more privileges. I cannot believe you have kept so quiet. Especially after your money ran out."

A guard arrived with a pair of large snips. "You want me to take the shackles off of old Malbouche?" he asked incredulously.

"Just do it," La Roche ordered.

It didn't take long until the chain between his ankles lay on the ground. David would have kicked his leg high to the side, but didn't trust his balance any longer. And he felt too tired for such activity.

Still, he squatted down to view the pink, raw flesh, and rubbed it. Pain resulted, a good pain. He couldn't rise on his own. Too much had occurred. The guard helped him to his feet.

"What will you do with your freedom?" La Roche asked.

David looked down at himself, so broken, dirty, and foul-smelling. Hardly earl-like these days. "A bath, please?" That was a start.

"There's a tub out back. I'll find you some clothes." He handed David the document.

David reached forward and ran a shaking hand across the heavy, fibrous paper. The inky words, black and fuzzed around the edges, sent another shaft of bright light into his soul. Freedom.

"Hard to believe, is it not?" La Roche asked, seeming almost jovial now that the emperor's signature had placed them on equal footing. "Fortune has smiled on you, Malbouche."

David nodded. His throat felt too thick for trivial responses. He let himself be led around to the back of the bungalow where a servant drew a warm bath. David stumbled into the small wooden cistern, not remembering when his last real bath had occurred. Holding tightly onto the rim, muscles quivering, he lowered himself into the almost scalding water. His throat issued a groan from deep down as the water covered his bruised, scraped body, sucking him into a state slightly more than conscious, slightly less than spiritual. The water was changed three times before his hair shone and his skin had been liberated from the grayish tinge that had not completely left him for seven years. The constant itching he had endured was almost gone as well, he realized as he toweled himself dry with the slow, gentle blottings of an old man.

La Roche provided a pair of gray wool trousers and a clean white shirt.

"You will be given a coat for the journey home, when you leave St. Laurent," the servant explained, handing out the clothing piece by piece as David shook them on.

The colony's barber had gone to the mainland, so David pulled back his hair with a piece of twine and made his way onto the porch of the bungalow where La Roche ate breakfast. David eyed the toast and jam.

La Roche, dressed as well, pointed to the chair opposite. He called to his servant. "Fix up a plate for his lordship, Loic." Then he turned to David. "Your old friend, that Door fellow, would have had a statistic for what's happening this morning, eh?"

The servant set a plate of toast and jam before him.

"Probably." David spread the jam. He stuffed half a piece of toast into his mouth at once. The taste of the sweet mashed berries on his tongue closed his eyes at the ecstasy of it. The texture of the toasted bread, rough and stimulating, triggered something deep down, tickled a portion of something gone long dormant.

"A half of one percent imprisoned on Devil's Island are pardoned by the emperor," La Roche laughed, imitating Becket's tones. "So you were innocent, eh?"

"No, sir. As guilty as most, more guilty than some."

"Well"—La Roche shrugged—"I've finally found an honest man on Devil's Island, and he's leaving."

David finished his meal, feeling more like himself than he had in a long time. A bell rang down at the landing. The transport from the mainland had arrived.

"It's time you go home, Malbouche," La Roche said. "I will accompany you. I love to see women cry."

"Yes, sir."

David walked down the steps into the dappled sunlight. His shackles were gone. He could eat real food like meat and eggs and cheese. No one had the right to beat him any longer.

"The human animal is amazingly resilient, Malbouche," La Roche said. "You'll do just fine."

The ferry trip across the choppy channel, the boat literally pulled along a rope extended across the water from island to mainland, gave him excellent cause for nausea. But David didn't care anymore. He bid adieu to the island. The first leg of the journey home had begun.

He could see the dock easily once they were out in the middle of the channel. La Roche had been right—a beautiful woman awaited him. Camille had gained some weight, but her hair, still that beautiful, peculiar shade of blond, infused with an almost pink tinge, remained the same.

And her clothes. Good heavens!

Well, life must have changed severely for Camille, or else she chose her most serviceable garments for the journey. Her plump figure, a surprise surely, and more pleasing to him somehow than the thin one, was sausaged in a plain brown dress with a high neck. She must have felt like a capon roasting in parchment in such a getup, but, not surprisingly, she appeared cool and confident as she stared out across the water, delicate hands gripping a carpetbag in front of her.

As they grew closer he could take in her features. Still the same lovely little nose, the same green eyes with dark lashes. The mouth stretched wider than he remembered and her cheeks appeared softer, fuller, and less sculpted. She had ripened to womanhood, a gentle, pleasing, skirt-swaying womanhood.

She caught sight of him and lifted her hand in a wave. The smile that had charmed the noblemen of France made him gasp. *Oh, dear God,* he thought, an informal prayer of thanks. *Could it be that she still loves me?*

⁓

Camille knew David immediately. But only by his mouth. If it hadn't been for the harelip, she would have never recognized this white-haired, tiny, stooped man who limped painfully down the gangplank next to that pig of a man she'd spoken to yesterday. He was so bent and ragged now, like a toy animal with a wide stuffing leak—still recognizable, but not nearly so large and no longer able to sit up straight on the chair.

What shall I say to him?

In the time it took for him to step onto the landing Camille remembered the haughty man he'd once been. Oh, he had been devilish, to be sure, but in a likeable manner. Most people couldn't help but like David Youngblood. At least in the crowd in which she used to run. The way he used to throw himself on couches, draping his leg over the arm. His drawl. His sense of humor. His temper. His pride.

It looked like all of that had deserted him long ago.

But those had never been the reasons Camille had loved David Youngblood. Camille had seen the boy inside. The lad who had been shunned by his good-looking parents, sent to live at a cold castle called Greywalls in Scotland. The lad raised by the servants. Camille loved him for the way he had nestled in her arms, the way he had cried out in his sleep, sometimes in anguish, sometimes in a cloying sadness that made the blood rush to her heart so that it ached and throbbed and pulled at her.

He stood before her now, and she wasted no time gathering him into her arms. "Oh, my lord," she whispered, resting her cheek upon his bony chest and crying. "Oh, my lord. What have they done?"

"Camille." He breathed her name.

"Yes."

"Elspeth?"

"She's fine. Living in London now with Lord and Lady Youngblood."

"That's good. Keep your arms around me."

He said nothing else, just loosely settled his hands on her hips. David barely moved. Silence swelled the air around them, and she waited for him to draw back.

"I'll never let you go again, my lord," she said as guards and convicts milled around her, shifting bloated eyeballs in their direction.

He refused to pull away. And so she decided not to either. If they had to stay there until nightfall, well, so be it. She'd waited seven years to hold him like this, not fooling herself even once that he would be the same David.

The hot sun melted them together by their own perspiration. His hair smelled clean and sweet, and though the white had well overtaken the auburn, she couldn't help but smile at the queue in the back. In fact, she rather liked it. Made him look like a well-seasoned, overcooked swashbuckler who had endured too many years on the high seas, had seen too many days with too little food, had been in too many brawls in too many taverns.

It would be only a matter of time before he'd be laughing and joking with her. Just like old times. Old times for tired old souls given new life by a loving God.

Ten minutes passed, fifteen, and he finally moved. David lifted a trembling hand to her face and muttered three words. "Let's go home."

She cupped his cheek with her hand. "The ship sets sail the day after tomorrow, my lord. But there's an inn we can stay at for the night. Here in St. Laurent."

He didn't look her in the eye as he said the words, "I have no money. I used it all."

She chuckled, knowing she had to be as normal as possible to bring him back to the David Youngblood who could sizzle the very air around him. "It's my treat."

Wrapping an arm around his spare waist, she brought the other one around to meet it, clasping her fingers together. She looked up into his face. "I never stopped loving you, my lord. I just wanted you to know that. I just wanted to make sure you knew that, so you didn't have to guess."

He nodded, took the first step forward, and they inched their way down the dusty street.

CHAPTER ❖ EIGHT

David, relieved the inn porch didn't collapse beneath them, didn't protest when Camille led him into her dim room. He just let her prattle on like an only child at her birthday party. Her voice soothed him as she bubbled at a rolling boil about everything he had missed, her chatter a patch of sunlight in the gloomy surroundings. He didn't hear much, just scraps of conversation, snippets of "this and thats" held together by the silky thread of her velvety voice. Wonderful to hear, but concentrating on anything but his freedom proved impossible.

"Lie on the bed there, my lord." She guided him to the small mattress dumped on an iron bedstead in the corner. "Sleep if you wish, and I'll find something to eat. You must be starving."

Food, yes. "Meat, please." Something to chew on. Something that didn't fall apart on his tongue after the first good chomp. "Anything but bread and broth."

Camille sat down next to him. She smelled feminine, like wind over flowers, and the cool of her touch refreshed him as she took his hand. Could it really be as she said, that she had never stopped loving him? "Camille." Her name from his lips to her ears was ecstasy. He laid his head in her lap, just what he needed now. Softer, rounder. So nice. Yes, just what he needed.

She slid down the twine that held his ponytail and ran her fingers through his hair. "I've always wanted to do this," she said. "But before, I was afraid to assume."

Please assume.

He opened his eyes and stared up at the soft bosom directly above him, then the pointed chin. She looked down at him, and he realized that all her rough edges had been rubbed away, inside and out. "Don't stop," he said.

"All right."

There *was* an intimacy to her action, he realized. It was more than sex or passion. It was about steady commitment, about expressing the broadest, fullest of loves in the smallest, gentlest of ways. About freedom from time and money and expectations.

After an hour, she said, "It's getting late, my lord. Shall I find us some supper?"

He'd soaked in as much contact as she would allow, he guessed. "All right."

"Would you like a bath first, some coffee or tea, while I'm gone?"

Tea! He'd almost forgotten about tea. He struggled to sit up. "Yes, some tea."

"Still an Englishman to the core." She stood to her feet, smoothing her skirt over her hips. "I'll go round up a pot of hot water. I brought the tea with me, you know. Actually, your sister suggested it when I dropped off—anyway, I'll be right back." She hurried out into the corridor.

David watched her leave the room. Dropped off what? He'd have to ask her later. He plumped the pillows up against the wall and lay down. If he never saw another hammock he'd be a happy man. The feel of a mattress beneath him, however lumpy, comforted him. Nothing like Camille's lap, though.

Her weight gain could mean only one thing. That she had forsaken her old life. Good for her. Good for them both. Not that he had any room to judge. Heavens, no!

Details began to court him once more. For so long he had seen the same familiar surroundings, the same broad leaves and muddy paths, nothing new on which to rest his eyes. He looked around the room. A cold fireplace punctuated an already filthy wall. The windows suffocated under a thick layer of grease. The low, bowed ceiling threatened to relieve him of his consciousness at any moment. The splintered washstand begged to be burned. But the tiny table supported something most precious. *My Bible!*

With quickening joy he made fickle footing on the uneven floor, stumbling as he scooped up the small, worn volume. He needed this more than anything right now. More than tea, more than meat, more than Camille. He opened the cover to find Miranda's elegant handwriting, remembering the day she had given him ownership of the precious book. Below it he read another message, scrawled in spidery, timid writing—with Chinese underneath! He translated the French words.

Today Camille found Savior. 25 March, 1869.

He felt his skin constrict, goosebumps prickling his arms. Camille hadn't changed. Camille had *been* changed. Praise God! He thought of their past, the way he'd desired her body and her beauty. But he'd seen Camille as ambitious, even aggressive at times, and he always wondered about the sincerity of her love, whether it was based on respect and admiration, or diamonds and champagne. Could he have loved her then anyway? Probably not.

And now it appeared they had been elements of a grander design. They had needed to be whittled down and fattened up on their respective pilgrimages to become the people God had created them to be.

He fell to his bony knees and lifted up his hands.

The sun warmed the room as he prayed, and an exhaustion of years overtook him. Feeling a thankfulness so deep it swelled his heart with gladness, he crept back onto the bed, pulled the threadbare blanket around him, and fell into a penetrating, healing sleep.

⌒

"You've been asleep for almost two days. We've missed our boat, and it's almost supper time."

The room came into focus as David opened his eyes. It took him several seconds to remember where he was, to recall his freedom. But she sat there, staring at him intensely with those startling green eyes. "Camille." The sight of her was as refreshing as the sleep. Right now he felt he couldn't get enough of either.

"I've been watching you sleep," she whispered. "I held you in my arms last night, *chéri*. I couldn't sleep myself for disbelief."

"You found me."

"I found so much more in the bargain. I found my heart once again." She knelt by the bed and took his hand. "Oh, my lord, I missed you so."

"I thought of you all the time, Camille. Your memory kept me going."

"Even when your sentence was over and you weren't freed?"

"Well"—he smiled—"I do believe God helped out there as well."

"He helped me too, my lord." She pointed to the Bible, once again lying on the small table. "You saw inside?" she asked, her face now red.

Camille embarrassed? He sat up straight. "Yes."

"And?"

He felt life beginning to speed up once again, and he held out his arms. Camille wound her arms around his waist and burrowed her head into his chest.

David breathed in her scent again. "And I think that we belong together, Camille."

Her voice vibrated against his shirt. "I've always known that, my lord."

He pulled her up to sit beside him, then reached out to touch her white, smooth cheek. "What did you possibly see in me all those years ago, Camille? It's so hard to understand now."

"I saw the man I see before me now. I saw the man you were made to be."

"I'm not what I once was." He sighed. "It's been a long journey. For both of us."

Camille nodded, her eyes dropping. "I'm not the same woman anymore, my lord. There's much you don't know. There's so much to tell you about my journey."

He kissed her cheek. Ah, so right to feel her skin beneath his lips. It calmed him even more. "We have time."

"How about that tea I promised you yesterday?" she asked suddenly, springing to her feet.

"I'd love it."

"I just got a pot of hot water before you awakened. I was feeling thirsty myself."

"No wonder I woke up," he said. "You know me and my tea."

She pulled a sack of rich black Darjeeling from her carpetbag and spooned the leaves into a simple, earthenware pot obviously retrieved from the kitchen downstairs.

He watched in fascination. Just to see a feminine form was like an elixir. Many more cups of tea, many more kisses on his cheeks were coming his way if he had any say in the matter. "Imagine you coming all the way to French Guiana," he said.

She turned, her smile more beautiful than he had remembered. "Imagine me *not* coming!"

"Now that you are here, I can't imagine why I didn't once hope that you would."

Her eyes rounded in horror. "You thought I left you to die here?"

"Considering the way I behaved toward you, is that so unbelievable?"

She shook her head. "No. But two years is a long time to wait to be rescued."

Handing him a teacup, she told him the story of Peter Metery. Not at all surprised, he said when she finished, "I'm glad you didn't sell yourself for that document, Camille."

"You wouldn't have wanted that."

"You're right. Now the old David . . ."

Camille stirred sugar into her own cup of tea. "Those days are behind us, my lord."

David knew truth rested in her words, but he'd lived redeemed for over seven years now, and he knew the past always returned in one way or another, and some matters were too serious to ever be left behind for good.

"You say we missed our boat?"

"Yes. But I've booked passage on another one. It leaves in five days. We'll have to go home by way of New York City." Her eyes danced. "I love New York City!"

"Well, then, Camille. New York City it is. But not for long."

She shook her head. "No, my lord. We both have a lot to come home to."

That night, after hours of quiet conversation and a short walk into town, they lay atop the covers, mosquito netting shielding them from the night buzzings. He should have slept well, but sleep failed to come. Restless, Camille sighed often and smoothed her skirts every few minutes. Back in the old days this situation might have proved too tempting, but not tonight. He was simply happy to be alive and free.

With a full stomach, at that!

"Are you awake?" he asked, out of politeness, not because the answer eluded him. He wanted to talk with her, to fill in the silence of the darkness he had come to dread.

"You know I am," she said. "I'm still not used to all these bugs. Why aren't you sleeping? I'm sure you have years of sleep to catch up on."

He took her hand in his and stared up at the ceiling. "I'm finding I don't wish to sleep. I can't quite get used to the fact that two mornings ago I was sleeping forgotten in my hammock, and tonight, the moon is mine, the air is mine, and you are mine once again."

Her voice held a smile. "All three have always been yours. Even on Devil's Island."

"Hard to believe that there."

"I imagine so."

"So what kept you occupied all of these years?" he asked.

She practically jumped off the bed at his question, then gave a wilted laugh. "Just surviving. You know my way. I traveled quite a bit. As I said I would. Stayed for a year with your sister Adele and awaited your return. Then my plight in Paris began. I told you about that."

"Peter Metery."

"May he rot!" Camille snapped.

David laughed, knowing right then her green eyes glowered in the darkness. "It was a lonely time for me too."

Camille breathed in deeply. "I didn't say I was lonely, did I?" Her voice held an apologetic yet defensive tone. A tentative hesitation.

David felt his stomach tumble. Here it came, the truth of all those years. Unfortunately, he didn't know whether he yet possessed the strength to receive it or not. Some days deserved to be void of harsh realities. He changed the subject instead. "I have a job ahead of me when we get to England."

She breathed a sigh of relief and turned to face him, supporting herself on her elbow. "Is it something we can do together?"

He remembered the perfect face of a dead man. A young man. An innocent man. "There was a man here named Becket Door," he began. "He was unjustly sentenced."

"Was he freed?"

"Yes, in a way. God took him to heaven."

Camille put a hand on his arm. "Let me guess."

Seven years later and she still knew him so well. Only recently back in each other's company and they were starting to feel like a pair of old slippers.

She continued, her voice dropping in a conspiratorial tone. "You're going to clear his name."

"Precisely. You amaze me."

Her laugh rang out and the person in the next room pounded on the thin wall. "Be quiet!"

They clapped their hands over their mouths. And he told her the story of Becket Door. By the time the tale had graduated to old news, Camille was crying. "The poor man," she said, sniffing as she rooted in her pocket for a handkerchief. "But what can we do?"

"The first thing we'll have to do is get married."

She sat up straight. "What?"

David experienced a moment of hesitation, then plunged forward. He hadn't survived the better part of a decade of torture to be shy now. "I'm asking you to marry me. Unless I've become so distasteful, Camille. I know I'm not the virile specimen I once was, but, you *did* say you still loved me down at the dock."

He waited.

Oh, blast!

"Did I make a mistake in asking you that question?" he asked, alarm raising his scalp.

Camille burst into loud, ringing sobs. She threw herself into his arms and covered his face with kisses. "It wasn't a mistake," she blubbered. "It's only that I never thought I would ever hear such words from you addressed to me."

She cried louder and more furiously, a violent maelstrom of emotion revolving again too quickly to remain oriented. It spun them together. He kissed her hair, her cheeks, her forehead, her eyes, and finally her mouth. But she would not be silenced. And he could no longer contain himself.

He began to cry with joy.

"Be quiet, I say!" the man behind the wall yelled again.

But David knew the fellow would be sorely disappointed. These cleansing, wonderful, thrilling tears of happiness, relief, and belonging needed to be spilled. And he refused to make them stop. If Monsieur Contrary over there wished to start something up, so be it!

As prepared as Camille had been for David Youngblood's state when they met at the dock, she was equally prepared for a quick bounce-back. For David Youngblood had always done more than survive. He survived with panache.

They'd talked into the dawning of the day, and by the time the sun had distanced itself completely from the horizon, he'd even regained his drawl. Oh yes, David Youngblood surely knew how to survive. And yet the arrogance had faded somewhat, as

73

if a refining had been achieved from all he'd endured. It hadn't burned away the amusing parts of him, thank God. It hadn't lent him a piety that could have never been convincingly owned by such a man, and it hadn't stained him with a judgmental cast. Simply David remained. Still flawed and malformed, still wont to have his own way, still able to pull her along in the tide of his enthusiasm.

Five days later, they boarded the first available ship, a merchant schooner named *Crimson Skies*. Anything to get away from this place, anything to get home. And yet, the past few days had been tender. Getting to know one another once again. Slow strolls. Simple meals. Holding hands and kissing softly. Chuckling at remembered jokes from long ago.

As they embarked, Camille noticed people muttering behind their hands. She'd quite forgotten the reaction David could cause. And now, he looked even worse! But no mind there. She knew he was smarter, braver, kinder, and more resilient than all of them.

They found their cabin through no help of the crew.

David frowned. "Are you sure there weren't any other berths?" he asked, eyes scanning the tiny chamber furnished with only a bed, a table, and a chair.

"No, my lord. I'm sorry. Frankly, I thought we could make do. With my limited finances . . ."

David's mouth dropped. "You financed all of this yourself?"

She nodded. No one had offered to help, and she hadn't wanted to ask.

He groaned in disgust. "My family! Sometimes I have to wonder about them."

"Oh, no, my lord. I didn't have a chance to see Lord and Lady Youngblood before I left, and Adele . . . well, they're not exactly well-heeled, you know."

"I promise you, I'll repay every penny when I am reinstated as earl."

Camille shook her head. "You know it isn't necessary. It's all Claude Mirreault's money, anyway."

"No one deserved that treasure more than you, Camille. Oh, well," he continued, "I suppose there's only one thing we can do about these sleeping arrangements." He examined the small fold-down bed attached with chains to the wall. It would be very cramped quarters, indeed. A pleasant prospect, but . . . "I'll be back in just a moment. You wait here."

Camille looked around her, and joy so exquisite filled her that she began to cry. *Ciel!* But she seemed to be crying at everything these days. And yet, her happiness could not be contained. She wanted to throw open the porthole window and scream out her feelings. *I love him!* She hugged herself. *I love him, and he loves me!*

CHAPTER ❖ NINE

David and Camille stood on the deck of the soon departing vessel. A consternated captain took a final drag on his cigarette and flicked it overboard, the burning tobacco separating from the remainder of the paper. "All right, then, if you insist! Let's get it over with. Do you, David Youngblood, take this woman, Camille . . . what did you say your last name was?"

"Poulsson," she supplied.

David was stunned to realize he had never heard her last name. "Poulsson?"

She shrugged. "Yes. Not a very pretty one, I'm afraid."

He put his arm around her and pulled her to his side. "Well, you won't need it much longer." He welcomed her sweet kiss.

"I like the name Youngblood so much better."

The captain clapped twice and cleared his throat. "If you don't mind, Romeo and Juliet, I have a ship to sail?"

"Of course." David laughed. What an amusing way to wed, and considering Camille was the bride and he was the groom, it was only fitting. He saw their future as anything but normal or traditional.

"Well?" the captain said. "Do you take him? Although a pretty girl like yourself with this fellow . . . makes me wonder how much money the man has back home!" His smoky laugh grated like the scrape of mismatched gears.

David felt Camille stiffen. *Oh, dear,* he thought, remembering the temper that didn't show itself often but when it did . . . watch your head! "It's all right," he whispered. "Let it be."

She stomped first her left foot, then her right. "No, it isn't all right! For your information, Captain . . . Captain . . . whatever your name is. David Youngblood is the earl of Cannock and doesn't deserve to be insulted this way. And he is the most beautiful man I've ever known."

The captain glared at her. "Look, Miss Pullson, I have a ship to sail. An American ship. You can all check that nobility malarkey at the door. I don't need morality lessons and I don't need to know who's who or what's what. I just want to shove off! Now are you getting married, or aren't you?"

David leaned his mouth down toward her ear. "Let it be, *chérie.*"

Her body relaxed and she melted against him, putting her arms around him. "Oh, David, you've never called me *chérie* before."

He kissed her. "And you've never called me David, *chérie.*"

He kissed her again. Oh, dearest God in heaven above, his heart expanded painfully with love and gratitude. She moaned high and soft against his lips, obviously experiencing the same intoxication, and she pressed her body tightly against his.

The captain threw up his hands in disgust. "I give up! When you're ready to be married, come get me. But don't make it for another few hours until we're well at sea. You Europeans!" And he stomped off.

David pulled his mouth from hers and they laughed and laughed, tight in each other's arms. The sails squealed up the masts, the boat eased from the dock, and they hurried aft. Devil's Island lay behind them now.

Forever.

A strange panic pierced him. But only for a moment.

They sat together and watched the island slowly fade from view, as a nightmare fades with the reality of the progressing day.

"Thank God," he voiced his thoughts as the island finally disappeared.

"Thank God to be sure," Camille said softly, resting her head on his shoulder. "It's over now. And we are finally together."

He took hold of her chin and examined her pale green eyes. "I haven't told you this yet, Camille Poulsson. But it's a fact now. I love you, *chérie*."

For seven years she had haunted him. She overwhelmed his heart, his mind, his soul. She belonged to him. And now, he would keep her by his side forever.

"I love you," he said it again, delighted to hear the words come from his mouth, to feel his lips freely form the most godly statement he'd ever uttered.

Camille cradled his face with either hand and she leaned forward, tenderly kissing his ragged mouth.

"Let's find that captain," David said. He stood to his feet and held out his hand.

Camille placed hers in his and allowed him to pull her along in his urgency. Then he stopped, put his hands on her shoulders, and turned her to face him. "Are you sure you want this, Camille? I'm a tattered, broken man. Making love with me won't be like it was before, you know. I'm not strong like I was. I'm not so bold as I was. I'm just a . . . a scarecrow now, really."

She laughed and patted her hips. "If you can accept me as a little partridge, I can certainly accept you as a scarecrow!" Her eyes turned serious. "David, I've wanted this for years. You couldn't possibly know what I'm feeling right now."

"Tell me."

"I'm feeling as if I've lived in a cave and finally I'm emerging into the light."

"Then I do know how you feel, *chérie*. Take my hand, my love. We'll go there together."

Camille nestled into him, praying that they wouldn't fall off the narrow bunk now that they lay side by side. She giggled softly, relishing in the feel of the naked flesh of his chest beneath her cheek. Skinny and scarred, he was still David, the only man her heart had ever loved. "I'm glad there's no moon tonight."

"As am I," he confessed. "I'm too old for the trysts we used to have, *chérie*."

"It was different tonight, wasn't it? Good different. I wish—"

He cut her off. "It's foolish to wish such things. We've been given a second chance to love the right way."

She liked that. The right way. It made it so clear. "There are many who'd disagree with you on that one," she said.

"Well, they're wrong." His voice filled with strength, and he raised himself up on one elbow. "We've been through both ways now, Camille. And now we know there's a purity in the act itself, a trust, a giving away of the heart. God never meant it to be used for gain."

The sharp pain of regret stabbed at her. "Or sold for profit."

David leaned forward and kissed her cheek. "As I said, it's foolish to wish for a different past when it simply cannot be given to us. We have each other. We understand each other. And for me, that is more than enough." He lay back down on his back and pulled her head back to rest on his upper chest. "To think that you gave up your life and waited for me for seven years. It astounds me."

He deserved the truth. He deserved to know about Lily. In fact, she knew she should have revealed the truth before the captain pronounced them man and wife. But she couldn't find the right opening in their conversation.

Juste ciel! What a wobbly excuse!

How could she justify what she had done? How could she explain that her very betrayal had made her the woman he now needed?

"I have a child now," she blurted out, raising her head up to look into his eyes. "Her name is Lily and she's six years old and she's the daughter of Evariste Lyell!"

"Camille—"

She felt the dirtiness of her past surface as it would many times until the day she died. "I know I betrayed you. I know I said I would wait. But I cannot deny this child to you any longer. I cannot deny that she has defined my life, that she is the most beautiful, the most wonderful thing that ever happened to me. And yet I cannot deny that what I did was something you might not be able to forgive." Camille suppressed the tears gathering behind her eyes. "I should have told you before this. Right away."

David stirred beside her and took her hand in his own. "Camille, please, don't rant so. Just tell me what happened."

The last thing she wanted to do was drag up all that muck. "A week after you left he called me to him. He was so sad, and I was so sad, and we got drunk and—"

"You were drunk? Well, I know how that is, *chérie*."

Kissing the back of his hand, she closed her eyes, bowed her head, and said, "I wish I could claim that excuse to its fullest measure. But I remember the night. I remember that I decided to do it, David. I tried to drown my own sadness, the lost feelings that were haunting me."

He placed two fingertips beneath her chin and gently tilted her face back up. "Open your eyes, *chérie*, look at me. I am your husband."

She obeyed, and when she saw the love, the acceptance in his eyes, her heart thundered inside of her.

"What happened after that?" he asked.

"I never saw him again. Even when I realized I was pregnant. But I tell you, I was relieved . . . *relieved* when I realized I was to have a baby. It was as if my destiny had been decided and the life I had led for so long was undeniably wrenched away from me." She caressed his face. "I would never want to hurt you, David. But I must be honest and say that God used my sin that night to bring me to himself. I needed to be chastened like a naughty child. Can you begin to understand what I have done?"

"It's a little late for that, isn't it?" he drawled. Then laughed. "Oh, Camille. For heaven's sake! Who am I to judge? I'm the lowest of the low, the vilest of the vile! Do I understand how God can use the consequences of our sins to bring us to himself, you ask?" He put his arms around her. "*Chérie*, if anyone understands . . . it is I."

Relief threatened to overwhelm her. "You're not angry I didn't tell you this before we were married?" she asked. "You aren't upset with me?"

David hugged her tightly, his hands finding the small of her back. "I'm only upset because you didn't feel you could tell me right away. You know me better than that, Camille."

He was right. She did. But she'd been so afraid he'd leave her.

"I was many things, *chérie*, back in the old days, but a hypocrite wasn't one of them, and I've never been much of a judge either." He chuckled. "Mainly because no matter how bad I judged someone to be, I was even worse!"

His laughter pulled her into his obvious forgiveness. "We were quite a pair then, *chéri*. Quite a pair!"

"And we still are. We're just a different suit now. From a completely different deck." She spoke as the card player she once was.

"Diamonds then," he said.

"Hearts now," she followed.

"Of which you are the queen," he said, kissing the palm of her hand. "The queen of my heart anyway."

She belonged to him. He belonged to her. "I've waited a lifetime to be loved like this, David. And I know that you have too." Oh dear, crying again!

He brushed away her tears with the pad of his roughened thumb. "You know me well, *chérie*."

The waves rocked them to sleep, and their embrace held strong through the first of many nights.

Book Two

"Why do we make ourselves more strict than Christ. Why, holding obstinately to the opinions of the world, which hardens itself in order that it may be thought strong, do we reject, as it rejects, souls bleeding at wounds by which . . . the evil of their past may be healed, if only a friendly hand is stretched out to lave them and set them in the convalescence of the heart?"

ALEXANDRE DUMAS *FILS, CAMILLE*

Chapter ❖ Ten

Two months later. Blackthorne. Cornwall, England. September, 1869

As moonless as their wedding night had been, the night they arrived at David's home in Cornwall the sky provided them with a clear moon, sailing high, dazzlingly potent. Blackthorne squatted before them, a gothic, brick, hunchbacked manor house that David had never liked as a child. Not that he'd spend much time there. Not like Adele, who called it home.

But somehow, knowing Adele and her brood had resided there for years now, the gargoyles looked less menacing, and the pointed towers less . . . pointy. Ivy, running riot over the structure, glistened with moonlit dew, a waxy, vegetative sheen that moved in the breeze like friendly hands waving hello.

"I can't believe that man wouldn't bring us to the door," Camille said crisply, regarding the coach driver who'd let them out with a "Next time wait until the morning, why don't you?"

They had deserted their baggage down by the wrought iron gate, trusting that no one would steal it. "Can't blame the fellow, *chérie*. Not many people ask for transport in at three o'clock in the morning."

Camille didn't try to hide her annoyance. "Well, you *did* make it worth his while, David."

David didn't know why he was so bent on defending the man. "Yes, but it's not an easy drive from Penzance to Blackthorne."

"So he kept telling us. Seemed easy enough to me."

He decided not to press the matter further. But he found he loved baiting her at times. She looked so attractive with her arched brows knit and her shapely lips pursed. Truth now, the long journey had tired both of them. They had to sojourn a week in New York City before booking passage on a suitable ship. Not all bad, that. He'd supplemented his La Roche wardrobe with two new suits of clothes and some shirts, as well as a decent pair of shoes. Surprisingly, Camille had refused to buy a new dress. If it wasn't made in Paris, it wasn't made for her! He liked that about her too.

David found he liked many things about his new bride that he had never known before. She was the third of four children. Her father, not a farmer as he had always assumed, spent his life running a grist mill. Her mother, having married socially beneath herself, possessed a temper that kept the children playing out in the yard most of the time. And that same mother embroidered garments with such skill the Paris couturiers waited in line. But David appreciated most Camille's natural way with the children aboard ship and the way she rubbed each toe when she took off her shoes at night. That she still had a doll from childhood, a collection of scraps named Fifi, touched him at his core. He loved to watch her brush her wavy hair and pinch her cheeks to pink before she climbed into the bunk with him.

Only twenty-eight years old, she had been but a babe of sixteen when he ushered her into the life of a kept woman. She'd always looked and acted in such a mature manner.

And now, with weeks of marriage behind them, he found certain things got on her nerves. Like now, with this silly driver. He'd never realized how annoyed Camille could become at trivial matters, but he found it adorable and amusing. He'd never seen anyone talk to inanimate objects the way she did. "Oh, you horrible corset!" she'd say when trying to squeeze her waist down an inch or two. Or, "Why did I ever think you would hold up this mop?" to her hair comb.

That heavy "mop" preceded him down the path, and he reached out and touched a soft curl. The woman comforted him merely by being alive.

With heavy feet, they climbed the steps to the front portal. "Shall you or shall I?" he asked, pointing to the bell cord.

Camille touched her index finger to his chest. "You do it. The way I feel I may pull the place down with it."

"All right. Let's get ready to wake up an entire household."

He reached for the weathered cord, curled his fingers above what used to be a silky tassel but looked now more like the head of an unkempt afghan hound, and tugged. Nothing moved at first, and he realized he hadn't yanked hard enough. So, making the most of his body weight, gravity, and both of his hands, he pulled down again.

Camille jumped at the loud gong of a large bell, then the sparkling jingle of many smaller bells, and finally a mid-range tone. They all faded off together. "What kind of a doorbell is that?" she asked, mouth wide open.

David shook his head. "I don't know. But I'm not surprised, considering I've more than my fair share of eccentric predecessors. I'm not sure anyone has used it in years!"

"We always went in around back," Camille admitted.

Two minutes later, the door flew open and there stood Mr. Smythe, wide-eyed with alarm. Adele, her face as round and pale as the moon, scuttled up beside him, candle in hand. "Who's there?" she said at their silhouettes.

"Just an ex-convict and his lady love," David drawled and stepped forward.

"David!" his sister screamed, and rushed at him with the force of a tidal wave, nearly knocking him back to Devil's Island.

"Is home!" Mr. Smythe finished his wife's thought.

A reunion indeed, Adele cried at least half of her weight in tears, and Mr. Smythe drew his lips down toward his chin and sniffed.

Camille whispered to David, "I'm going to find my Lily."

And he nodded, unable as yet to extricate himself from Adele's embrace. He would swear her ligaments had atrophied into this position, and wondered if he would ever be free!

"Oh, David," she wailed, her tears soaking through his shirt. "I thought you were dead. Dead! And then we got your message from New York saying you were alive!" She finally pulled away and blew her nose with a resonant "quank." "I can't believe you're here. Camille said she would find you, but I didn't believe her. I thought it was an empty hope, I'm loath to say. I just can't believe you're here at Blackthorne."

"In the flesh." Mr. Smythe sniffed again.

David couldn't believe it either. As younger siblings they had been separated for the most part, but Adele had always written him letters, sent cards and pictures she'd drawn. She had always wished she had been strong enough to buck her parents' decisions and demand to be with her brother.

"May I come in, then?" he asked with a laugh.

Mr. Smythe, whom David had always liked although never quite understood, sprang into action as Adele, yanking off her nightcap, pulled her brother inside. The children all sat upon the great staircase, eyes round and curious.

"Children! Children!" Adele yelled happily, tying her red robe around her puffy middle. She reminded David of a female ghost of Christmas past, pale and rotund in the dim light, exuding happiness and warmth. "Come, come welcome your Uncle David home."

"To Blackthorne," Mr. Smythe said, his eyes still brimming with tears.

David found himself in the middle of a huddle of dark-headed children, little hands and bigger ones patting him in various places on his back and legs. Adele began crying all over again.

Good heavens, David thought. For years he'd never shed a tear, had surrounded himself with people who cried at nothing. *And now I'm stuck with a bunch of weepers.*

God bless every single one of them!

Camille, oblivious to the ruckus going on downstairs, hugged Lily tightly to her. She had scooped her up at the top of the stairs and had gone right to the room they had shared over a year before. Still warm from her covers, the child smelled of a recent bath and the bluing from the sheets. Her blond curls, soaking up her mother's tears, brushed against Camille's chin.

Lily bounced with delight, and when Camille let her go, she sprang to her feet, hopping around. "You're home, *Maman*! You're home!"

For someone to whom love had once been a simple transaction, this flood of feeling was overwhelming. "I told you I'd be back soon!" she cried, standing to her feet again and grasping Lily's hands.

"Soon! You were gone for four months!" the child scolded. "I missed you so, *Maman*."

"But Aunt Adele took good care of you, didn't she?" Camille asked, hopping in time with the child from foot to foot.

"Yes, and Mr. Smythe taught me to read perfectly well now!"

"He did?"

"Yes. And I'll tell you another thing. Five plus five equals ten!"

Camille clapped her hands. "Wonderful! So I see you've come along just fine without poor old me."

Lily turned serious and stopped her dancing. "*Maman*, don't say such silly things." She brightened again. "Is that the man you were looking for?"

"Yes. That's him downstairs right now with the rest of the family."

Lily crossed her arms and leaned forward. She smiled up at her mother, mouth closed, head dipped. "Can I see him?"

"Of course you can! But I have to tell you something first, Lily. Something quite serious and very important."

Lily took her mother's hand. "Well, then, I suppose we should sit down on the bed," she said soberly.

Camille let out a laugh. "Oh, Lily. I can't believe I'm back here with you. And in our room too!"

She looked around her at the room they had shared. Dusty blue curtains drawn aside at both windows let in the moonlight. The faded blue counterpane was pushed down in a tiny U at the top where Lily had escaped the covers when the bells had rung, the imprint of her small body still visible. The open wardrobe displayed a disorganized mess, shoes and dirty laundry jumbled on the bottom, but she could see two clean dresses hanging from the rod within.

"You've been happy here?" she asked her daughter.

"Oh, yes. We've taken lots of walks, learned lots of things. And Aunt Adele makes everything such fun. Even the chores!"

"Chores?"

Lily giggled. "Oh, *Maman*. Surely you didn't think I'd not have to help out?"

Camille had always hoped her daughter would be raised more gently than she had been raised herself. But obviously, the chores had done her some good. Pink with health, she had even gained a little weight. Not a surprise in the Smythe household! "What did you do?"

"I helped pick the cucumbers and lettuces, and I darned the socks."

"Indoor and outdoor work, I see."

"Yes."

"And which did you like the best?"

Lily thought for a moment. "Outdoors, because I always thought that maybe you were outdoors that very moment and we were sharing the same big room!"

Camille held out her arms. "Oh, come here, you imp, and give your mother another hug."

Lily eagerly complied, then pulled back and sat down beside her mother on the bed. "So what is the 'sitting-down' problem?"

"The man I went to find—"

"David Youngblood."

"Yes, him. Well"—she fought for an easy way to say it and found none—"I've always loved him, so I married him on board the ship home."

Lily shook her head. "But I knew that already!"

"What? How?"

"Aunt Adele said to Mr. Smythe"—her voice took on Adele's tone—"'Mark my words, Mr. Smythe, if my brother's alive, he will bring Camille home with a ring on her finger. I just have a feeling about it.'"

Camille laughed.

Lily continued. "And Aunt Adele wouldn't lie."

"No, my dear, she certainly wouldn't."

Lily hesitated. "I heard the older children talking about him. They say he's . . . ugly, *Maman*. Is this true? I couldn't much see him downstairs."

Camille's heart broke, like it did countless times when she'd heard such criticism of her beloved's face. "It depends on what your definition of ugly is. *I* think he's rather beautiful. His eyes are just like his sister's, but his hair is the loveliest shade of red you've ever seen. Well, it used to be anyway. There's a lot of white in there now."

"But they told me his mouth—"

"Is deformed. Rather like a rabbit's mouth." Maybe the child wouldn't be so put off if she thought of it like that.

A long shadow fell across the floor from the doorway. "Talking about me, I see?" David said.

Both Camille and Lily jumped. "I'm sorry, David," Camille explained, hoping he wouldn't be angry. "Some of your nieces and nephews were—"

"Don't say another word. Let me explain it myself." He walked into the room and leaned down on his haunches in front of Lily. "First of all, I want to introduce myself. I am David Youngblood."

"My new father," Lily said.

He took her small hand in his own and sat down next to her on the bed. "Yes, that's right. If it's all right with you."

Lily giggled. "He's as silly as you are, *Maman*!"

"I was born just as you see me, with this very mouth. It isn't very pretty, I know. But it doesn't hurt, and I stopped letting it get me into trouble years ago. You can stare at it all you like and even touch it if you want to. And then, we'll just go on from there once you're used to it."

Lily looked up at Camille, who nodded. David had certainly chosen the right tack with this curious little one. "May I, *Maman*?"

"Of course, Lily." She reached up her own hand and touched her husband's mouth with her index finger. "See? To me this is most precious, because it is a part of him."

"And you love everything about him. That's what true love is, I think. That's what Mr. Smythe says when Aunt Adele says maybe she should stop eating dessert." She put her other hand on her mother's thigh. "This is the man you used to cry about in our bed at night, isn't it?"

Camille never knew Lily had heard those sad moments when she'd succumbed to her loneliness. "Yes." She felt David's simple touch on her back and their eyes met above Lily's head.

Lily reached up and touched the exact spot on David's mouth her mother had touched. "You've pretty eyes, my lord," she said.

He laughed. "So I've been told. I stopped looking into mirrors years ago."

With a shrug and a smile, she put her hand up to her mouth. "I've never liked them much myself. I'm too short mostly, for one thing."

David smiled at Camille. "She's charming, *chérie*. You've done a wonderful job with her so far."

"*Merci*," Camille said.

David pulled the two of them into his arms and yanked them back on the bed, where they toppled over into a heap. "I've waited my entire life for this moment," he whispered in Camille's ear.

"So have I, David."

"So have I!" Lily chimed, displaying her acute sense of hearing.

"We'd better watch what we say around that one," David laughed, hugging them tightly as the moon disappeared from view and the new day began. "She's got quite a set of ears on her!"

Much later in the day the children busied themselves with croquet. Well, some form of croquet, anyway. They used no wickets, for they had been bent into all sorts of other strange contraptions, or used years ago to jerry-rig doors and lock windows. They dug several holes in the weed-stricken lawn and proceeded to play a sort-of golf, only there were obstacles between the tee-off and the holes.

Six children in all shouted and laughed and vied to be first, but they finally decided that Lily, as the youngest, would start them off.

David watched as he sat on a wicker chair and drank a good strong cup of tea.

He missed his Elspeth. Bethie. Already he had sent a messenger to London to notify his uncle Tobin and Miranda, his wife, of his return and soon arrival to the town house. They were taking the earliest train out of Penzance in the morning.

Adele emerged from the house with a tray of scones and jam. "Cucumber sandwiches coming out shortly! Very shortly!" she called. They'd eaten breakfast only two hours before, but the old cook at Blackthorne was so happy to have someone "distinguished like his lordship" to cook for, that the kitchen fire in the stove was not predicted to die down anytime soon. Good news, that. He had much catching up to do. Camille, on the other hand, tried her best to resist temptation by refereeing the game.

Not Adele! She opened up a scone and slathered two large spoonfuls of jam. "So here you are, back in England. Safe and sound. Fortune must have been watching over you, little brother."

"As she always does," Mr. Smythe said, standing nearby, hand around his walking stick.

David prepared his own plate. "Fortune had nothing to do with it. Only God can keep a man alive on Devil's Island, Adele."

"Oh, I think we can all use our share of good luck," she said with a wink. "Don't you?"

From what he remembered, Adele had her own peculiar brand of religion. Mr. Smythe bore a fascination with the thoughts of fairies and gnomes, and they both had a rather childish view of spirituality, hoping against hope that "magic" really did exist in the cosmos and touched them regularly.

He watched Camille with pride as she turned around to face them, threw up her hands, and cried, "*Zut alors!* I have no idea what this game is even about!" She tromped back up to his seat. He pulled her onto his lap, kissed her neck, and handed her half of his scone.

"You're no help at all, David Youngblood," she said, taking a bite.

He leaned into her and nuzzled at her neck, breathing in her scent. "I rather like you like this, *chérie*. There's more of you to love."

Adele snorted. "Heaven help us! If you need me to watch Lily for an hour or so whilst you go to the newlywed's ball, I'll be glad to do it. Glad to."

"Help in any way we can," Mr. Smythe said.

David and Camille laughed. "I think we can at least wait until after dinner," he said, picking up Camille's hand and kissing the thin gold band he'd bought in New York at Tiffany's.

Adele noticed the sweet gesture. "Now you need to give her a proper ring, Cookie. With lots of diamonds. Lots."

David winced, and Camille let out a hoot. "I'm sure if your brother never sees another diamond for the rest of his life, he'd be a happy man!"

CHAPTER ❖ ELEVEN

"Papa!" Elspeth screamed David's name as the open carriage pulled up to the town house on Grosvenor Square. Flinging open the door, he stumbled out of the vehicle and met her halfway up the lofty expanse of marble steps.

"Bethie!" he returned the greeting, sweeping her petite form up into his arms and holding her against him like a baby, though her eighteenth birthday had come and gone. She felt so solid, such a part of him. And she had changed so drastically. The deformation they shared was still evident, painfully so. But she'd piled her thick brown hair upon her head most dramatically, and eyes once childish and round had elongated and deepened. And those thick lashes. By heavens, they rivaled even Camille's!

So Tobin and Miranda had taken good care of her, for she appeared healthy and well-dressed in an afternoon gown of pale buttercup.

He set her down, the gesture too much of a strain on his back. What had he been thinking?

More tears all around. As expected. Weeping sentiments and "I missed yous" whispered between them as she clung to him commanding him to never leave her like that again. "I won't,

Bethie," he promised, each word as true as mortal man could ever make it.

At the top of the steps Miranda and Tobin greeted him with loud cries. The interim Lord and Lady Youngblood. If he had not bounced back so quickly from his stint in captivity, surely all the love and warmth that had rained upon him since his arrival in England would have done the job.

"Tobin!" he cried, pulling his uncle, only seven years older than himself and as rumpled as usual, into a great hug. Then, "Miranda!" Just the same as he remembered, only clothed in finer garb, Miranda had grown radiant under the light of her husband's devoted love. The port-wine stain still eclipsed half of her face, proving once again that this new generation of Youngbloods welcomed anyone accepting enough to have them.

"David!" Miranda cried. She hugged him to her, though her belly, rounded with child, clearly impeded the blatant display of fondness they had always borne one another.

Lily, out of the carriage now and tugging on his coat, said, "Can anybody say anything else but names around here?"

They all laughed.

"Come into the house," Miranda invited. "We've held supper for you until later."

Camille! David remembered. He had left her in the carriage. She sat there quietly waiting, and he hurried back down the steps. "Forgive me, *chérie*."

"There's nothing to forgive. I've just never been much good at jumping down from carriages."

He reached in and helped her alight. Miranda appeared, wisps of blond hair blowing about her face. "How wonderful to see you again, Camille. And how wonderful that you're part of the family now. Welcome to this crazy clan of the Youngbloods."

Camille smiled. "Thank you. And how is your brother? David talked so fondly of him on the way back from French Guiana."

Miranda slid an arm through Camille's. "Matthew's still preaching up a storm at the same little church in Scotland."

"And Sylvie?" Camille asked, looking at David to see his reaction at the mention of the woman he had literally killed for, but who had never returned his love in the same fashion.

David didn't flinch, but he caught Miranda's knowing glance in his direction. He took his wife's hand.

Miranda, always the peacemaker, answered simply. "She's doing well. Keeping busy with Eve and the twins."

David wanted to ask about these twins, for Sylvie had been expecting when he was exiled, but knew better than to say a word. He led his wife up the steps, thinking her by far more graceful than Sylvie had ever been and not at all naïve. For some reason he found that endearing, yet at the same time something solid to which he could cling. As if the grace that saved her had been far deeper than the grace that pulled those of pure lives into the bosom of a shining eternity. They shared that kind of grace. They shared the beauty of an utterly foul life turned fair.

Miranda, in her chatting mode, pulled David from his thoughts. "As far as I'm concerned," she was saying to Camille, "the more Youngbloods the better. This family could use a little diluting."

David howled with laughter. "That's an understatement if I've ever heard one, Mira. We need a complete gutting and redecorating."

Elspeth rolled her eyes.

"Speak for yourself." Tobin bowed to Camille as they entered the airy town house. He took her hand and kissed the back. "It's lovely to see you again, my dear."

Camille dropped a small curtsey. "As it is to see you, my lord."

David felt proud of his wife in that instant. True, she seemed a bit reserved, a bit shyer than usual, and later he would find out why. But for now she rose to the occasion with aplomb. He placed a possessive hand at the small of her back, and she seemed to relax. "*Chérie*, I'd like you to meet my daughter, Elspeth."

Elspeth stuck out her hand, a stiff flipper extended toward Camille. "I can't tell you what a surprise it was to get the news that my father had already married."

Camille took her hand. "It's lovely to meet you, Elspeth."

Elspeth gave it a single, hard shake, and let go. "Well, nothing personal, Camille, but I thought that finally I'd have Daddy to myself."

David turned to his daughter, surprised at her forthrightness. "Oh, Bethie, there's plenty of me to go around."

Elspeth stuck her hand through her father's arm and pulled him through the door. "I should say so," she said, throwing her voice over her shoulder. "You must have married the girl for you then, Daddy. At least from what I've heard. She must feel like the lucky lady."

David tried to see the expression on his wife's face, but Elspeth dragged him toward the library where he supposed that long ago discarded copy of *Tom Jones* awaited them.

"I'll catch up with Miranda, *chéri*!" Camille called after them. "Come, Lily!"

"Finally," Elspeth said. "I thought I'd never get rid of her."

"Now, Elspeth." He should have reprimanded her further. But how could he? He'd deserted her many years ago, and she had every right to be angry. Unfortunately, she wasn't directing her anger where it belonged.

They read together. He put his arm around her, and she laid her head on his shoulder, emitting sigh after sigh of happiness. Finally, after an hour, Miranda came in. "Supper will be ruined if we hold off any longer, you two. It's time to wash up."

Elspeth leaned forward and kissed her father. "I'll meet you in the dining room."

"Save me a seat next to you!" he said, patting her knee and rising to his feet.

After washing up in his room, he meandered down to the dining room. The fresh smell of the flowers mixed with the aromas wafting up from the kitchen made David realize a hollow hunger. He'd gained some weight since leaving the island, but still had far to go. Unfortunately, no matter how much he consumed, he knew he would never return to being the man of fine form he once had been.

The meal was eaten to the accompaniment of all the stories he and Camille had related to the Smythes. Mouths opened in horror at some points, smiled with laughter at others, and more than once tears brought on grave silences. And then Lily started to chitchat. One thing he had learned about the child in the past few days, she couldn't abide extended silences.

Tobin finished eating first. He ran a hand through his wild, auburn hair, the same hair David used to possess, and wiped his mouth. "That was a fabulous dinner," he said, always one to enjoy the taste of good food.

"I hope you didn't get too comfortable, Tobin," David drawled. "You'll be out on the street now that I'm home."

Tobin laughed. "Gladly, I hand it all back to you. The operas have done well enough. A few months ago, Miranda and I began plans on a house in the village of Broadway. A lovely spot. It should be ready by November."

"You may stay with me as long as you wish, you know that, Tobin."

Tobin held up a hand. "Oh, no! Miranda and I are looking forward to the country life. We inhabited Greywalls quite regularly, you know, and are planning to go back there until the house is finished. With our brood it will be much too crowded here."

Miranda rolled her eyes. "We're just simple country people at heart, David."

Tobin agreed. "My music flows from me with ease there, and Miranda feels the same way with her librettos, don't you, my dear?" He turned to his wife and laid a hand over hers. David thought it such a good idea he did the same with Camille, still awfully quiet.

"Yes," she answered. "Bethie liked it there too, didn't you?"

Elspeth shrugged. "I suppose. Although with Angus always hanging about, it could get annoying at times. But London is fascinating for me now." She turned to her father in excitement. "So we'll be staying here?" With her tone so eager, David knew better than to refuse her request.

He took his hand off of Camille's arm and placed it on Elspeth's. "Yes. Camille and I have much to do in London. In fact, our work is very much cut out for us."

Tobin sat forward. "Going to take your fisticuffs to 'the Lords'? Good for you, I say."

David nodded, leaned back into his chair, and got comfortable. "Yes. There's much I have to get done. I've been given my life back and refuse to waste it as I did the first half."

"Not many people are turned completely around the way you were, David," Tobin agreed.

David could have gone on all day about God's grace, but he wanted to get to the matter at hand. The time had come for his new mission to begin. "Tell me, Tobin, what do you know of Becket Door?"

Tobin raised his eyebrows. "The murderer?"

David didn't want to go into it all just then, so he asked, "Has he been at all exonerated over the years?"

"No." Tobin shook his head. "Not as far as I've heard. His brother Cyprian made a brilliant political career after that mess."

That didn't surprise him. "A phoenix out of the ashes, eh?"

"Precisely."

"And what of Lady Charlotte, Becket Door's wife?" he asked. He set his knife down and pushed back his plate.

Tobin eyed David knowingly. "She married Cyprian years ago. A year after his brother was exiled."

Camille gasped and David turned to her, shaking his head almost imperceptibly. He began to plan as the servants set dessert before them. But the apple charlotte suddenly held little interest. "We have to make our way back into society, and the sooner the better."

Tobin stuck a fork in his dessert. "The *Times* will love it. It will be front page. 'David Youngblood reappears after a seven-year disappearance—beautiful wife in tow! And naturally, the man has something up his sleeve.'"

David picked up his own fork and spun it by its handle between his index finger and thumb. "Do you know this Cyprian Door?"

Tobin shook his head. "He's a very powerful man now. Good friends with the Prince of Wales."

"I see."

"A good political ally for you, perhaps? Or is there more?"

"Perhaps. But I'm not saying a word yet."

"Well, all the best in the Lords, then. It's your funeral, David. Like going into the lions' den."

An apt description. "Every day is my funeral, Tobin. I just have to decide whether I want to mourn it, or make the most of it."

Miranda reached around Tobin and patted David's hand. "If anyone can do it, David Youngblood, it is you."

Camille suddenly wiped her mouth and stood to her feet. She looked pale and strained. "If you'll excuse me, the journey has taken quite a bit out of me. Would you all be offended if I took a little rest?"

David jumped to his feet. "I'll go with you, *chérie*. Forgive me for being so callous to your needs." Blast it, but he enjoyed this attentive husband role. True concern for his wife was such a new thing and so many men complained about it, but he found it ultimately gratifying.

"It isn't you, David," she said, turning to go. And as she walked away, only David heard her say, "It's me."

CHAPTER ✦ TWELVE

The truth? Camille not only felt shy and subdued and tired and overwhelmed, she felt miserable. As they had ridden up to the town house, this grand, beautiful home, as lovely as any dwelling in Paris, the horrible reality had trounced upon her. She was Lady Camille Youngblood, countess of Cannock.

For the past two months it had all been future tense, unreal and far away. Miranda Youngblood was the countess of Cannock, and she, Camille, was not. Simple.

Zut alors! A courtesan comes to town. And a famed one at that. What had she been thinking? Was she supposed to just walk into British society, head held high, extend a hand, and say, "Oh yes, I'm the new Lady Youngblood, and most likely I've slept with your husband or at the very least a friend of his!"

Even Elspeth knew better. The young lady's attitude pained Camille, but who could blame her?

She hated her own husband just then—a fleeting hate for what he had done to her all of those years ago, introducing her to other libertines just like himself who had come across the water, escaping their straightjacket of a country for a fortnight of folly and debauchery in the City of Lights, presenting her at parties like some painted pony, some exclusive, delectable confection.

The *truth*? She could have gone back home to her father's mill, but she didn't. She chose her life, and she chose it willingly. She had no abusive family to blame for her sinful past, no set of dire circumstances that seemingly forced her to make immoral choices. The *truth*? She wanted the money, the jewels, the fame, the men who raved over her beauty, sought to possess her, though for but a while, with their precious gifts. The *truth* was, she had no one to blame but herself. Not David. Not her mother or her father. Just Camille Poulsson.

It was the loneliest moment of her life.

Lady Youngblood!

How can I do it? she asked herself, wondering why she had ever thought she could pull this one off.

"Oh, God," she prayed, "let him come to me now. I need him to show me the way. I need him to show me what to do."

At length she slept. And when she awakened, she found herself curled up with her husband.

The fronts of his knees touched the backs of hers, and his arm draped over her tummy. He slept deeply, and the breeze from the open window jostled his silvery red curls. She turned in his arms to face him and he moved, mumbled, then settled back down.

"I could never hate you for long," she whispered, reaching out and laying a hand on the curve of his neck. "I love you so."

He slept on and she watched him, watched *over* him, she felt. Perhaps he needed her on some level or other. Perhaps things weren't as they really seemed to be when examined front-faced. Perhaps he had been given to her by God for safekeeping and not the other way around.

She pressed her body to his and kissed his jagged mouth. He stirred, breathed in deeply, and opened one eye. "Yes, my lady?" he asked, voice raspy and sleepy and warm.

Camille chuckled. "I couldn't resist."

"I'm glad about that."

"Did you sleep well?" she asked, noticing that the sunlight reaching through the window had turned to gold and that the shadows cast by the bedposts stretched long and distorted. "Have you been up here long?"

"Half an hour, or thereabouts. After reading with Elspeth, I suggested a nap after the trip. In fact, she said she'd take Lily over to St. James's Park."

"I'm sure Lily will love that."

"I'm sure she will, the way she was hopping from one foot to the other." He reached out and laid a warm hand on the curve of her hip. "That's a lovely dress, Mrs. Youngblood, but seeing as we have some time together . . . just us . . . I was wondering if I might refresh myself on what's underneath it."

Camille looked into his eyes and saw the desire flash over his gray irises like St. Elmo's fire. But it wasn't like before, for love had laid a true foundation. "Well, then, my lord, why don't you do something about it?"

To her delight he did, taking his time as David always did, his loving an art. A slow, languorous art. Sweet kisses deepening to passion. Tender caresses becoming smooth and purposeful. She succumbed to the delight of being with him, the joy of knowing that from the moment on board ship when they had been pronounced man and wife, this act they had shared many times before was made sacred. The beauty of God's imagination was now theirs to enjoy to its fullest.

By the time their sweat had cooled, an evening storm covered the setting sun, watering the gardens of London and beyond. Camille blew a soft sigh and turned her face into David's chest. Planting a small kiss, she tasted the salt of his skin.

"What has you concerned, *chérie*?" he asked. "You've been so quiet since we arrived. Is it Elspeth?"

"Not really. Her reaction was exactly what I expected."

"What then?"

She didn't want to confide in him, but as he was the only friend she had, she did, pressing down the tears and speaking as though relating a purchase at the market. As she spoke she arose from the bed and stepped into her clothing. When she finished, setting her doubts and fears on display, he patted the mattress next to him.

"Sit," he commanded, taking her hand. "I don't blame you for being overwhelmed, Camille. In fact I completely understand."

"How could you, David? These are your people we're about to descend on."

He shook his head and rubbed the back of her hand with his thumb. "They're not my people, Camille, and you know it. They've always despised me and you know that too."

"Aren't you afraid they won't accept us?"

His laugh possessed a bite. "That's the last thing you should worry about, *chérie*. I'm richer than a man ought to be, and my family lineage goes back to some Norman noble long since dead. It doesn't matter to these people whether or not you're a monster, as long as you have the right credentials."

"That's a shame, if you really think about it."

"On a larger scale, yes. But we, my dear, will shamelessly use it to our advantage."

Not enough. "But what about me? Your friends will recognize me, and it will be spread all over London that David Youngblood married a whore."

"They'd better not say such to me!" he said, eyes lighting up with battle fire. "If they know what's good for them, anyway."

Camille felt weary. "David, you can't fight everyone's wars. Not mine, surely. And perhaps not even Becket Door's."

He stiffened. "Is that what this is really all about? I promised him, Camille."

"I know," she whispered. "I'm sorry."

"Like it or not, it's the course set before me, *chérie*. And you can help me with it, or not. I leave that choice totally up to you. But it's something I have to do."

Camille knew no true choice existed. She would be by his side. "Then I will have to do it with you, I suppose."

"Those pesky wedding vows!" He smiled and sat up.

"But David, I don't want to live a flashy life. I want to help you, but first I am Lily's mother. She doesn't deserve to be raised inside a scandal."

He kissed her. "I'll gladly accept your help no matter the form. But now the bigger question is, where are my pants?"

She bent down and saw a pant leg flowing from beneath the bed. She whipped out the garment and threw it at him. "Life with you won't be boring, will it?"

His saucy grin filled his eyes with humor. "Not even for one bit, *chérie*."

"Not ever?"

"Not ever."

"Maybe one hour a week? For sanity's sake?" she begged, remembering the lovely days of Lily's childhood.

"Camille, you really are a delightful woman."

Delightful or not, the future still concerned her. "What if they don't accept you, David? What will you do then?"

"Oh, they'll accept me, *chérie*. They're too polite not to. Don't forget, you're in England now. It's not like Paris. No one likes to make a scene over here." He pointed to his shirt at the foot of the bed.

She handed it to him. "But won't we be seen as eccentric?"

He shoved his arms into the sleeves. "I've always been seen as eccentric."

"Now that's something I can easily believe!"

Lily burst through the door and declared that the cook had just pulled a cake out of the oven and there was a big piece for everyone.

Juste ciel!

CHAPTER ✦ THIRTEEN

Absolutely not!" Camille stomped her foot, the veil of her elegant green hat flapping behind her in the stiff breeze. She felt ridiculous standing out there on the street, everything blowing about like flags, her skirts pasted against her thighs. The English and their exercise. The English and their fresh air. *Zut alors!*

A beautiful dappled mare clopped around from the stable at the back of the house. Pretty enough to be sure, her deep brown eyes, so satiny and gentle, took Camille's breath away. But she was still a horse. "I've never been on one of those things, and I'm not about to start now."

David's mouth dropped open. "Never ridden a horse? I can't believe it."

"Well, you'd best start trying. I'm not getting on that thing. I don't even have a riding habit!" *Please God*, she prayed, *let that be enough*.

He patted the horse's flank. "Oh, come now, *chérie*, Peach is a darling little creature. Gentle and easy to ride. She won't throw you. I can promise you that."

Miranda, looking fetching in a riding habit the color of newly ripened lemons, stepped forward. "You could ride Mister Socks. He's Tobin's and my favorite."

Mister Socks? What kind of comfort was that supposed to be? Camille searched in vain for some support somewhere. Perhaps a bit of common sense might serve her purpose better. "Do you honestly want my first ride ever to be in St. James's Park on our debut day?"

David looked at Miranda, who nodded her head. "She's absolutely right, David. And besides, she would look so lovely in the black phaeton. I'll drive, and I'm sure Lily will be glad to go along, which would look awfully sweet and domestic. I'll go get her."

"I'm glad somebody can see some sense around here," Camille grumbled. "Mister Socks, indeed! *Ciel!*"

By the stance of his eyebrows, David still wasn't happy, but he conceded with, "All right, but only if I can ride alongside."

Camille waved a graceful, white gloved hand. "You'll get no argument from me. And perhaps Elspeth will want to come along in the carriage." Perhaps she could make friends with the girl.

"Oh, no. Not enough room," David said. "There's only one seat, and Miranda will have to drive from that. You can sit on one side of her and Lily on the other."

Camille couldn't help but admire Miranda. "Imagine! A woman driving a phaeton through St. James's Park! Perhaps I might learn to do something daring like that someday."

"As if traveling alone to South America fails to fit that description," David drawled. He slapped the middle of his riding crop into the palm of his hand. "Elspeth is riding along with me, anyway. She told me last night that she's come to love riding over the years. In fact"—he leaned forward—"Tobin told me she's quite the expert horsewoman. She was the best at Harrowgate." He referred to the boarding school near Oxford that Elspeth had attended the past three years.

"Sounds like she was the best at almost everything there," Camille observed, thinking of the conversation the night before when Tobin and Miranda gushed over her successes while Elspeth blushed and said, "I wish the fuss would die down so Daddy and I could get back to *Tom Jones*."

At that David had taken her in his arms and squeezed her tightly. Before the night of the murders at Greywalls, over eight years ago, they had been reading *Tom Jones* together, he explained later to Camille.

"I waited seven years to see what's happened to the rascal," Elspeth said.

"You did?" David's brows raised. "You really waited for me?"

That, of course, stabbed a knife into Camille's heart, but she knew the remark had not been slipped in to wound her. Still . . .

And now this morning Elspeth came hurrying down the steps in a plum-colored habit, a top hat with a black ribbon crushed down upon her brow. "I'm ready! Hoooo!" she blew. "I was trying not to be late, but for some reason I couldn't get my boots fastened. I guess I was too nervous."

Miranda smiled gently at her niece as she emerged with Lily. "Too nervous? Whatever for?"

She rolled her eyes. "It would take all day to tell you that! Oh, good, here comes the phaeton." She lifted Lily up into it as it came to a stop, much to the child's delight. "Camille, you're riding in there, aren't you?"

David laughed. "For some reason, Bethie, you sounded just like Mrs. Wooten! What's happened to my sweet old housekeeper? Still up at Greywalls?"

"You couldn't pry her away from the place," Miranda said.

"I'm going to do exactly that," David said. "I want the Wootens with us wherever we are."

Miranda nodded. "I can certainly understand that. I'll send them a message right away. But the fact that she'll know you're safe and that you'll be waiting at the other end of their journey south will certainly help."

She climbed in with a bit of difficulty and David's help, settled her skirts, took the reins, and beckoned to the others. "Come on! I promise I won't get into an accident. You'll be quite safe."

"It's a lovely vehicle," Camille said.

Miranda waved a hand. "Tobin had it shipped over from Boston. He can be very odd."

"Well, wherever it was made, I'm proud to be seen in it." Camille allowed David to help her up the step to the carriage. As she leaned in he patted her bottom. She turned and he smiled, his eyes mischievous and hopeful. Into his ear she murmured, "You're insatiable, my lord."

"So I've been told," he said softly. "And you are irresistible."

She raised her eyebrows. "So I've been told."

"Off we go, then!" he called as a groom helped Elspeth onto her mount. "Everybody ready?"

"As ready as I'll ever be," Camille said, grabbing onto the side of the carriage as though it was careening over a waterfall.

"I must say"—David looked over the decidedly female group before the horses set out down the street—"I'm completely outnumbered here and utterly delighted to be so."

Miranda laughed. "It makes complete sense, if you think about it. David Youngblood emerges once again, surrounded by women!"

Everyone joined in on the joke, including Camille. Hoping this new life, this new David, didn't prove too good to last.

The group moved forward, Elspeth claiming her father's attention immediately.

⁓

David tipped his hat and tipped his hat and tipped his hat some more. He couldn't remember the last time he had this much fun.

Oh, shock had drawn fabulous expressions on their faces! Wonderful! If he could have made a Daguerreotype of these images for future perusal, he would have loved nothing more. Some couldn't even collect themselves to nod as they passed. They gaped. They gasped. They dropped their jaws, dropped their reins, and one elderly man whom David failed to recognize even dropped his false teeth. Magnificent!

"David Youngblood? Was that really David Youngblood?" he heard the duchess of Angley say to her mother as he passed their carriage.

"Who else has a face like that?" the old woman, obviously hard of hearing, shrieked in reply.

And certainly the conversation went on from there, but, too much in his glory, too busy frightening the rest of the crowd, he failed to overhear. Oh, such fun. He turned around and winked at Camille. Poor dear. With that strained, tight face she exhibited, he doubted whether *anybody* would even recognize her.

Gerald Raines, the viscount of March, a man David had schooled with at Eton, passed by, examining him incredulously. "Perhaps it's not David Youngblood?" March said to a pretty redhead riding beside him. "He was never a happy fellow, and not nearly that skinny."

"It is I, Gerald!" he called over. "Back from the dead."

March shook himself and politely tipped his hat. "Welcome back from wherever it was you were, David."

"Thank you," he answered, and they passed completely. Ever as before. The two knew each other, but only in passing. He had always liked March, but always from afar.

David lagged behind, now riding beside Camille's spot in the carriage. "See, *chérie*?"

"They *are* polite," she agreed.

"Too polite," he said, then clicked his tongue against his teeth and trotted up next to Elspeth. "Hello, my dear."

"Oh, Daddy. You really are still a dashing sort, aren't you? I'm glad you're still so *bon vivant*."

"Some things never change." He decided to ignore the crowd for a while. A little bit of demureness might do some good for a spell. He had to keep them guessing, an utter necessity, he had decided as he lay sleepless in bed the night before. "So, you enjoyed your school, Aunt Miranda tells me." Miranda chatted next to Camille, discussing the sorts of things women discuss, he guessed. Probably their hair.

Elspeth rolled her eyes. "She's been so proud of me. Just like a mother, you know."

"And Uncle Tobin?" He had always worried about that. Tobin, an artistic type, might have thought Elspeth novel for a while, but having to look at her for years ... well, he hadn't honestly known if the man could rise to such an occasion.

Elspeth smiled. "You needn't have worried, Daddy. He's been lovely. He's taught me to play the pianoforte and even wrote a song for me. Quite a lovely song. Scottish and lonely. You know the sort. Makes you think of pipes and haggis and skinny little women mourning skinny little half-starved corpses on the field of Culloden." Her dry tone tickled him.

David gave her a warm pat. It appeared she had inherited more than his mouth! "So you were happy?"

She nodded. "I still am. Only more so now that you are home."

"That's good, child."

He realized just then that she had lost her Highland way of speaking. How sad. They rode along chatting like they had never been separated. Heavens, but the love he had felt for her as a child, the love that God had literally used to awaken his soul from the black sleep of a living death, grew stronger than before.

"Good day, Elspeth," a man greeted as they rode along. He wasn't young. He wasn't old. But he was frightfully thin, and even though it was hard to judge a man's height when he was sitting on a horse, he seemed very small. Definitely around the same age as himself, David guessed.

"Sir Keir," she returned, dipping her head and saying nothing more. In fact she kept her eyes purposely from his, purposely straight forward.

He passed them without another word.

Intriguing. He didn't know that fellow. "Who was that? Sir Keir who? And perhaps you should have introduced us, Elspeth?" He stole a glance at her. Blast it if the child wasn't blushing from neckline to hairline!

"It's really nobody, Daddy. Really."

Nobody? Really? Hah!

David knew those "nobodies" usually turned out to be giant "somebodies." But prodding her about it now would do no good. He remembered one thing about the younger set—they didn't volunteer information to their parents unless pried out of them with red hot pincers.

Hmm. It didn't seem that long ago that he had been that age himself.

A cheerful yet abrasive voice called his name, stealing his thoughts from the miniscule Sir Keir. "David Youngblood, you sorry villain! I thought you were dead!"

David looked up with expectation. A voice he hadn't heard since his days in Paris, a voice he'd never forget, issued from a face the size of a mutton roast, the voice of a fellow Oxford graduate. "Merlin Pencraig, you haven't changed a bit. You're still as fat as an opera singer and four times as loud."

Elspeth demurely dropped behind and rode beside Lily. David breathed a prayer of thanks. One couldn't begin to predict what Merlin Pencraig, Lord Cardigan, an impulsive, irreverent Welshman, might articulate.

Merlin, swathed in perfectly cut garments, reined in alongside of David. "Where were you, old boy? We'd heard you'd been acquitted of all charges in France. Some other fellow confessed, eh?"

"That about sums it up." He'd already purposed to say as little as possible.

"Then where have you been?" he asked, spit polishing a small smudge on his saddle horn. "Holed up in some harem in the far east with thousands of women at your beck and call?"

Go west instead and make it thousands of men, and you may be onto something, David thought. "An extended stay in the tropics. I was married there, you know, and we have a daughter. There in the carriage."

Merlin looked behind him, then turned back, his mouth open. "Camille?" he said softly, trying not to laugh. "You married Camille?"

David threw him a harsh look. "Camille. And beside her is our daughter, Lily. And if I were you, Merlin, I'd not say another word. You seem like a chap who knows what is good for him."

Merlin's black eyes danced and he held up a large hand even wider than his impossibly broad smile. "You'll get no arguments from me. I ended up marrying Absinthe O'Shea, you know. And if I had it to do over, I'd take beauty over reputation any day. You can't possibly imagine what it's like waking up to *that* face every day."

Remembering the aforesaid Absinthe, too smart for her own good, anemic, myopic, flat-chested, and large nosed, David laughed. "You have a point there. Not to be offensive, old boy."

He rubbed a thoughtful finger along his black sideburn. "You'll be the most envied man in England. We all wish we had the guts you have. What do you say we get together? How about some cards with the others?"

David shook his head. "Those days are behind me, old man. I have children to take care of now. A wife."

"Ah, the whole blasted routine, eh?"

"The whole *wonderful* routine."

"My goodness, man, the heat of the tropics must have addled your head."

David chuckled. "You couldn't know the half of it!"

Merlin's raspy laughter mingled with David's, then he said, "Well, I hate to think that nothing more will come of this reunion. Absinthe may kill me for this, but we're having a dinner party tomorrow night and I'd love for you and Camille to come. I'm sure two more guests won't upset the stew pot too much. How about it?"

"Hmm." David acted as though he had to think about. "Well, as we have just arrived in town, we don't have a full calendar as of yet, so, I believe I'll give you a hearty yes, Merlin. What time, then?"

"Eight o'clock. Out at Pencraig Manor. I'll send round directions. Are you still at the same house your parents inhabited?"

"Yes." He tipped his hat. "Much obliged. We'll be there. Anyone else of note coming?"

"Depends on who you ask. Off I go! Ta!" Merlin cried, and galloped off to catch up with his party. David rode on, pleased with the outing so far. Things were coming along quite nicely, if he did say so himself.

CHAPTER ❖ FOURTEEN

iranda, you're simply no help at all!" Camille's light tone spilled over with laughter as she examined herself in the bedroom mirror. "You look like the type that would know everybody!" Although Miranda had much improved in her appearance since they'd said good-bye at the train station in Paris all those years ago, she'd obviously done so to make herself more beautiful to her mate and not to please society.

She'd done a good job at it too, no longer pulling her hair back in that severe marmy bun. Full curls curved sweetly around her face and tumbled down her back from exquisite jeweled combs. Her clothing was simple and elegantly cut, fashioned out of exotic materials and sparingly trimmed. And her earrings always looked as if they had come from a foreign land.

When Camille asked about who might be attending the dinner party, Miranda shook her head. "We've never been much for socializing with the *beau monde*, Camille. I'm sorry. Tobin has his kooky friends, and they are lovely enough for the both of us."

Camille waved her hands in exasperation. "But you're the countess of Cannock! How could you escape all that?"

Miranda laughed. "I *was* the countess of Cannock, and I didn't escape all that, I merely refused to engage myself in the battle."

"As I said, you're no help at all."

Camille took one last, assessing glance. It was good to have all her clothing back, and she knew that the gown she wore, a masterpiece of resonant emerald, had been a wise choice on many fronts. It deepened and intensified the green of her eyes. It created a slimmer silhouette. And, cut to enhance her shoulders, it provided the perfect backdrop for the stunning set of emeralds given to her years ago by Count Rene de Boyce. She wouldn't give them up. They served to keep his memory alive and her raging guilt as well. And after that final conversation with the countess . . . well, she felt her eyes beginning to swim, that was just best left to die. It was too heartbreaking to ponder for long.

"You look perfectly lovely," Miranda said, tucking a stray curl into Camille's updo. "I'm sure you'll have a wonderful time."

"I'm just going to go and eat, smile, and leave all the talking to David."

"Well, he's certainly never at a loss for words."

Lily ran into the room and pounced onto the bed. "*Maman*! Ooooh, you're so pretty! Can I come too?"

Camille laughed, leaned over, and hugged her daughter. "I'd certainly like nothing more, but you have to stay here with Aunt Miranda and Uncle Tobin."

"Will Elspeth be here?" the child asked, starting to jump.

Miranda shook her head. "No. She's gone to a meeting of her literary society."

"Literary society?" Camille asked.

"It's a group of overly educated girls that love nothing more than to get together and dissect poetry."

Lily stood still, screwed up her face. "Yuck."

Camille, herself uneducated, had to agree with the child. She only spoke English because David had taught her so she might communicate more effectively with her clientele. Sometimes she wondered how she could be married to such an intelligent man like David and how they could love as they did after all they had been through. She wondered about a lot of things, like how she'd been convinced that going to this party fit into her description of helping out quietly.

That man!

Miranda grabbed Lily's two hands in her own and the child jumped off of the bed. "I thought we'd all go down to the river and watch the barges. You might even get to see the queen on her way to Hampton Court."

Lily giggled. "Oh you're funny, Aunt Miranda. Aunt Adele told me she lives nearby in Kensington most times!"

Miranda plonked her hands on top of her head. "I'm found out. Well, you'll just have to make do seeing regular folk, then."

Lily clapped. "They're the best kind!"

Camille heaved a weighty sigh. "The gallows await. I might as well get it over with. And I'm sure this Lady Absinthe will be most disagreeable if we are late. At least that's what David thinks."

"Oh, don't worry about her"—Miranda waved a graceful hand—"if she gives you trouble just look at her and be in awe that anyone can look that much like an owl."

A distinct autumn tang thinned the air, so Camille bundled Lily up in a hat and shawl and flipped a black velvet wrap around her own shoulders. Tobin and Miranda each took one of Lily's hands and set out for the long walk to the wharves, their two eldest children, both boys, walking behind them.

"Let's sing!" Lily chimed as they stepped out of the door.

"Sounds like a grand idea," Tobin's deep voice answered, and Camille closed her eyes as the sound of his baritone washed over her. The night breeze carried away "Sing a Song of Sixpence" as it ruffled the small choir's hair.

Camille watched from the front door as Tobin and Miranda lifted Lily by her hands and swung her little body to catch up with their long strides. She squealed with delight over the simple game that Camille could have never done with her alone.

"Ready?" David asked behind her.

Camille turned at the sound of his voice. "My goodness, it's the old David Youngblood come to haunt me!"

"Do you like it?" He patted his chest. "I was at my tailor this morning demanding he take in my evening clothes. I think he did it out of sheer fright!" He held up two triumphant fists. "I seem to be having the same effect on everyone."

"It's as if they'd made up their mind you were gone for good, and up you go and reappear, blast them." She mimicked his tone perfectly on the last two words.

He hugged her to him tightly, lifting her feet off of the floor. "*Chérie*, you get more charming each day. And that must be terribly hard to do since you are already the most charming woman in existence."

"Put me down. You'll muss up my dress," Camille complained, but didn't move out of the circle of his arms. "Are you sure we have to do this?" she whispered. "What difference does it really make? We could fix up the house in Cornwall and have a wonderful life with Adele and her brood. There'd be children for Lily to play with and Elspeth would enjoy—"

"Shhh." Tenderly David tilted her chin up with gentle fingers. He looked so deeply into her eyes she became almost uncomfortable. "Without this, I have no purpose."

"Isn't it enough to love your family and do some good in the House of Lords?"

"No."

"I knew you'd say that," she said, pouting.

"Keep your lips like that for long, *chérie*, and you'll get them kissed."

She smiled at his remark and got her lips kissed anyway.

"Off we go, my love?" he asked, excitement brightening the edges of his voice.

"Do I have a choice?"

"Always."

"I choose to be with you tonight, then. I'd hate to think I spent two hours getting ready for nothing. But this is the first, last, and only party I'm going to with you, David." She pushed against him as he began to nibble her neck. "Let's go then. It's a bit of a drive, isn't it?"

He took her hand and led her out of the house and down the steps. "It is. But it's a nice night for a little ride."

She let him help her into the closed coach. Keeping hold of his hand she turned, her face peering out of the door. "Why are you so compelled to do this?"

"It's an urging I can't explain, *chérie*. Why does a man feel compelled to do anything?"

The Pencraig country home, as unique as the Youngblood estate in Cornwall but meticulously maintained, cast numerous yellow eyes into the heavy twilight. Built centuries ago by a very rich, but very obscure baron, Merlin had snatched it up at a wicked price several years before. Or so he told David as they climbed the steps from the entryway upstairs to the ballroom. "It suits my name, does it not?" he asked, sweeping a hand in front of the whimsical stone facade.

"It does look like something Merlin himself might have designed," David admitted.

"No dancing, by the way." Merlin seemed to reassure himself more than David and Camille. Looking bigger on foot than he was on horse, Merlin Pencraig was truly a Welsh giant. Dark hair, eyes, and skin, towering height, and teeth so crooked yet white seemed to characterize his very nature. And voluble! The man was louder than a gong.

"It's a lovely home," Camille said softly, squeezing David's hand for support.

David's heart broke for her then. She'd had many clients, and he knew she wouldn't remember them all, but Merlin Pencraig could not be forgotten by anyone.

Merlin graciously took Camille's hand, bowed over it, and kissed it. "Welcome to my home, my lady."

Camille's eyes brimmed with tears. "Thank you, Merlin," she whispered.

He'd never mistreated her as some of the others had, David knew. It could have been much worse.

"Your secret is safe with me," he said to both of them.

By this time they stood at the doors to the ballroom. David offered up a quick prayer for direction, as well as discretion, breathed in deeply, and entered the room. Taking note in a glance of the fiery chandeliers, the copious floral arrangements, and an excruciatingly long table punctuated at even intervals down the center by flaming candelabra, he immediately began taking inventory of the guests.

Camille tugged on his arm. "Over there. Is that Lady Absinthe?"

David nodded. "It certainly is," he whispered only for her ears. "And I do believe her eyes have become even rounder over the years."

Merlin waved his wife over. She shook her head in minimal, rapid sweeps and resumed her conversation with two gentlemen in military uniform. "She's really not that bad if you don't have to live with her," he quipped.

Merlin went off to circulate and David held onto his wife's hand. Certainly decorum might frown upon the way he entwined his fingers between hers and kissed her hand frequently, but he didn't care. She'd always been ready to comfort him, to support him when no one else would. He longed to treat her with the same respect.

Soon the group gathered about the table. He figured its length could be measured in yards, not mere feet, and the dinner began with a buzz aimed in their general direction. Not surprisingly, Lady Absinthe had seated them in a "minor corner." A few knighted merchants and some business types chattered all around them, men and women who knew little about them.

Delightful!

Thrilled to be seated near an earl and his countess, the guests blushed with pleasure as David made them feel as if they were the most important guests of the evening. Camille tried to follow suit, joining in on the genial conversation as servants delivered course after course from the kitchen. The chef was obviously trained in France, Camille noted to David with relief when the first course, a mushroom veloute soup, arrived.

The main course, a souvarov of partridge, tasted so heavenly that Camille unsuccessfully stifled a soft moan. Stuffed with foie gras and truffle, the bird was browned, then finished off in a casserole. She'd had her cook in Paris make it for David years before.

"It's all I can do not to swipe my finger across the juices left on the plate!" she whispered. "There's no better taste in all the world than a good demi-glace."

Dessert, even more amazing, was a work of art. A large, intricate set piece, a pastry imitation of the Parthenon, held court on the table over chocolate truffles and caramels, toffee and candied fruits. Biting into a caramel, his wife rolled her eyes heavenward. "I'm glad I came after all, if only for the food!"

"I don't remember seeing you at any parties before this, my lord," said one fellow, a very skinny banker named Maynard Pymore, who obviously believed in investing every penny he earned. "Do you, Gertrude?" He turned his razor-thin nose toward the woman sitting next to him.

His wife, equally de-blubbered, and sporting an odd topknot near the front of her head, nodded. "'Tis true, Maynard. Begging your pardon, my lord and my lady, but I don't remember either of you."

David smiled, wanting to add, *"And I'd remember a face like yours anywhere!"* Instead he managed to say, "We've been abroad for seven years."

"Upon my word!"

"Heaven's sake!"

"Isn't that remarkable?"

And so on and so forth. The exclamations blew across the table and back from the little group like toy boats across a shallow pond. David enjoyed the people around him, knowing Camille was much more at ease with the bunch at this end of the table than near the overdressed, twittering violins up at the respectable end of the room near the garden doors.

By the time the meal ended they were unofficially crowned as celebrities to the bourgeois denizens of the nether regions. They had found out that no, the baron and baroness of Dividen were not, in fact, in attendance that night. They also learned that Charlotte had been elevated to the position of lady-in-waiting to the queen. And apparently a favored one at that, and isn't it good to have friends in high places?

Camille leaned forward. "Why is she favored?"

A rotund man named Frederick Dormerthwaite, who had already declared with delight that he was a good friend of Tobin's, readied himself to answer, stifling a belch. "Bless me, my lady, but her majesty just hasn't been herself since the Prince Consort, God rest his soul, passed away. Has been in mourning for years."

The emeralds at Camille's throat sparkled as she nodded. "So I've heard."

Mrs. Dormerthwaite, as rotund as her mate but more gelatinous, jumped with jiggling vigor into the conversation. "But now," she whispered, her dark eyes round and somewhat amazed, "it's gone beyond the normal!" She fiddled with a five-strand necklace of black pearls the size of ripe cherries that crowned a bosom so grandiose David could only begin to speculate as to what manner of device allowed such blatant defiance of gravity. Not that his thoughts remained there for long, for her next statement proved flabbergasting. "She's started having séances."

"Really!" Camille laid a hand on David's arm. "She doesn't seem to be the type. At least where I come from."

Dormerthwaite wiped his mouth. "From where anybody comes from. Bless me, but I remember the day she was crowned. So young and fair, and now to see her reducing herself to this."

"She's still a good queen, by and large," Pymore the banker said, Gertrude nodding her agreement in the manner of a half-starved chicken, topknot bouncing front to back like the head of an unfortunate doll being given a good shake.

"I'm not saying she's not! Especially the large part." Mr. Dormerthwaite defended himself with a chuckle, running a hand over hair whiter than Merlin's teeth. "But you cannot tell me you think she's the same old girl she once was. See here, she hides herself away in Scotland more than usual, refuses to stop wearing black."

"I think she's still feeling guilty over the Flora Hastings scandal," Mrs. Dormerthwaite said.

"Oh, for heaven's sake, Mary," Dormerthwaite said, irritated, "that happened over thirty years ago!"

"But it was a terrible thing she did to the poor woman," Gertrude agreed.

Camille leaned forward. "What happened?"

Blast it, but she was doing a bang-up job getting information! The women took over.

Mrs. Dormerthwaite told the tale, with Gertrude the banker's wife supplying forgotten details. Flora Hastings, thought pregnant out of wedlock by the queen, was "raked over the coals" most unkindly by the fledgling monarch. The fact that Victoria suspected the father was "that Lord Conroy," her mother's controller, who had tried to take political advantage of Victoria years before during an illness, "didn't give poor Flora Hastings a leg up."

"Fact was," Mary Dormerthwaite finished up, "poor Flora was a virgin, and the swelling of her stomach was the symptom of an illness that killed her not long after."

"How horrible!" Camille gasped.

Gertrude nodded. "Indeed. You can imagine how the queen regrets treating a dying woman as she did."

"No, I cannot imagine," Camille said, turning to David. "Poor girl. To be so unjustly accused."

He shamelessly used the opening. "Now imagine how I feel about Becket Door," he whispered softly. "Three years in hell together, *chérie*. He was all I had. I was all he had."

After dinner, the men gravitated to the library for their port while the women slung on their wraps for a stroll in the torch-lit formal gardens behind the mansion. David entered the library with Dormerthwaite on one side and Pymore the banker on the other.

The large room, anchored on either end by large, hooded fireplaces, sported stuffed game looking as if they had tried to ram their bodies through the walls, but had been ground to a halt by their shoulders. David had never been much of a game hunter, really. He'd never wanted to work that hard to eat. Except for fishing. True sport, indeed.

He lifted a cigar from the box proffered by a footman. Another handed him a glass of port. This had to be done, he assured himself. A means to an end if he wanted to become active in the Lords. He'd be retreating into countless libraries before he hung up his horsehair wig for good at the ripe old age of eighty-two. Or so he hoped. Praying for a duplicate span of years of the ones he had already been given, he thought perhaps he could live one good year to redeem each rotten one he had let molder away on the refuse heap.

Merlin Pencraig hailed him from near the fireplace. "Come join us!"

David excused himself from Dormerthwaite and Pymore and approached them, trying not to look too eager or too reticent. He watched his world distinctly changing shape, like a child's face, full of cheeks and lips one year, thinned down the next.

But when I became a man, David thought, *I put away childish things.*

"Good evening, gentlemen," he greeted them, bowing like the gentleman he had been born to be, fitting into the scene almost as easily as a hard-boiled egg fits into its porcelain cup. Hard boiled, hah! An apt description for an ex-convict!

Merlin introduced him with a whack between the shoulderblades. And he found himself in a circle of illustrious peers. A duke, two earls, a viscount, and a marquise.

"We were just discussing the new game that appeared last summer out at Beaufort's," Merlin caught him up to speed.

"At Badminton?" David asked.

"Precisely," said Lord Aaron Campbell, an older man with the sparkling eyes of a twenty-year-old. "Fine game. If you like that sort of thing."

David accepted a light for his cigar. "What do they call it?"

"Badminton, of course!" Campbell said, and everybody thought it riotously funny. "You wouldn't expect something original from Beaufort now, would you?" he drawled.

David knew Campbell only a very little from Pratt's gentlemen's club, another venture of recreation started by the duke of Beaufort. "Does he still haunt Pratt's regularly?"

Merlin replied with a nod. "Oh, yes. And Sophia Pratt is still running the place." He drew in heavily on his cigar. "So tell us, David, being in the tropics so long and all, what made you quit your native land? Was it that messy do in France?"

Tread carefully, David. Don't lie, but don't carry a torch about it either. "Actually, yes. Quite trying, as you can imagine. Until Richelieu confessed. I had to get away. As soon as the boat left harbor, I realized I wouldn't be coming back anytime soon."

Gerald Raines, the viscount of March, the man he had seen in St. James's Park, shook his head wearily. "Blast it, Youngblood, I cannot say that I blame you. Sometimes I want to leave England so badly I can feel it in my teeth."

"Why not go then?" David asked. But knew the answer. March would soon inherit the earldom of Sutton. Or so he hoped, David guessed.

March swirled the garnet liquid in the firelight. "Same old story. The old badger refuses to die. Just lies there taking last breath after last breath."

It could have sounded callous, but David knew it had been one of those situations where everybody had been praying for relief for years. Once a man of dignity and charm, the old earl had been reduced to nothing more than a body to be fed and changed. It was one of the ways of God David didn't understand before his repentance, and still failed to understand now.

March had always been a good fellow. Very reliable, an unremarkable but dedicated student, and a dutiful son. Even though he had secretly admired Gerald, it was this type of fellow David used to publicly avoid like a pair of thrice-worn socks. Now, he realized men like March could teach him what he needed to learn.

"Well," David continued the conversation, "I can recommend an extended time abroad. Especially in the tropics. But I don't think I was ever so glad to see England's green and pleasant lands!" He quoted Blake and felt his heart go fond.

And for the next fifteen minutes, they prodded him with questions regarding the exotic places he had been, David only admitting to being in the northern part of South America. They seemed satisfied with his answers, in awe actually, of the sense of adventure David seemed to have when compared to their own inability to roam to outlandish destinations for any extended period of time. David's old reputation worked in his favor.

The conversation glided into the world of investments, and David learned that gold had been discovered in Wyoming just two years before and that diamonds had recently been found in South Africa. "The world is just one gigantic treasure chest, ready to burst wide open." Merlin grinned. "And I'm ready for it when it does."

David found out he had missed much in the seven years of his imprisonment, and the peers were more than happy to fill him in on even the most minor developments.

"There's carpet sweepers now too," the earl of Blandford reported. "My wife has the maids all over the house with these little gadgets, whirring back and forth."

"No more banging rugs over the clothesline?" David remembered the way he'd helped Mrs. Wooten and the housemaids at that most enjoyable of tasks. At least to an eight-year-old.

"Not so often," Merlin put in. "Absinthe swears by them."

Such mundane matters. David wanted to cry he was so glad to be home. They informed him of the new Pullman Cars, "Black Friday" on the London Stock Exchange three years previous, the new *Whitaker's Almanack*, and that just before he arrived home, debtors' prisons had been abolished.

David waved his cigar in the air. "High time for that! Now there was a law that never made sense. Put a man in prison for debts, so he can't work to pay them off."

March agreed. "There's been a great deal of reform since you've left home, Youngblood."

When the time to rejoin the ladies arrived, March pulled him aside. "I assume you'll be joining us in the Lords?"

"I'm thinking about it. I mean, surely, I'll do so eventually, but I was wondering if I might wait awhile. Get my feet more accustomed to the political terrain."

March shook his hand, eyes warm. "I'd be honored if you'd join me Monday morning at my home in Lambeth. I'll answer any questions I can. With Gladstone just becoming prime minister last year, it could prove to be a fascinating discussion, I'm sure."

David noticed Lady Absinthe Pencraig looking through the open doorway of the library, staring his way. She lifted her hand in a falsetto wave, and he returned her gesture with a slight bow.

"Are you Gladstone's friend or his foe?" David asked, turning his attention back to March. Not having much political opinion one way or the other just then, he had to admit he'd never been much interested in such. Time to change his ways, especially if he planned to get near Cyprian Door.

Gerald shook his head. "I'm not going to answer that tonight. Can I count on you, then, for Monday morning? Ten o'clock?"

"Be delighted," David answered. "But now"—he spied Dormerthwaite and Pymore looking his way—"I must see to my friends."

The men heartily welcomed him back, and they ambled out into the gallery that connected all the main rooms of the house. The women blew in from the garden in a waft of freshened perfume, chatting and laughing and looking decidedly breeze-kissed.

Camille entered. David's heart stopped, proving once more that the most beautiful woman in the room belonged to him. A woman who had sailed the seas to courier him back from the gates of hell.

I love you, he mouthed in her direction. She rewarded him with a smile that not only tilted her mouth, but gentled eyes that looked only at him, loved only him. It pleased him to know that if her body hadn't exactly been virginal, her heart had never been given to another man. She didn't believe that could be enough for him, but it was.

Camille felt like an apple pie without vents, baking away in a dry oven, juice bubbling, and about to split open at the very top of its crust. She couldn't wait to tell David what she had heard! Finally, after David introduced her to the men he'd met during the port stage of the evening (recognizing none of them, *Dieu merci!*), the group began a slow disassembling. They bid good-bye to the Dormerthwaites and the Pymores, not that the banker and his wife even began to live up to that name, as Mary Dormerthwaite pointed out with a chuckle. Gertrude didn't seem to mind the jest. She just circled her hands around her waist and whispered that she never did much care for food, even before marrying tightfisted Maynard.

David helped Camille into the coach, spreading a soft wool lap robe found beneath the seat. After bestowing a kiss on her eyebrow, he climbed in beside her. The caring physical contact sent a thrill through her. David had learned what so many men she knew had failed to realize. He knew that the key to unlocking her deepest passions needed to be turned by everyday kindness and caring. He had created a masterpiece of love from a thousand tiny strokes: tender kisses, holding her hand, a cup of tea, even tucking back her stray locks of hair. He gave her significance and worth, and in turn she had given him everything she possessed.

Once the horses were on their way, they turned to each other and said simultaneously, "I have so much to tell you!"

CHAPTER ❖ FIFTEEN

"You go first," David invited.

Camille, happy to comply, took his hand in hers and set their wadded fingers in her lap. "Well, we finished the conversation about the séances."

"It's hard to believe the queen is taking stock in such nonsense."

Camille didn't think so at all. "If you loved somebody the way she loved her husband and you thought there was a chance, no matter how remote, that you could communicate with them once again, wouldn't you try?"

"Not in that way. It's witchcraft. No matter how debased I was, *chérie*, I had too much sense to dabble in that sort of thing."

"I agree. I'm not justifying it, David. I'm just trying to understand the poor soul, that's all. Anyway, it seems that she's become quite obsessed with the idea. Believe it or not, Lady Pencraig joined our little discussion when Mary Dormerthwaite called her over."

"You talked with Lady Absinthe?"

"Yes. She's every bit as uppity as she seems, but she loves to be the one who knows what's going on!"

"Not surprising. Merlin's the same way."

Camille hadn't felt this excited in years. "Anyway, in connection with the séances, Lady Absinthe brought up the name of none other than . . ." She hesitated for effect, waiting for him to fill in the blank.

He did. "Charlotte Door!"

"Precisely." She clapped her hands.

He took her hand back in his. "And what does Charlotte Door have to do with it all?"

Camille almost shouted the answer. "She's serving as the queen's medium!"

"You've got to be joking!"

"No. So it isn't any wonder she'd be the queen's favorite. Isn't it amazing? These Doors get increasingly more interesting, don't they?" she asked.

"Becket did say she was a bit eccentric, but a medium?"

"Of course, Lady Absinthe swore us to secrecy right there."

"A vow you proceeded to quickly throw away," David laughed.

She swatted his arm. "I know, I know. It wasn't the right thing to do knowing all the while I'd tell you, but there you have it. But that isn't the most exciting thing!"

"There's more?"

"Just before we left, she pulled me aside and invited me for tea this coming Tuesday. Just a little gathering, she assured me, of women she thinks I'd like to meet. A *quiet* gathering."

"What is *that* all about?"

"Apparently, according to Mary Dormerthwaite, Lady Absinthe surrounds herself with beautiful women as friends, though she herself is less than pretty. You are going to rise up with the cream of society, she knows this, and she's marking her territory. Or so Mary said."

David looked perplexed. "Really? You think so?"

"Of course. The Dormerthwaites aren't stupid. You were the talk of the party, whether you realized it or not. I saw all sorts of people looking your way and speaking in low voices as they did so. And don't pretend you didn't notice." Camille knew better.

Both knew how to take the temperature of a party with a very exact thermometer.

"I can't pretend with you, *chérie*," he laughed. "So, are you going to this little tea party?"

"Yes. You see, Charlotte Door is Absinthe Pencraig's best friend."

"Ah-hah."

Camille, honest to a miserable fault, had to admit that, "I can think of nothing more ridiculous than spending an afternoon with a bunch of priggish women like Lady Absinthe Pencraig. But"—she hurried to add—"since it's to be a quiet gathering ..."

David began to snicker.

"And what do you find so amusing?"

"You. Miss Quiet Life, indeed. Camille, you'd never be satisfied for long with a regular life. You need excitement, intrigue. You need more than suppers and shoes and shopping. You're already in completely over your head."

Zut alors, he was right. Not that she cared to admit it just then. "I'll do nothing to compromise Lily's well-being."

"I know that too, Camille."

Later as they walked up the steps to their bedchambers, she asked, "Ready for bed?"

David chuckled. "I'm always ready for bed, *chérie*."

She turned and watched him as he followed her up the steps, turning down the gas sconces on the wall beside him as he did so. She savored the sweet domestic moment, knowing that David Youngblood was incapable of making life any more normal than this. "Did you lock the door?" she asked.

"Blast," he grumbled, turning around and shuffling back down the steps.

Sunday morning arrived much too soon. As hard as getting out of bed proved to be, Camille still looked forward to their excursion to worship at Westminster Abbey. Elspeth pleaded a headache, so they ate a quick breakfast in the conservatory off the back of the house and found themselves standing at the back of the massive church not an hour later.

"I haven't been to mass since I was a child. My mother's sister, Aunt Genevieve, died from a fever, and after that *Maman* refused to go. She was always one to blame God for everything. I did used to go to Notre Dame every so often, when I'd let the guilt creep in."

David put his arm around her and drew her close to his side. "There, now," he said with a sigh. "This is much better."

"What will it be like?" she asked.

"Truth to tell, *chérie*, I don't remember much myself. With Mrs. Wooten we just went to the small parish. I guess it will be all hymns and Scripture and robes and the like."

Camille still felt shy about plunging into the whole church affair. "Perhaps we could just stand at the back for now?"

He smiled. "All right."

Organ music, pleasant and soft, reminded Camille that monks had once spent their lives here. The bells rang in quick changes, something she'd never heard in France. "How beautiful!" she cried as the first hymn began. More eager now to join in the worship she felt her throat swell. Not that she could carry a tune, or had a keen sense of timing. In fact, when it came to music, Camille could claim only the ability to let herself be transported by its beauty. Worshiping along in her head and in her heart had to be enough. Surely there'd be something unholy about unleashing her voice upon those around her. She already had too much to answer for!

David's singing voice proved more than pleasant. Camille realized she had never heard him sing before. Yes, quite pleasant. But then, the Youngbloods seemed to be a musical lot.

She looked upward, wishing for sky but seeing only a series of pointed stone arches cued one behind the other from nave to apse.

The architecture wasn't nearly as astounding as that of Notre Dame, but the soaring ceilings, gothic arches, and carved pillars towered impressively on their own. The windows cast their colors on the stone floor, the blue from the robe of some apostle edging slowly over her foot as the service wore on. She found her mind wandering and fiddled with the prayer book in her hand. Neither reading the words nor understanding them, she felt an irritation begin to simmer inside of her. She became increasingly annoyed by the drone of the prayers and kneeling and standing, kneeling and standing.

All in all, by the time they re-entered the coach, her mood represented no brief trip to heaven. In fact, contrariness had worked her into a lather. "Get up there quickly now, Lily!" she scolded. "There are other coaches waiting to pull up!"

Lily's eyes rounded and she allowed her stepfather to help her into the vehicle. Camille followed, feeling terrible about the state of her emotions, but ready to explode. She chose the seat next to Lily in hopes of making up for her impatience. "Hurry, David. Get in!"

He climbed up, looking all arms and legs as he seated himself across from his wife. "Blast it, Camille, but you've found yourself breathing a foul wind," he drawled.

"I didn't understand a word they said in there," she snapped. "Not one word."

He leaned forward and squeezed her knee. "To tell you the truth, I found it a little cold myself. And the dean's voice . . ." He raised a hand to his mouth and pretended to yawn.

Lily was not put off, however. "I thought the organ played prettily. And did you see all of those tombs! It was spooky. Why do they have dead people in God's house?"

Camille didn't know, so she turned to David, arms crossed over her bosom. "Well?"

"I guess it's because they wanted to be close to God, even after death, Lily. They pay lots of money to be buried there."

"But isn't God everywhere?" the child asked, brows drawn together by some invisible thread.

"Yes," he said.

"And once you're dead you're dead, so why does it matter if you're buried in a church?"

"It doesn't," he said decisively and looked at Camille. "Do you want to go back there?"

"Not if I can't understand anything!" she said, still highly irritated. "I knew we should have gone down to the mission with Tobin and Miranda," she grumbled.

David held his hands up. "I wanted to go with them. You were the one that wanted to see—"

"I know that! But you did nothing to convince me otherwise."

David sighed, smiled wearily, and turned to Lily. "Did she get like this often before I came back?"

Lily shook her head, her blond hair beating at her cheeks. "I think it's something she only does for you."

"Well, then," David said, sitting back against his seat, "I suppose I should count myself privileged. It's not every man that so thoroughly gets on the nerves of his wife."

Camille couldn't help but laugh at that and brightened immediately. "So we'll go with them next week?"

"Why not? You won't be the first noblewoman slumming it down at the East End."

"When it comes to slumming, I could teach them a thing or two. And I'm not noble."

"You married me, didn't you?"

She crossed her arms. "You, my dear, are anything but noble, and no one knows that better than I do."

Camille gazed out the window as they turned the corner of their street. "Oh, look!" She pointed in the direction of the house. "Elspeth must be feeling better. There she goes, on her way to the park."

Elspeth rode away on Mister Socks, accompanied by a groom.

The coach stopped. "Good," David said. "I'm glad her headache is gone. Shall we go inside and have our dinner, then?"

"I'm starving!" Lily cried.

"I am as well," David said. "It seems that all the food I eat now is a gift from heaven."

"And it wasn't before?" Lily asked, clearly puzzled.

"Oh, it was, to be sure!" David said, stepping out of the vehicle and lifting Lily down. "I just didn't realize it."

Camille rested her hand in her husband's and stepped down onto the street. "I decided I'm done being upset for the day."

He caught her round the waist and pulled her close. "I love you, *chérie*."

Looking up into his eyes, she said, "We have a good life, David."

"We do, thank God."

A voice interrupted their moment, and Camille watched as David's face practically split in two with a smile at the words, "Master David!"

"Mrs. Wooten!" he cried, running up the steps to where an older woman dressed in black held her arms open wide.

Camille watched the exchange. *So this is Mrs. Wooten.* The woman who for all practical purposes was David Youngblood's mother, the only source of love he had known for many years.

She appeared to be all a mother should be. Short, round, and smiling, she patted David fondly as they embraced. A pudgy hand reached around to caress his wavy hair. When her fingers found the ponytail at the back of his head, she pulled back in horror. "Master David, get in this house right now and let me take a scissors to your head! I've never seen the like!"

David turned to his wife and winked. But the sheepish expression on his face was unmistakable. Camille doubled over with laughter and followed them into the house.

CHAPTER ❖ SIXTEEN

Monday morning possessed air so clear and clean David felt as if his lungs had been scoured of any and all objectionable substances that may have slithered their way down over the years. The streets of London had been pumping business for hours, and so had David, for that matter. He'd been reading back issues of the *Times*, trying to get a proper feel for the erosion the political landscape had experienced since he had left England. His father had been very much a Conservative member of the House of Lords—when he bothered to show up. Let the Oxbridge set run the nation, Eustace Youngblood proclaimed. Give the everyday Englishmen a vote and you'll be sorry. To the late earl of Cannock, the only good peasant was an ignorant one. And don't even get the man started on the topic of that Evangelicalist Lord Anthony Ashley, the earl of Shaftsbury! Religious people drove him mad.

For years David had agreed.

But now he had experienced slavery firsthand—laboring day after day for someone else's gain and having little or nothing to say regarding your own future, your very life. The feudal system had died long ago, so they might as well bury the bloke! He prayed Viscount March felt the same. Gladstone seemed to be a proponent of more rights for the average citizen. While David suffered in French Guiana, parliament had passed the Reform Act of 1867, granting all landowners and men who paid at least ten pounds a year for a furnished room, the right to vote.

But as Robert Lowe had remarked, "We must now educate our masters." And now a great debate raged regarding an Education Act. For the people to vote, they needed to be educated, informed, and the process needed to begin post haste.

Made sense.

Yes, he looked forward to this meeting with March. David knew himself well. Knew he needed to throw himself headlong into something more constructive than just Becket Door. He had begun following the path to trustworthiness and honor, but hunting these traits could never be enough. Nothing would satisfy him until he had overtaken them, capturing them for good in the hinged jaws of his own convictions.

Anticipating the meeting before him, he left the house early, kissing an adorable, snoring wife just before setting out. He decided to ride west by the river up to the Tower Bridge, cross over the Thames, and travel south, then eastward into Lambeth. Viscount March's home rested near Lambeth Palace. Not horribly grand, but very comfortable and impeccably tasteful, it echoed its owner. It would be just like the March family to put their town home there and not in London proper.

He was whisked into March's study, where his hat and coat disappeared at the hands of a quiet footman. On a small table near a green leather sofa sat some of the latest books he'd heard Elspeth mooning over. *Crime and Punishment*, and *The Idiot*, both by Dostoevsky, and a book by Wilkie Collins called *The Moonstone*. According to Elspeth it was a detective story. Fancy that. Never heard of the like. He picked up a copy of the latest offering of his favorite novelist, Victor Hugo, published only that year, entitled *L'Homme qui rit*.

"Do you like Hugo as well?" a voice said from the door.

David turned to see March, dressed casually in tan riding breeches and shirtsleeves, entering the room. "Yes. I see you have his most recent work."

"Haven't read it yet."

David lifted the book shoulder level. "May I? I promise I won't up and off with it for good."

March laughed. "Please do. And then you can tell me what it's about. I don't have time for fiction much these days."

"Who does?" David set the book down and quickly studied the man before him. Viscount March, a friendly sort of man with facial muscles that relaxed into a happy expression, had a long chin at the bottom of his face and wavy, heavy brown hair at the top. In between, his features skewed a bit to the left, as though someone had taken a needle and thread and basted up the left side of his face, then pulled slightly. Pale hazel eyes, clear and forthright, looked on the world unafraid. At least it seemed that way to David. His eyelashes were so long, David could only be thankful March had to lug them around and not himself.

"Forgive my state of dress," March apologized, "but Monday is my catch-up day. Having endured all the social activities of the weekend, I find myself here in my study for most of the morning as well as the afternoon. Correspondence and reading dispatches. That sort of thing."

"No need to apologize," David said.

March came around to the couch. "Have a seat," he invited, doing the same. "Campbell will be joining us a bit later. You'll have much in common with him, I believe. And he's certainly not the type to hold a man's past against him. I've sent for some tea, if you don't mind."

"Mind? It would fill the bill." David had read more about Lord Aaron Campbell since he had seen him at the Pencraigs. A real workhorse in the Lords. Distinguished, yet known for his sense of humor. And David couldn't help but notice at Pencraig's manor he had a first-class drawl, even more admirable than his own!

March laid his right ankle atop his left knee. "I've been looking forward to this visit ever since the Pencraig's do. It's astonishing to see you after all of these years, David. But then, I shouldn't be surprised. I should know that where you are concerned I should expect the unexpected."

"True enough. And what have these years held for you, March?"

"I was married about four years ago. Lady Portia Witheridge. A great friend of my sister Monica. Did you know her?"

David shook his head no.

"Anyway, she passed away two years ago."

"I'm sorry to hear that," David said, not completely surprised. March's eyes had echoed a loss. "How?"

"Childbirth."

"Good heavens. And the child?"

"Still with me. She lived, praise God. Two years old now and the very image of myself. Or so my family tells me all the time."

"You must be thankful for her."

"Most days, yes. Other days, she makes me miss her mother so badly I wonder how I will cope with my duties."

David could only imagine the viscount's loneliness. True, he had been lonely on Devil's Island, but March endured a loneliness of the soul. He could only pray that he'd never have to live a day without Camille.

"After Portia died I threw myself headlong into the political scene. For something to do, you know, to keep my mind off of her."

"Certainly." David nodded.

"I've come to see things differently now that I'm getting older. One hits one's fortieth birthday and realizes it's now or never."

David slapped a hand onto his thigh. "I'll heartily agree with that!"

"So the House of Lords has become my home away from home, so to speak."

"Yes, I was reading back issues of the *Times*, trying to get a more accurate picture of what is going on. So tell me, were you at all involved with the Reform Act two years ago?"

The tea arrived on a heavily laden cart. March stood to his feet and dismissed the maid, saying, "It's all right, Lorna, I'll take care of it from here. Sugar?" he asked.

David declined, saying a little milk would be lovely, however.

As March fixed the tea, David eyed him. He had become quite a man since college days—a respectable gentleman, quiet yet strong—qualities David would have to work at owning.

He handed David his tea, then raked a hand through his hair before bending to fix his own.

David took a sip of the strong brew, wondering how he made it all those years on Devil's Island without it. "So you were going to tell me about the Reform Act," he prodded.

"Oh, yes." March took a quick sip, then set his cup on the table beside him. "I'm a supporter of Gladstone. My father would be most upset with me, but . . ." He shrugged.

"If my father knew the way I felt about my own nobility, he'd come back from his grave to strangle me," David said.

"So you're with us then?" March asked. "You've read about the Education Act?"

"A little. I'd like to know more before I make a commitment about which party to associate myself with."

"Of course. Load your plate up first, though, Youngblood. You may be here a while."

"Gladly." David picked up two scones, spooning some jam and cream onto his plate, and stacked up several sandwiches. "Now, what's entailed?"

March took only one scone and a bit of jam.

"Let's sit at the table and spread out," the viscount suggested, and they moved to the other side of the room, where a large library table squatted amid walls of bookshelves. "There's a great deal to tell you."

David was pleased he'd had the foresight to read up on some of this beforehand, for March gave him little license for running mental rumination. He heard about new school districts, assessment of the needs of the elementary schools, ratepayers electing school boards.

"And, women should be allowed to vote for the school board," March went on to say.

"What?" David asked. "Women voting? I've never heard of such a thing."

"What's wrong with it? They're the ones raising the children. They should have a say in it all. Most assuredly!" His normally white skin ruddied up.

David held up his hands. "I'm not saying I'm against it, Gerald. It's just new to me. That's all."

March laughed a squeaky, embarrassed laugh. "Sorry, David. It's just that, well, I guess I feel so strongly about this because Portia did. She would have made a fabulous MP."

"Must have been quite a woman."

"She was. There's much more to discuss, though. And if you'd like, I'll arrange for you to meet Gladstone soon."

David agreed that would be a fine thing. The sooner he got involved in the workings of the country, the sooner he would catch up with Cyprian Door.

"I also would like you to meet Lord Ashley," March said.

"Actually, I would love that. I've read a lot about him, and I do believe I now have much in common with the man."

March's brows raised. "You? How is that?"

David knew he had a right to act surprised. Lord Anthony Ashley had done so much to help the poor in England, had brought on reforms in coal mines, in factories, had even championed the cause of the "climbing boys"—chimney sweeps who were dying in heated flues and falling horribly sick in the lungs. "Lord Ashley does all he can to help people because he believes that the Lord is soon returning. He wants as many people to be ready for it as possible."

March shrugged. "Well, we all have our different motivations, I suppose. And you? You believe all that?"

"I do now." David set down his teacup.

"As I said, I shouldn't be surprised at anything you say or do, Youngblood."

"Would you like to hear about it?"

March shook his head. "Not today, David. Too much to do."

David pointed a finger at him. "Someday, though. Promise me someday."

The viscount forced out a wary laugh. "I'm sure you'll pursue me as relentlessly as the hounds of hell, eh?"

"More so."

March bowed his head slightly. "All right, then. I promise I'll hear you out someday. Just not today."

David sat back. Good enough. He'd make sure that Gerald Raines lived up to his word.

Aaron Campbell arrived not long after. "March," he called as he came through the doorway, a newspaper rolled up under one arm, the other arm straightened over the top of the cane upon which he leaned, "if that tea's not hot, you'll wish you'd never awakened this morning! I am *not* in a good mood!"

"Lorna!" Gerald called. "Hot tea!"

Obviously no need for decorum with these fellows! David felt right at home. And he watched in fascination as Lord Aaron Campbell threw the newspaper in a heap on the table, shrugged off his coat, and cast it carelessly over the arm of the sofa. Ah, yes, most interesting. Though Campbell was sixty-five if he was a day, David knew he'd found a compatible soul. And when he said, "Blast it, but I do believe if my Maria keeps me up late one more night I'm going to have to send her packing off to Scotland until the sessions are over!" David let out a hoot. Stood to his feet. Held out his hand. "David Youngblood, sir. An honor to see you again."

Aaron's clear eyes, the color of deep aquamarines, squinted up with humor. "The honor is mine. In all my born days, I never thought I'd find anyone more roguish than I was as a young man. But you, sir, shredded my reputation to bits, thank God!"

They shook hands and a friendship was born.

Campbell took off his hat, straightened his short, faded blond hair, and pulled out a chair. "Blast this arthritis!" he complained as he sat. "A chair is my greatest friend and my worst enemy!"

"I know what you mean," David said, lifting up his own cane.

"Isn't it just awful being a prisoner to your aches and pains?" Campbell asked. "But you're such a young man to be experiencing such ills—"

Gerald Raines cleared his throat, clearly ready to set down to work. "Shall we, gentlemen?"

"Oh, by all means, March"—Campbell waved a hand—"don't mind our little ills. We're all ears now, aren't we, Youngblood?"

David sat down with a grimace and relaxed back into his chair, his back throbbing already from the time he'd spent on the hard seat. "Proceed, gentlemen."

"Can I give you a lift home in my carriage?" David asked Campbell as the meeting adjourned.

"That would be a good idea." Campbell nodded. "I'll just send someone round to get my horse later."

"There are some things I'd like to discuss with you."

"I can tell. Shall we, then?"

March looked on in triumph. David knew March felt responsible for a lot of matters, that he believed he held the fate of millions in his hands, that he believed he could put people together who could do far more good when joined than they could ever do alone. "Go on, gentlemen!" he laughed. "Compare war stories. You know I have nothing in common with you on that score!"

They exited through the front door. Aaron Campbell and David turned around at the same time saying, "Thank God for it, March!"

David's eyes met Campbell's, and they laughed their way down the steps into the waiting vehicle. Campbell painfully settled into his seat, but said no more about his arthritis. David sat across from him and arranged his hat and papers.

"I suppose this meeting was planned not only by Viscount March, but by God himself," Campbell drawled.

David said nothing. He couldn't judge by Campbell's tone whether or not he was serious about his reference to God. Well, he'd make sure. "I believe nothing happens that God does not allow. And so yes, I agree with you."

Campbell's hands kneaded the top of his cane. "One young man, one old. I take it then, you are a follower of God? One of those 'fanatical' people who believe that 'he is, and that he is a rewarder of those who diligently seek him'?"

David relaxed. "Yes. And you?"

Campbell leaned forward and placed a hand on David's shoulder. "He, and only he, is the reason I am alive today. For he pulled my feet from the mire of my own foolishness and set them on a rock."

The words washed over David as if he had been in a desert. But surely this man's sins didn't match his own? "I wish I could only claim foolishness as my singular fault, my lord. I was an evil man." Could he trust Aaron Campbell with the truth?

The distinguished man nodded his head. "I hired a man to kill my own brother. My twin."

David ordered his driver to take the long way home.

CHAPTER ❖ SEVENTEEN

Despite Elspeth's soft snicker when Camille walked down the steps ready for the tea party, Camille was glad she had chosen the coral-colored day gown with the smart little hat.

"Good-bye, Elspeth." Camille smiled, pulling on her white gloves. "Are you doing anything special with your day?"

"Oh, no. Nothing planned. But that's all right. I've grown used to being alone." Elspeth crossed her arms, eyes sparkling with challenge.

Camille let her smile drop from her lips. She hoped her eyes looked kind, but she couldn't be sure. Elspeth made her nervous, made her doubt herself like she'd never done before. She so wanted the girl to like her. *Juste ciel*, but they were going to have to put up with each other for a very long time. "I'm sorry. It's hard to wait, and then when the wait's over to find that things weren't what you expected them to be."

"How would you know? You waited, and you won the grand prize for your efforts."

"Your father?"

Elspeth nodded. "Precisely."

"Well, on that, *ma chérie*, we agree. He is a most cherished prize. And one I do not deserve."

The carriage was announced.

"I'll see you at supper tonight, Elspeth. All right?"

"Will Daddy be there?"

"Of course."

"Oh. Well, then, I'll be there too."

The cool carriage ride out of the city refreshed her. She thought about the previous conversation with Elspeth. They had quite a rocky road ahead of them. It wasn't going to be easy for either of them.

A quiet, yet dignified butler showed Camille back to the verandah overlooking the spacious, parklike lawns of the Pencraig's estate. Absinthe greeted her warmly, introducing her to the two other women already present. But the formalities were dispensed with quickly, and Camille settled in to listen, allowing Absinthe to pick her a cup of tea.

She flicked a fallen leaf from atop her shoe. Most of the other women assembled for an afternoon at "Merlin's Cave," as she and David joked, appeared almost dowdy compared to herself. English clothing. She suppressed a shudder and forced a wider smile to her face. So far Charlotte Door had failed to show, a keen disappointment.

She dropped another lump of sugar into her second cup of tea and continued to observe the scene before her. Shining on the verandah of the house, the September sun warmed their hats and their cheeks. The flowers in the formal garden faded almost before her eyes.

Four ladies in all flocked together, and she'd been introduced most kindly by Lady Absinthe to the lot of them. To her relief, this interesting gaggle of women spoke of their travels, their family, the political scene. Camille, content to remain quiet, deemed it wise to gauge the real purpose of these gatherings. Recreation?

Or more.

Best to stay mute, until asked a question. Gertrude's statement had been on the mark. Each was very much a beauty in her own right—other than the group maven, Lady Absinthe, of course. But even she arranged herself as attractively as she could in a gown the color of crushed blackberries and a daring bit of kohl lining each eye. Sapphire earrings dangled almost to her shoulders.

Lady Absinthe, done serving the others, poured herself some more tea and sat down, her skirt ballooning with air as her bottom made contact with the chair. "Your dress is charming, Camille. Paris?"

Camille nodded.

"Worth?" she asked.

"No. I used to frequent Monsieur Worth, but I found a wonderful woman who will soon be all the rage."

"Her designs are certainly unique." The remark issued from between the pretty lips of Viscount March's sister. Monica Raines, unmarried as of yet, proclaimed herself more than ready to vote for one of the school boards Camille had heard David discussing with Tobin after his visit to the viscount's home. He'd spent another entire afternoon with Lord Aaron Campbell, and it had changed him somehow. But David could not yet speak of it. Camille understood.

"Anytime I see a woman doing well in business for herself it makes me warm all over!" Lady Absinthe said.

Camille hated to admit it, but she enjoyed being in this group of headstrong women. Normally she liked men infinitely better than women, had never ceased to find them fascinating. It was why she had been so good in her profession. But she didn't know such women as these existed, opinionated about things that mattered, well-informed, strong in and of themselves, not because of the families into which they had been born or the men to whom they were attached.

And certainly, Lady Absinthe surprised her most of all. She'd been most welcoming when Camille arrived, had introduced her around the group as if royal blood trickled somewhere inside of her.

"Well, you certainly have a way with fashion." Monica reached forward to fill up her plate with cucumber sandwiches. "I daresay we could all use a little help in that area. Except for Charlotte of course."

"Charlotte?" Camille leaned forward, playing the innocent.

"Charlotte Door!" Absinthe supplied, and all the other women nodded. Almost reverentially. "She's a regular of our little group. But she's going to be late. Her fashion sense is hopelessly eccentric."

"But she does possess a certain style," Monica said.

Camille seized upon the moment. "Well, tell me about her, then. She must be fascinating to cause such a ruckus among this group of less than mundane women." There. Judging by the sudden smug set to their mouths, she could tell they liked that.

The fourth lady spoke. An older woman, in her mid to late fifties, if Camille guessed correctly. Georginia Stiles, a former ballet dancer and the wife of the duke of Farnesworth, looked the most stylish of all the English women, though definitely prone to too much jewelry and lipstick. She'd been bucking convention for years, no doubt.

Absinthe already warned Camille that the woman also loved to hear and broadcast "juicy bits." "Don't say anything you don't wish for all of London to hear!"

Utilizing a speaking voice full and warm, she picked up the conversational baton. "Charlotte is most unusual, Camille. She was born and raised in India, you know."

Camille remembered David's warning. "And how did she come to leave India?"

Georginia fiddled with a golden brooch sporting a miniature of an African child pinned on the high collar of her dazzling gown. "She married Becket Door. He was visiting her family. It's quite a juicy little story."

Juicy.

"Becket?" Camille played dumb. "Isn't her husband named Cyprian?"

"Oh, yes! There's the intrigue of it!" Monica Raines's eyes darkened.

"Did somebody say 'intrigue'?" A voice as smooth as marzipan spoke from the doorway leading into the house. "I love intrigue."

Camille turned and beheld one of the most exotic women she had ever seen. Surely that said something!

"Charlotte!" Absinthe immediately arose from her chair. "You've arrived just in time. The tea is still hot."

Charlotte Door crossed her lithe, brown arms. "Tea! Whenever are you going to learn, Abby? Just get me a scotch. Neat."

Absinthe yelled for a servant.

Charlotte's request failed to shock Camille. After one look at Charlotte Door, clad in a sari of blood-red minted with small coins of gold thread, only the curious should be expected. Her features were undeniably English, of the thin variety. A long, thin nose, heavily lined eyes—hardly sloe shaped—and slight cheekbones brooded over a pointed chin. Her broad, high forehead supported a braided crown of hair the color of black peppercorns, streaked with cayenne. A spicy woman.

"She sunbathes in the nude," Monica, seated next to Camille, whispered.

Lady Charlotte heard. "That's right, Monica dear. I can't survive a day without it. Even in winter."

"You must certainly stand out in a crowd," Camille said.

"It may seem like a drastic measure." Charlotte picked up a bunch of grapes, pulled one off, and bit it in half. "But not all of us can have a face as perfect as yours, darling. Camille Youngblood, I presume?"

"Yes."

She began to peel the remaining half of the grape. "Absinthe told me you'd be included today. I'm sure you could tell *me* a story or two, darling. I may look like I've lived a fascinating life of abandon, but it must be nothing compared to yours."

Camille felt the blood rushing to her head, but she remained cool, willing her heart to slow back down. "It was just a way of life that's over now."

"But traveling all around the world must have been fascinating!" Absinthe's sallow skin grew pink. "Merlin says you were all over the world."

Relief flooded her. "Well, not the entire world."

"Where then?" Charlotte pulled a cushion off the remaining chair, set it on the ground next to Absinthe, and lowered herself down to a cross-legged position in one sinuous movement of silk against skin.

"Oh, yes!" Georginia cried, "Do tell us all about it!"

Absinthe's dry tone crackled in the air between them. "Georginia is an insatiable busybody, Camille. But she knows so much about what's going on in the ton, we wouldn't dream of having a gathering without her!"

Georginia's bottom lip ripened. "I'm just curious, is all."

Camille laughed. "I was in Tuscany, Greece, Rome . . . South America."

They all gasped.

"South America!" Georginia's earrings flagellated her jaw. "My goodness!"

Charlotte ate the remainder of the grape. "By all the gods, you make my growing up in India seem mundane."

Camille doubted whether Lady Charlotte or anything she did could ever be classified as mundane. The golden thonged sandals binding the woman's feet could only be described as extraordinary.

Charlotte noticed the direction of her gaze. "You like these? I'll bring you a pair next time."

"Next time?"

Absinthe smiled, leaned over, and patted Camille's knee. "We're here every Tuesday, my dear. And if you're invited once, it means the invitation stands."

Monica crossed her legs. "Needless to say, Abby here is careful with the screening process. We trust her implicitly. She was right about Charlotte, wasn't she, Georgie?"

"Perfectly in*sight*ful!" Georginia agreed.

Camille had no idea why she had been invited in the first place. "So why am I here? I'm new to London. And I'm the wife of David Youngblood, for goodness' sake. Hardly a respectable gentleman."

Georginia Stiles chuckled deeply. "If you haven't noticed, we're all renegades in one way or the other. We're all unconventional women married to unconventional men. Sisters in oddity and strength."

Monica cleared her throat and tossed her loose, bright red hair over her shoulder.

"Or we're *about* to be married to unconventional men," Georginia corrected herself. "Monica is wedding Lord Percy St. Dennis in October, a widower who used to be married to the type of woman we all despise. Petty, snobbish and—" Georginia fought for the word.

"Pale!" Absinthe cried.

"Dead." Charlotte said, eyes glowing. "And at her own hand."

Georginia's eyes softened in pity. "Lady Sharon became very sick." Her voice grew faint. "She was losing control of her functions, and one day they found her in her bed, arsenic powder on her lips."

"How very sad." Camille acted sorry, but having only known of the woman's very existence the moment she found out about her death, true sorrow eluded her. It didn't matter what stratum of society one found oneself in, certain niceties were expected.

Monica finished the last of her cucumber sandwiches and set the plate on the table. "Let's not talk about her. She treated Percy horribly, her children horribly, every one she knew horribly. And she got the death she deserved. Finally, Percy gets to be happy, and he deserves that."

Juste ciel! So much for niceties!

Obviously, the discussion had ended.

Charlotte stretched her legs out in front of her, crossing them at her very thin ankles. Three golden bracelets around her ankles brushed together like wind chimes. A footman arrived with a glass of scotch on a silver tray. "You were speaking of intrigue when I first came in. Continue, please." Charlotte took the drink without a thank-you and gulped down a healthy swallow. Camille could recognize stage presence anywhere.

Absinthe complied happily with Charlotte's wishes. "Camille knew nothing of your previous marriage. I told her you were originally married to Becket Door."

Charlotte chuckled and reached for another grape, beginning, Camille soon realized, a ritualistic way of eating grapes. She bit it in half. "It seems I opened the wrong Door back in India."

"What happened that you should now be married to his brother?" Camille asked, her voice sounding a tad bit high to her own ears.

"My first husband killed his parents." She began to peel the other half with her incisors.

"Really!"

"Oh, yes." More peeling. "Wanted the title and the money and couldn't wait for nature to give them to him. Murdered them in cold blood when we were all on holiday in the south of France." Charlotte Door looked Camille straight in the eye, then her face crumbled and tears filled her eyes. "It was horrible."

Liar! Camille thought.

Georginia touched her arm. "There now, Charlotte. It was years ago."

"I know. But moments like that are impossible to get over." She ate the grape anyway, and began to move her feet quickly from side to side, an agitated bobble of golden sandals.

As Monica drew a handkerchief out of her pocket and handed it to Charlotte, Camille assumed a look of sympathy. "What happened to him?"

Charlotte sniffed, wiping off the heavy eyeliner along with her tears as she chewed. "Cyprian pulled what strings he had in the French government and had him sent to a penal colony in French Guiana instead of to the guillotine."

"And how did you come to be married to his brother?" Thank goodness women were naturally curious! Nobody seemed to suspect a thing, Camille noted with relief.

"We fell in love right away, lived in sin until an annulment could be granted, and married as soon as we got word."

"*Zut alors!*" Camille couldn't help herself.

Absinthe looked at her sharply.

Charlotte shrugged. "At least I'm honest about it."

Camille agreed with haste. She hadn't listed alienating Charlotte Door on her agenda for the day. "There's certainly something to be said for that. Especially here in England."

Monica nodded. "Especially if you are a woman."

Charlotte took another swallow of scotch, picked another grape. "So that's my tragic tale. We all have them. Georginia used to dance before royalty before breaking both legs. Monica eats opium. And Absinthe is a closet Impressionist, for heaven's sake, who writes the most depressing poetry you can imagine."

Camille laughed, relieved to notice none of the others minded their secrets being scattered about like weed seeds over a freshly fertilized field. "It seems I've found myself in colorful company."

Absinthe rolled her eyes, which was quite a sight. "My dear, you have absolutely no idea!"

When the time to leave arrived, Absinthe pulled Camille aside. "Stay for a bit after the others leave. I wish to talk to you."

They waved the ladies off, three impressive carriages slowly rolling down the drive. Absinthe sighed. "Truth be told, I'm glad Charlotte was late. It enabled us to get *some* worthwhile conversation in."

This statement surprised Camille. "I'd noticed it all turned to shoes and Charlotte Door after she arrived."

They walked back into the entry hall. "Come into my study. It's at the back of the house."

"You have your own study?"

"Oh, yes. Who do you think is behind Merlin? That man couldn't think his way through the morning fog! For all practical purposes, I am the MP."

The surprises kept surfacing!

Absinthe's study was a magical room. Walls papered a dark blue with golden stars offset gilded furniture. Every bit a woman's room, it nevertheless lacked feminine frills and pastels. "It's my favorite room in the house." Absinthe pulled the tortoiseshell comb from her hair, the thin brown waves falling softly around her austere face. She looked quite different altogether—surely not pretty, but appealing in a gauzy, Celtic way.

"It's like nothing I've ever seen."

Absinthe pointed to a golden yellow sofa opposite from her desk. "Have a seat. And feel free to put your feet up on the butler's table. Take your shoes off if you want."

Camille very much did want, and she complied to all three of Lady Absinthe Pencraig's invitations.

"I know practically everything there is to know about you, Lady Camille." The words came out without warning.

"Oh? And what is that?" Camille looked away.

She lifted the lid of a hinged box on the left-hand side of her desk. "That you've slept with my husband, and almost every other nobleman in Europe. Cigarette?"

Camille waved a hand. What could this woman be up to?

Absinthe's face fell with disappointment. "You used to."

"Before Lily."

"Ah, yes, Lily." Absinthe leaned down and undid her own shoes, pretty beribboned affairs that Camille had noticed earlier. Shoes spoke reams about a person. "I don't smoke them myself." Doubled over at the waist, Absinthe's clear, high voice transformed to somewhat of a grunt.

Camille felt that familiar impatience. "What's this all about, Lady Absinthe? Is this some sort of drama? Some sort of '"Come into my parlor," said the spider to the fly'?"

Not put off in the least, Absinthe stood up from her chair at the desk and tugged on a bellpull near the doorway. She perched next to Camille on the couch. "I know what you were. I don't tell you this without a purpose."

How frank. "And if your purposes don't coincide with mine?"

"They will."

"Funny," said Camille. "I would swear you are . . . oh, what is it you English say about threats and veils?"

"A veiled threat," Absinthe supplied.

"Yes, that's it. Just tell me what you want from me and be done with it. If you truly know my past, Lady Absinthe, you know not to dress up the issue." Brave words, but Camille realized her back was wet with perspiration.

"You mean skirt around the issue?"

Camille waved an impatient hand. "Yes, yes."

"And, please, Camille, call me Abby. We're probably going to be spending a lot of time together."

"Why is that?"

"I want you to convince your husband that he should align himself with the liberal party."

"Why should I?"

Absinthe leaned back into the upholstery of the couch. "Because we women have taken a backseat long enough."

"What is that supposed to mean?"

"Don't you realize what we were saying out there? This Education Act is just the beginning. Voting for school boards, running for school boards! It won't be long until we are given the vote, until we can stand in the House of Commons and the House of Lords on our own two feet as our own person."

Ciel! It sounded as if the woman was winding up to give a speech. "You mean women serving in parliament?"

"Why not?"

"Well . . ." Camille tried to make her brain hurry. "To be honest, I can't think of a good reason why they shouldn't."

"There! You see? And this is just the beginning! There's no good reason why we shouldn't be allowed to serve the people. But we need the votes of enlightened, forward-thinking, dare I say unconventional men. Like the earl of Cannock."

A servant stepped into the room. "Yes, ma'am?"

"More tea." She turned to Camille, then laid a hand on her knee. "Is that all right with you?"

Camille nodded, hoping that there'd be no tray of sweets to go with it. Her willpower was completely dilapidated, and she'd eaten more at the tea with the ladies than she used to eat in an entire day.

The servant curtseyed and left.

Absinthe turned her attention back to Camille. "Do you know what our queen actually said about us?"

"Who do you mean by us? Women?"

"No, not all women. Feminists. I rather like that title, don't you? I'm not sure who coined it, but I wish it had been myself. Sounds modern and strong." She set her feet on the table, relaxing in a way that reminded Camille of David. "Anyway, she doesn't like us at all, mind you. But then she doesn't have to, she already has a place of prominence."

"So . . ." Camille prompted lest she go off on another tangent.

Absinthe reached for a small leather-bound book on the table. "She said, and I quote—"

"Quote? Really?" Camille had to admire that. "I can hardly remember what I said two seconds ago."

She flipped open the book. "Oh no, it was in the *Times* and I copied it down right here in my diary."

"You have a diary?"

"Absolutely. I'm a chronic record keeper, of my thoughts, my actions, goals, everything. It's a disease, really." Her eyes sparkled with a sense of humor that had not previously come to the fore. "Now then, here's the quote." She tweaked her voice up several notes, raised her chin, and pursed her lips. Her nostrils flared in an attempt to imitate the queen. "'I'm most anxious to enlist everyone who can speak or write to join in checking this mad, wicked folly of Women's Rights, with all its attendant horrors, on which her poor feeble sex is bent, forgetting every sense of womanly feelings and propriety.'"

Camille's mouth dropped open. "Poor? Feeble? And she's even had children!"

"Yes! I can hardly imagine a man grunting out a baby after hours of labor. He'd look at his time piece after fifteen minutes of birthing pains, and say 'I'm finished now. Have my wife come and do something!'"

Camille laughed and started to add her bit, but Absinthe held up a hand. "I'm not done with my quote. She went on to say that 'feminists ought to get themselves a good whipping. Were women to "unsex" themselves by claiming equality with men, they would become the most hateful, heathen, and disgusting of beings and would surely perish without male protection.'" Absinthe sat back in triumph. "She said that. She did." With a snap, she shut the book and threw it on the table in front of them.

Camille thought of the past seven years. "Perish without male protection? Let the lady speak for herself!"

"Exactly!" Absinthe clapped. "You've got the idea, Camille, darling."

"Do the others in this tea club agree with you?"

"Yes. It's one of the reasons we meet. There's the 'Kensington Club,' you know. Barbara Bodichon's group. But they're so outspoken they can put people off. We prefer to be more subversive about it."

"Charlotte, too? She's in on this with you as well?"

Absinthe shrugged with a grimace and a nod. "She was a little harder to convince at first. She's very much an aristocrat, remember. To give more power to the people, women included, means chipping away at the aristocracy."

"But it must do good to have Charlotte in your camp."

"Precisely." Absinthe placed her feet beneath her, knees bent to the side. "Charlotte has quite a hold on her husband." She leaned forward. "Sexually speaking." The whisper was barely audible.

"You don't have to whisper about such things with me!" Camille said. "And why, tell me, is Cyprian Door so important to your cause?"

"He's one of Bertie's best friends."

"Bertie?"

"Bertie. The prince of Wales."

Confused again! "I thought the prince of Wales's name was Edward?"

"Oh, it is. But you know those royals with their ridiculous nicknames! Why, the queen herself was called Drina all during her growing up years. For Alexandrina. It's her first name, you know."

Camille didn't. But not about to let on, she said, "Abby, you're such fun. I got the wrong impression of you that first night at the party."

"Oh, that!" She waved Camille's remark aside. "I was mad at Merlin. Not twenty minutes before he'd related the entire sordid story of you and he, just as I was trying to get ready. His timing made me furious."

"And that was all? His timing? Not his past history?"

"Heavens, no! First of all, that was before we were married. Second of all, Merlin and I quit sleeping together over a year ago. He's never stopped his philandering, and so I finally told him if he's going to prowl around the hussies, his prowling days with me are over. Heir or not!"

Camille clapped her hands once, patted Absinthe's knee. "Good for you!"

The tea came and Absinthe poured. Once each cup brimmed exactly to its imbiber's liking, Absinthe raised hers in a toast. "To the future!"

"To the future!" Camille raised hers and they tapped them together, the china clinking musically. Interesting developments, indeed.

"Oh, I almost forgot!" Absinthe smiled broadly. "Remember that discussion we had regarding the queen's séances?"

"How could I forget?"

Absinthe held a hand up to her mouth, excitement raising her shoulders slightly. "Charlotte's taking me to one tonight!"

"No!"

"Yes! I've never been to a séance. Have you?"

"Tons of them!" Camille shook her head and waved a hand of dismissal. "They're as fake as you can well imagine, and only the grief-stricken or the most gullible of creatures can begin to fool themselves it's real."

Absinthe wrinkled her nose. "I thought so. Charlotte insists it's real."

"She's the medium."

"True. Anyway, I'll tell you all about it."

Camille sat up straight. "Please do."

"But promise you won't tell Georginia, or it will be all over London in two hours!"

"Georginia's that bad, is she?" Camille asked, setting down her cup.

"Absolutely. It's what makes her so interesting."

"It seems I've found myself in the midst of a fascinating little group."

Absinthe reached for the teapot. "Camille, you don't know the half of it!"

CHAPTER ❖ EIGHTEEN

David looked through the doorway of the dining room, focusing on the front door of the house. Where was Camille anyway? Supper should have begun fifteen minutes ago and she had yet to return. Elspeth was dining with a group of girlfriends and wouldn't be back until late. Blast it all, but his stomach gurgled like the hot spring at Bath! And he had reams of research to do tonight. March and Campbell had sent word to Lord Ashley, who was very favorable at the idea of meeting with David.

"Wooten!"

The aged man, a faithful family servant for years, husband of Mrs. Wooten, appeared with his hands tucked tightly behind his back. "Yes, my lord?"

"I'm hungry, Wooten."

Wooten tugged on his vest points. "Just a moment, sir. I'll return shortly."

Two minutes later Mrs. Wooten appeared. She planted her pudgy hands on her hips. "You're hungry, eh?"

"Yes."

"And you're wondering whether or not to wait for Lady Camille?" She took a dust rag out of her pocket and began dusting a chair back nearby.

"Actually, I wasn't wondering any such thing. I merely told Wooten I was hungry and he went and fetched you. He didn't say, 'I'll get your supper, sir,' or 'I'll set things out right away, my lord,' or even a 'by your leave, sir' which, I might add, is what a proper servant would have done. No, there was none of that."

Wooten cleared his throat. "Just trying to save you from yourself, my lord. That's all we're doing."

David wanted to feel irritated at the two overly protective servants, but he couldn't. He put his elbow on the table and rested his chin in his hand. "So you think I should wait for her, then?"

Mrs. Wooten didn't hesitate. She pulled out the chair next to him and sat down with a puff. "Well, it all depends on what you want later on tonight, lovey."

"Mrs. Wooten!" Mr. Wooten gasped.

David laughed. That anyone as stuffy as Wooten could be married to anyone as homey as Mrs. Wooten proved God's mysterious ways. "Don't pay her any mind, Wooten. She's been talking to me like this for years, and well you know it. All right, then, it's settled. I'll wait. Where's Lily?"

"Up in the nursery, my lord." Mrs. Wooten straightened the tablecloth to perfection. "Having her supper."

"By herself?"

"It's the way of things, my lord."

Wooten excused himself.

David raised his eyebrows up and down. "Well, I do believe I've thought of a way to win my lady's favor and eat as well." He stood to his feet. "Send my supper up on a tray to the nursery. I'll eat with Lily."

Mrs. Wooten stood up as well, blushing with pride. "Oh, you are still just as devious as ever, aren't you, Master David?"

"It's getting more difficult with every passing day." He patted her shoulder as he passed by. "Oh, and send up a special dessert. I'm in the mood for something sweet."

"As you wish, my lord."

David's hunger was justified. He'd again met with March that day and they'd eaten little. Much to March's well-concealed but nevertheless apparent chagrin, David decided he wouldn't support any party. He'd become a cross bencher, voting his conscience and not some party line. They could keep their traditions as far as he was concerned. England's government needed a stiff jab, and he would gladly help deliver the blow.

Even the queen's popularity had recently experienced an all-time low. March reported the monarchy had cost the people 400,000 pounds during the last year, and many wondered if it was worth it. Victoria had taken an official stance of neutrality, although it was common knowledge she couldn't abide Gladstone, the current prime minister, and his ilk. Everyone suspected Disraeli, previously in power, topped her list.

But she had a fondness for Aaron Campbell. "'You always remind me of my beloved Highlands,'" Aaron had related in a high, squeaky voice. Notwithstanding that Aaron was a lowlander with a very faint burr. Already, David would lay down his life for this man of God.

David climbed up to the top floor of the house and found Lily in the nursery. She sat cross-legged on her chair, picking at her food with a fork that appeared much too large in her tiny hand. Dressed in a white sailor dress, she seemed very English. Her hair, tightly captured by a large black bow, rested on the nape of her neck. "Lily?"

She looked up. "Hello." Her voice, soft and sad, twisted his heart.

He placed a hand on her head. "How's your dinner?"

"Fine, I suppose." She sighed, smashing her peas with the tines of her fork. "Not like *Maman's* soup."

"I'm having my dinner sent up here."

Her eyes looked up at him and a broad smile spread across her face. "That would be nice. Would you like to sit down?"

"I'd be honored." He pulled out a small white spindly chair and lowered himself. His knees practically met his chin. So he angled the chair instead and laid his legs out in front of him, resting his left foot atop his right knee. Poor Lily. Except for

Camille's trip to French Guiana, she'd had her mother's undivided attention all of her life. This must be new and not so nice.

He remembered all the nights he'd eaten alone in the nursery, and her loneliness wounded him afresh. "Where's Elspeth?"

"Gone off with her big girlfriends, I guess."

David knew he had to have a talk with his daughter later on that night. With Elspeth gone so often, they hadn't even had time to finish reading *Tom Jones*.

Wooten arrived with a tray supporting covered dishes. He served David there at the nursery table and withdrew right away.

"Yours looks much better than mine," Lily grumbled.

The child had hit that one on the nose. Her peas and pork pie couldn't compare to his leg of lamb with mint jelly, potatoes Anna, and currant glazed carrots. "Here, Lily." He took her plate and dumped its contents on the tray, then arranged portions of his own meal on its surface. "Does this look better?"

"Oh, yes!"

Her smile filled his heart to the bursting. "Have you said grace?"

She shook her head. "I feel stupid saying it all by myself."

So he said it for them, thanking God for the food and for Lily and that they could share their meal together. She echoed his amen and they began to eat.

He reached over and cut up her meat. "So do you like it here in London?" He knew the answer.

"I wish I saw Mama more, and everyone else is always so busy."

He cut off a piece of his own portion and put it in his mouth. The child needed companionship. He'd been thinking unclearly when he thought Elspeth would keep the child company. Elspeth, a woman now, intensely guarded her privacy. Not that it surprised him considering her malformation. But she did have a few good friends, and he wasn't about to keep her from spending time in places she found acceptance. Even though they'd been in London less than a week, he had hoped for more time with her.

"Is there room for a third?"

David turned at the sound of his wife's voice. "There's always room for you, *chérie*."

"*Maman*!" Lily sprang from her chair and up into her mother's arms. "I've missed you so badly today!"

Camille laughed. "It was only one day, Lily. I'm all yours tomorrow to do with as you wish. Where shall we go?" She set her daughter down.

She clapped her hands and danced her little jig. "The Crystal Palace!"

Camille sat down in the tiny chair next to David. "I don't suppose you'd like to join us."

"I can't. But I'll be home by early afternoon and we can go riding."

Lily cheered.

Camille scowled. "David, you know I don't like to ride."

"Well, I had an idea, *chérie*. How would it do if I took Lily riding with me and you made supper?"

"Supper? Me? Cooking down in that kitchen?" Camille acted shocked, but David could tell she liked the idea.

Lily pulled on her mother's hand. "Please, *Maman*!"

"What do you say, *chérie*? I haven't had your cooking since I've been home." The nights he'd sat in her kitchen eating bowl after bowl of soup and slicing up a loaf of bread to dunk in the tasty broth were too numerous to count.

Her nurturing instinct won the day for David and Lily and she crumbled with a sigh. "To be honest, I'd like nothing more. All this rich food we've eaten since arriving hasn't helped my waistline. All right. I'll cook for you, but only on the condition that you give the staff the night off. I don't want anybody looking over my shoulder."

David knew she tried her best to appear irritated, but she couldn't fool him. The sudden pink patches on her cheeks attested to the contrary.

Mrs. Wooten came in with another tray.

David jumped to his feet and took it from her. "Dearest Wifie Wooten, we're giving the staff the evening off tomorrow. You're free to do as you wish after two in the afternoon."

Mrs. Wooten's brows drew together in suspicion. "And what's this about, Master David?"

"I've a hankering for my wife's cooking."

She nodded, smug. "A better reason I've yet to hear. Well then. I'll have to make sure my Sunday dress is pressed and ready. Bless you, my lord."

Shoving the rag back into the pocket of her apron, she went away with a lighthearted step. As soon as she shut the door, they heard her voice calling, "Mr. Wooten! Mr. Wooten! Call the staff together right away! We're gettin' tomorrow night off!"

"Let's eat, shall we?" David served his wife her food. "I'm famished. And maybe you can tell us about your day."

Camille did, happily describing Charlotte Door. But he knew she left out details never meant for ears stuck on the heads of girls like Lily. More later.

~

Absinthe blinked in the dimness of the queen's private sitting room at Kensington Palace. A round table, brought in for the occasion, had been draped with a heavy black cloth. A single candle burned in the very center of the table. Charlotte had made sure its position was exact, acting in an odd blend of officiousness and mystery. She perfectly calibrated the room for contacting the dead. Impressive.

And so convincing.

Victoria watched it all from a straight-backed chair in the corner of the room. Her eyes glittered like jet buttons tucked deep into the folds of her padded face. Anticipation smoothed out her forehead. "Do you suppose he'll come again tonight?" she asked Charlotte as a servant turned down the gas lights in preparation. "I mean, with Lady Pencraig with us and all."

"Oh yes!" Charlotte had nodded. "In fact, your majesty, Lady Absinthe has her own powers with the world of the dead."

"Really?" The room now dark, illumined only by the flame of the single candle, Victoria stood to her feet.

"It's something I've been aware of for years, unbeknownst to even Lady Absinthe," Charlotte said as she helped the queen to a chair.

This was news to Absinthe, but she said nothing. She merely nodded, trying to look like Merlin might have looked in such a situation. And she didn't mean her no-good husband, either!

Queen Victoria sat down. "You're a good child, Charlotte. You've given me such comfort during these dark days."

Charlotte took the queen's hand and pressed it to her cheek. "It is an honor, majesty."

Absinthe thought she would lose her supper, which would be a shame since it was such a good supper. But she curtailed the nausea, forced down the disgust she felt at Charlotte's amazing thespian capabilities, and smiled.

What a crock! Absinthe saw Charlotte in a new light. What a liar! But she knew of Charlotte's ambitiousness. One couldn't be around the baroness of Dividen for long without realizing that. Two of a power-hungry kind, Charlotte sought more power for her beloved Cyprian, and Absinthe sought power through her not-so-beloved Merlin. The nausea turned to the urge to laugh.

"Join hands!" Charlotte proclaimed, her voice deeper and more authoritative.

I guess those pesky spirits must be stubborn. Absinthe shook her head.

"Let us begin. Close your eyes."

The three women clasped hands, providing the candle with a circular hedge of human flesh. Absinthe, not about to close her eyes, watched in fascination as Charlotte put herself into a trance, mumbling in a Hindu tongue, rapidly firing out syllables. Her voice echoed around the chamber, wooden yet commanding. Well, scary, actually, if one didn't know better!

The candle fluttered, and cold air settled around them. Rappings tapped like heels clicking, breezes exhaled, and automatic writing from some long-gone aunt seemed to be scribbled by an unseen, ghostly hand. All the normal spiritism fare. Impressive.

Charlotte knew what she was doing!

Absinthe had to admit Camille's tidbits had come in handy. She might well have fallen for this drivel without them.

"Oh!" the queen breathed, eyes still closed. "He's coming. My beloved Albert comes!"

Absinthe watched as the doorway to the queen's bedchamber opened silently and "Prince Albert" slipped behind the Chinese screen in the corner. How good to have friends in high places. Years ago she had determined to become the best friend Charlotte Door ever had. It hadn't been an easy road drawing the woman into a mode of confidence, but she had finally succeeded. And now the payoff had begun, but the final treasure was yet to be awarded.

She'd come back to more of these things. And that fat queen sitting there with a look of such rapt stupidity on her face, so vulnerable and wanting, could only be good for her plans.

CHAPTER ❖ NINETEEN

W alk with me."

Surprised at the request, Camille glanced across her pillow at the man for whom she'd come to breathe. Her fingers found the curls at his temple. "Like this?" She referred to their state of complete undress.

Beneath the covers, David ran a hand over her stomach. "Well, it would be nice, and we could certainly set tongues wagging even more fervently on our behalf."

She laughed and nestled into him, loving the way he always kept himself so clean and well-groomed, the way he took care of himself. Not like most of those Paris men. Wooh! "I rather think it's nice right here, don't you? And it is quite cool outside tonight."

"Come on, *chérie*. We could use the fresh air. And it's already near dawn. We could watch the sun rise."

He wasn't going to let up. Youngbloods never did. "Oh, all right, my lord. Let's get it over with."

Ten minutes later they shuffled forward in the darkness, comfortably navigating a path toward the river. David leaned less and less on his cane these days, she noticed with relief.

He expressed his concerns regarding the previous day's happenings. "It's going to be easier to get into favor with Cyprian Door than I thought. Politically speaking, that is. And yet . . ."

"Why does that trouble you?"

"I don't know, *chérie*. Perhaps I'm idealistic, but it's hard for me to comprehend a man so misguided in his personal life can be so dead-on when it comes to the issues. It makes me question my own beliefs a little."

"I may not be smart like you Youngbloods, but I do know that truth is truth no matter who believes it or why." She was enjoying the anonymity of the darkness, the deserted autumn night, and the sound of David's boots thumping on the cobbled street beside her. "It's probably not good to agonize over it for long."

"I suppose I need to talk with someone about it. Get some good advice."

It didn't pain Camille to know that he needed more counsel than she could give. *Ciel*, but she could hardly call herself wise! Talk about a life full of stupid choices. But that David loved her knowing that, loved her in spite of it and maybe sometimes even because of it, comforted her. "David, I think it's rather marvelous. It makes things so much easier. You can align yourself with Cyprian politically, and I can be infiltrating the mind of Charlotte Door."

"And get to know Lady Absinthe and the tea biddies in the bargain?"

Camille laughed. "Exactly. Absinthe knows all about our past. Not the Devil's Island part, but the fact that you sold me to her husband." She felt him stiffen briefly, then tighten the arm he had draped across her shoulders. "She means to use you, through me, to further her causes in parliament. She hopes to exact influence in the Liberal party by employing Charlotte's influence on her husband."

David shook his head. "I don't know, *chérie*, Cyprian Door has quite a reputation for being smooth and savvy. I can't imagine his wife is that much of an influence over him."

"You, my darling, have not met Lady Charlotte Door!"

They turned the corner of Grosvenor Place onto Buckingham Palace Road and headed closer to the Houses of Parliament. A while later, both lost in silence, they stood by the Westminster Bridge. The low moon shone down on the black waters of the Thames, its reflected orb shifting on the surface of the river.

"What do you think, Camille?" She watched as his eyes flitted over the moon-latticed water. "Are you still glad you married me?"

She turned to face him and wound her arms around his neck. "Of course, David. I wanted nothing else for many years."

He hugged her closely. "You're just what I need, my love."

"I always have been," she assured him.

"If I had only seen it at the beginning, think what trouble it would have saved us both."

She laid her cheek against his chest. "As we've said so many times, David, we cannot go back."

He sighed and she looked up at his face. A tear dropped onto her forehead. "I'm sorry, *chérie*. Can you ever forgive me for what I did to you?"

"I've forgiven you, David. How many times do I have to tell you that?" The man refused to hear her.

"As many times as I need to ask," he whispered softly. "It's what I've been learning from Campbell, *chérie*. That sometimes we do things that are so horrible we cannot ever make up for it. We just have to get through each day, take as many steps as we can, asking forgiveness along the way. Sometimes for the rest of our lives. For our own sake."

"I understand, *mon mari*."

They stayed by the river until dawn began to break.

Finally, he turned her toward the street. "Let's go home."

Camille wove her arm through her husband's, breathing in the still air of the city. "Do you remember Charles Blondin?" she asked.

His brows raised. "The French tightrope walker?"

"Yes. When was it he crossed over Niagara Falls? It must have been at least eight years ago."

"Eight? Oh no, it was at least ten, *chérie*. I remember because it was when you were in America with de Boyce."

She nodded. "Yes, that's right. It was quite a feat, what he did. Wasn't it?"

"Amazing. I've never seen the falls, but I can only imagine the bravery it took for him to do it."

"Or the stupidity."

David kissed the top of her head as they strolled. "And why does Charles Blondin come to your mind now, *chérie*?"

"I can't help but think we are trying to pull off something almost as impossible."

"We must be brave people, then."

"Or stupid." Camille suddenly saw the humor in it all. "Or both."

David stopped and looked at her in a manner so matter-of-fact she wanted to laugh. She loved it when his eyebrows did that. "When it comes right down to it, Camille, life is like that. With a little bravery and a little stupidity, anything is possible."

"I prefer to think of it as naivete, my lord." As if she could *ever* be called naïve!

"Whatever you call it, it merely shows how much we need God's guidance."

Camille stood on tiptoe and kissed his chin. "*Bien entendu!* Now *there* is something I can agree wholeheartedly with."

A while later, the burnished morning sun barely peeking over the black London rooftops, they turned onto their street.

"It seems quiet with Tobin and Miranda and their brood off to Greywalls now," David said.

"It does. But it's nice to have it be just us."

The smell of baking bread quickened their steps as they discussed the merits of an early breakfast. Camille noticed the front door of the house was just closing. So did David, for he dropped Camille's arm and went running up the steps.

"All right, Elspeth. Stop right there."

David didn't mean to sound so harsh, but nevertheless his somber tone felt stiff and overly controlled. What had the girl been thinking, being out all night?

Elspeth stopped dead, her hand clutching at the banister with such force her whitened knuckles looked as if they were about to split open the skin of her fingers like a molting snake sheds its skin.

She turned. "Dad."

"Did you have a good time?"

She nodded.

"Care to tell me where you were?"

"Do I have a choice?"

David wanted to laugh, but he allowed a very small smile instead. "Come to the sitting room with me, Bethie. I fear we have much to talk about, don't we?"

"Actually, we do."

She descended the staircase, past portraits of former Youngbloods with the same gray eyes that his daughter possessed, the same thick, wavy hair. A terrible thought attacked him with as much guilt as the remorse he had felt over his horrible sins. He'd never given her his name! All these years she'd lived as his illegitimate daughter.

But when could I have done so? He comforted himself as much as he could with the obvious.

"Would you fetch us some tea, *chérie*? Someone should be in the kitchen."

Camille complied, her relief at escaping the situation evidenced by the fast click of her heels toward the kitchen. He couldn't help but watch her graceful retreat in fascination, the way she unwound her shawl and threw it on the hall table, the way she smoothed back the wisps of hair that had been freed from her chignon by his loving the night before. Her alluring femininity complemented who he perceived himself to be. He needed her now.

David ushered Elspeth into the formal sitting room, the blue tones of the room grayed by the lack of sunlight. A polished walnut grandfather clock heaved its pendulum in a slow swing, its swaying brass circle catching the reflection from the two long windows at the front of the house. He'd never been fond of this sterile room.

Elspeth sat down on the ivory sofa and grabbed a round, needlepoint pillow, hugging it against her stomach. "I wasn't doing anything sexual in nature, if that's what you're worried about, Dad."

David couldn't hide his surprise. She'd read his mind. "Were you with a man?"

"A gentleman, yes."

"Elspeth, I don't need to tell you how this looks. Your reputation could be ruined." He reached for her hand.

"Dad, my reputation is ruined already by the fact that I'm your daughter. Any decorum I show is met with true surprise."

"The sins of the father . . ."

"Yes. All of that."

He reached out and caressed her cheek with his hand. "We haven't had time to talk yet, have we?"

"Not properly."

"No, not properly at all."

"There's so much you don't know about me, Dad. I've done a lot of changing since that day you left St. Ninian's Abbey for France. You said you'd come back and you never did."

"I wanted to."

"Well, yes. I suppose even I would be better company than a group of convicted felons."

He deserved that. "I'm sorry."

"I survived." She looked up into his eyes. "It's the Youngblood way, is it not?"

Oh, dear God. She was becoming just like him. He'd wanted things to be different for her.

He took her hand. "Will you spend the afternoon with me, then? There are no plans I have that I cannot cancel. Except for dinner tonight. Camille is cooking for us."

"Camille?" Clearly surprised, Elspeth pulled her hand away from her father's. "She can . . . cook? I thought women like her—"

Here we go. "Women like her? Elspeth? Are you saying what I think you're saying?"

She clenched her hands together in her lap. "My life was difficult enough *before* you brought her here, Dad. Now am I not only Elspeth Marquardt-not-really-Youngblood, illegitimate daughter of the murderer David Youngblood—and they all believe you bought your way out of that one, Papa, make no mistake about it—but then you show up with this Frenchwoman, clearly not of gentle birth, and there are rumors spreading that she was a kept woman! A nice way to say she's a common prostitute!"

A crash from the doorway splintered the air. There stood Camille, her skin gone to paste, her mouth open, while shards of china and pools of hot tea stained the carpet at her feet.

CHAPTER ❖ TWENTY

He jumped to his feet. "*Chérie!*"
Camille immediately dropped to her knees trying to pick up the pieces of hot porcelain, patting at the tea with her beautiful skirt. "I knew this was a foolish thing to try," she hissed, jerking her eyes up to burn into his. She was angry. Good. He couldn't bear it if she suddenly fell apart on him. "*Je m'en contrefiche.* These English and all their airs!"

Elspeth rushed forward to help, but David shook his head quickly. "Stay there, Bethie," he said. He turned toward his wife. "Let me help you."

David bent down, knowing that despite Camille's rants *en Francais*, she *did* care. She cared deeply what people thought of her, and always had.

They made quick work of the cleanup, and he picked up the tray as he stood to his feet. "I'll come with you, Camille."

She reached for the tray. "No!"

He laid a hand on her arm. "Are you all right?"

Her eyes displayed a lifetime of weariness. "I knew somebody would recognize me sooner or later, David. It only makes sense it is sooner. What will we do?"

"Well, we won't retreat! That's for certain."

"Well, I won't be brazenly paraded around as some cheap oddity either. No more parties! And I mean it, David. I may not have my virtue, but I do have my pride."

"Well, I won't let Elspeth get away with this comment, *chérie*. She hasn't been treating you with the respect you deserve."

She shifted her gaze to Elspeth who still sat on the couch. "*She* deserves more than this, *chéri*. I haven't enjoyed her little comments since I've come, I'll admit that, but, however disagreeable she is, she's done nothing to deserve all of this! She just wants you to pay a little attention to her, David."

He couldn't argue with that. "All right. I'm canceling all my plans for this morning and afternoon to spend the day with her. Are you still up to cooking dinner?"

"Up to it? I'm counting on it. I'm just about to go upstairs and collect Lily, and we'll go to market. That should make Elspeth happy as well."

He raised an eyebrow. "You won't mind being seen by the masses?"

She shook her head, eyes losing their ire. "How many women of quality will be out at this hour of the morning, and at the market at that?"

He leaned forward and kissed her fair cheek. "Someday we'll retire to the country, *chérie*, and we'll have a quiet, peaceful life."

She returned his kiss, but her eyes were sad. It wounded him deeply. "No, we won't. And you know it. You could never live a quiet life, David Youngblood. The fact that you married me despite who I was, despite the fact that I would eventually be recognized proves you've never been in for a quiet life at all."

"You're right, *chérie*."

"I always am."

He had to admit it. "You always are."

"Now, I'm taking this mess back down. That cook is down there. I'll tell him you and Elspeth want breakfast as soon as possible in the dining room and that in the meantime some more tea would be nice."

"Where will you be having breakfast?"

"At the market. We'll get some muffins there."

He laid a hand on her shoulder. "A splendid idea."

"It's just better if I get out of here for the morning, for everyone concerned."

She retreated down the corridor, through the doorway to the downward steps leading to the kitchen. Raking a hand through his hair, he returned to Elspeth, realizing that answering for his wild youth had become quite a pastime, realizing that some sins were never left behind for good.

Elspeth paced the floor. At least she hadn't changed so much that belligerence moved in. "Papa, I'm sorry." She walked to the window, pulling aside the sheer curtain and looking out at the dawn-gilded bushes. "If anybody should know how it feels not to fit in, it should be me. Did I hurt her feelings?" Her tone held just the right amount of obligatory repentance.

"Elspeth, let's dispense with the niceties." David sat down on the couch, draping a leg over its arm. "You've been terrible to her ever since we arrived."

"I knew you'd take her side."

"There are no *sides* to be taken here, Bethie. I'm on your side. So much so that to see you behaving like this raises all the fatherly hackles I possess. You can't treat people like that!"

"Oh, come on, Dad. She's only married to you for your title and your money. Everybody knows that!"

"Who are these 'everybodies' you keep referring to, Elspeth?"

"My circle."

"Oh ... what, a group of nineteen-year-old girls? Well, well. That's really saying something, then."

"You don't have to be cruel, Dad."

"Neither do you."

Elspeth slapped a hand onto the arm of the sofa and sat down. "Did you really expect another reaction? Really? I thought you were smarter than that."

"I suppose I was hoping in vain that you'd be a bit more accepting."

She laughed harshly. "Because of my face?"

"Of course."

"Oh, that's rich! If all that I've heard is true, you weren't an accepting young man at all."

"No, you're right there." He sighed. "So you positively won't accept Camille?"

"It's too soon, Dad! Did you really think it would be so easy?"

David examined her face, so vulnerable. "I suppose not."

"So what will you do? The entire ton knows about her past, Dad. If I were you, I'd move to Greywalls. For Camille's sake, and Lily's, if you have no regard for your own well-being."

"Camille knew this would happen eventually. She's more used to being part of a scandal than you could imagine."

"I've heard she was quite the rage in Paris a decade ago." She turned, her eyes filling with tears before she looked down at the hands she had folded in her lap. "She must have been an exciting woman," she whispered. "And she's so beautiful, Dad. I can see why you fell in love with her."

David's heart melted beneath the weight of his daughter's burning pain. "Oh, Bethie." He took her into his arms. "Those aren't the reasons I love her." He supposed it did good to talk to his daughter like this. But Elspeth understood things that no one else ever could. "She loves me. And has for years. With this face and all."

"And she stuck with you, Dad." Elspeth pulled away, crossed her arms grudgingly, her voice dropping. "You've got to hand that to her. If nothing else."

"How could I not agree."

"She's a good mother to Lily. And she's strong and certainly a woman with opinions of her own. At least, that's what Aunt Miranda told me."

His smile felt extremely broad as he looked up at his child. "And you like that in a woman? Why?"

She grabbed the pillow. "For some of us, our opinion is the only thing that is respected. So if it is strong, well-informed, and logical, then so much the better."

He never really thought of Camille as well-informed and logical. Strong? Yes. "So have you found a niche, Bethie? A place where you are accepted? You talk about these friends of yours." He sought to get her off the subject of Camille and onto the one topic most young people enjoyed discussing.

"Boarding school was good for me that way. There were several girls there who latched onto me right away. Maverick types, you know."

"What about the other girls?"

"You mean the belle-o-the-ball types?" She held up a hand. "Thank you, but no. Not my type. Never were."

"Did they hurt your feelings?"

She chuckled. "Dad, that would imply that I actually cared what they thought."

He laughed. "Good. I wish I had felt that way. I'm afraid, deep down at times, I did care what those types thought."

"It was a different set of circumstances. I had Aunt Miranda and Uncle Tobin to bolster me up before they sent me out into the big, wide world. And to tell the truth"—she leaned forward—"I'm so much smarter than the average society creature I would have been bored silly as one of their compatriots."

He was glad she gave herself credit where it was due. "So Miranda taught you well, then?"

"Wonderfully well. I graduated top of the class!"

He clapped. "That's my girl."

"*And*, even though you were such a scalawag, apparently you had a reputation for being an intelligent one. Everyone would always say, 'Oh, see Elspeth Marquardt, there, she's so smart, not that I'm surprised! She's David Youngblood's daughter. Shame he didn't live up to his potential!'"

Youngblood's daughter.

"Elspeth. There's something serious we must discuss. You've never been made a Youngblood officially. Is that something you would like? To be an official Youngblood?"

Her voice was wry. "I don't know, there's something mysterious about being illegitimate." She paused and David thought she was going to refuse. "Of *course* I want to be your official daughter! It's what I've wanted all of my life. But how are you going to go about it?"

"I have no idea!" he laughed. "Some kind of adoption, I suppose. They probably won't allow you to be called Lady Elspeth."

"Who cares?" She threw her arms around him. "I'm already known as your daughter, anyway. It'll be good just to know for me, in my heart, that you wanted to recognize me as such."

He kissed her cheek. "And now, almost official daughter, we have something else to discuss."

"Last night?"

"Yes. Do you want to tell me where you were?"

She looked up at him, arms still around his waist. "Do you promise not to get angry?"

"I promise. Not much gets me angry these days, anyway. But if I promise not to get angry, will you promise to let me spew forth fatherly advice?"

She sat back and put out her hand. "Sounds like a fair deal to me."

They shook on it, David feeling so warmly loved, so comfortable. His daughter had such confidence, such poise, despite her deformity. And yet he knew, that no matter how the world seemed to accept her, she would always have him to understand her deep down. In a way, he was glad he could understand, even if it meant the curse of his birth defect. For the first time in his life, he didn't regret the way he looked.

Wait. Make that the second time. *This mug got me off of Devil's Island!*

Just then, Wooten arrived and cleared his throat at the door. "Excuse me, my lord, Miss Elspeth, but breakfast is ready in the dining room."

181

"Thank you, Wooten." David rose to his feet. "Well, Bethie, shall we continue our conversation over breakfast?"

"Oh, yes! Whenever I'm nervous all I want to do is eat!"

They laughed together and he offered her his arm as they wove their way to the dining room. Eggs, kidneys and bacon, mushrooms, toast and jam were laid out on the sideboard. David made sure there was no china surface showing through the food on his plate. Elspeth heaped a large mound of eggs onto hers and three pieces of toast.

"Your appetite has picked up from before." She pointed to his plate and bit down into her toast.

"I lost almost four stone in French Guiana. And I'm trying to gain it back again."

"Well, if you keep eating like that you're sure to succeed."

They bantered for a while longer until Elspeth finished her toast and eggs and let out a long sigh. "I might as well get it over with, if you don't mind."

Not even halfway done with his first plate, he agreed. "So where were you?"

"With Sir Keir Faraday. But it's not what you might think, Dad. There's nothing like that between us." Her tone sounded almost disappointed at that fact.

"And where did you meet this gentleman?"

"A mutual friend."

Elspeth went on to explain that Sir Keir, knighted for his studies in the field of biology, graduated from Cambridge. Introduced to her by one of her former schoolmates, he was a dedicated scientist from "a good, upstanding family." Hard-working, kind, attentive, "a genius, Dad," naturally, he wasn't handsome "in the normal way," but there was something very pleasing about his straight black hair and pleasant demeanor. "You'd think he'd be arrogant, walking around with a brain like that stuffed inside his skull, but he's nice. A truly nice person."

"Sounds like he hung the moon," David said wryly.

"Dad, it's not that. Really. It's simply that I've never met any-body like him. He says things I've never heard before, not with all the religion that's always been so prevalent here at home with Uncle Tobin and Aunt Miranda."

New ideas. Hmm. "So these are scientific ideas?" He never had much of a head for science. He'd always been a man of letters, really.

Yes, they were. David had never been much interested in biology, but what Elspeth went on to speak of was fascinating, and yet so contrary to what he had been taught, to what he had found to be true in his own life.

"It explains so much!" Elspeth's eyes shone with excitement. "It's all just forces of nature combined with the passage of time, Dad. You, me, what we look like, our abilities. It all makes so much sense now." She went on about how she had always been disappointed with God for making her like he did, how she was angry at him for sentencing her to such a difficult life.

David had some trouble understanding why this would be any more of a comfort. Either God directly caused things to happen, or he allowed them even though he had full power to step in and take action. Either way, God was God, and man was man, and you had to either accept him, or reject him. But he certainly couldn't be redefined. "So you don't blame God now? You aren't angry at him anymore?"

She breathed in deeply, looked up at him, and closed her eyes. "How can I be angry at something I no longer believe in?" Her hands twisted her linen napkin into a wrinkled ball.

"Oh, Elspeth," he whispered. "I'm sorry. I'm so very sorry."

God forgive me, he prayed. Would his sins never cease to keep creeping upon him, strangling those he loved with its thin cord of guilt?

Apparently not.

"Papa?" Elspeth's voice pulled him from his self-berating. "There's something I need to ask you. It's probably a good thing all of this came out into the open."

If what she had to say bore any resemblance to what had already come to light, he knew the remains of his breakfast would remain in their present form. "What is it, Bethie?"

183

"There's a house party going on near Oxford. It starts tomorrow. I and some of the other girls from the club have been invited."

"Your literary club?" This sounded relatively harmless.

"Yes. And others will be there as well."

"Gentlemen guests, I presume?"

"Uh-huh. Dad, Sir Keir will be there. I so want to go. By most social standards it's going to be dull. But we plan on discussing the works of Swift and Defoe, and even Charles Darwin himself is going to be there for the more scientific part of the stay."

David set down his fork. "The last thing I want is for you to listen to this man, Bethie. Especially if he's an atheist."

"Oh, he's not an atheist, it's Keir who's the atheist."

"Then my point is doubly valid. I suspect you'll be spending more time with this Sir Keir than with Charles Darwin."

"But—"

"I'm not done. Your head has been filled with ideas that can only bring harm to you. You've separated God from his creation because you can't come to grips with his plan for your own life. But at the same time, you're nineteen years old, and I think the decision should be yours."

Elspeth looked dumbfounded. "Really? You're not going to start preaching to me about propriety and the like?"

He rubbed his chin. "When have I ever preached to you?"

She shrugged. "Never, I suppose. But that's it? You're just going to give me the go-ahead? Just like that?"

He waved his hands in exasperation. "Elspeth? What would you have me do?"

She stood to her feet and walked over to the sideboard, putting some more toast on her plate. "I don't know. I just thought it would take more than this. I suppose I've been sneaking around the past week for no reason too, haven't I?"

"You could say that. A little openness and honesty might suit our relationship, Bethie. Even though I was a cad for so many years, I never was a sneak about it. Pour me a bit more tea while you're up, would you?" He was trying to act normal, unruffled, concerned yet not apprehensive.

She picked up his cup and poured from a delicate porcelain pot sitting on the table. "I just thought you wouldn't understand. I can clearly remember how important God became to you before you left."

"He still is."

"I figured that would be the case. And I didn't want to hurt you." She sat back down, her movements graceful and mature. "Just because I've stopped believing in God doesn't mean I'm heartless."

Hardly the point. Some of the nicest people David knew were atheists. "It's not me you're hurting ultimately, Bethie, with this rejection of the Lord, it's yourself." He sipped his tea. "It's obvious I've done great damage where you are concerned. Ignoring you for years, and then being exiled."

Elspeth laid a hand on his. "You know I forgave you long ago, Papa."

Her voice comforted him. His child. "Yes, and I clung to that on Devil's Island, I assure you. But there's something you don't know, Bethie. I gave you to God on that island. I asked him to be the father I couldn't be."

"Looks like he didn't answer your prayer quite like you thought."

"It's not that. It's just that he's not finished yet." He took her hand and reached out with his other hand, directing her gaze into his. "If God could bring a hardened sinner like myself to him, I have no doubt he'll do the same with you."

She pulled her hand away, eyes not unkind. "I think you'll be disappointed, Dad."

"God hasn't disappointed me yet."

"How can you say that? You were on Devil's Island for seven years! Seven years!" Her eyes glazed over with emotion. "You were born with this ... this ... ugliness, and you had parents that despised you! What do you mean God hasn't disappointed you yet?"

"I only exacerbated things by my rebellion. But I have peace now, Bethie. Since I found the Lord, I have peace."

She smiled half a grin. "Even in a penal colony!"

"Even there."

She wiped her mouth and threw down her napkin. "Well, he's disappointed me, Dad. All of my life. So it's either believe he exists and doesn't give a fig for someone whose form is so obviously fallen from the way things were created to be, or believe he doesn't exist at all. I would think the choice is obvious."

David looked down at his plate, trying to think of something wise and perfect, something Jesus Christ himself would have said had he been sitting in this chair, facing this human in such desperate need. Nothing came to mind.

He felt the warm touch of her hand on his shoulder. "I'm sorry, Dad. I don't mean to upset you. But you said we should be honest with each other."

Looking up into her face, he said the only thing that he was certain Jesus would say at a time like this. "I love you, Bethie."

And he arose from his chair and embraced her, willing the love he bore for this flesh of his flesh seep from his heart through his body and into hers.

She pulled back a few seconds later, the excited young woman dancing a dreamy waltz in her eyes. "I'll go pack right now! Sir Keir will be so excited." After rubbing her cheek against his, she ran out of the room, a graceful flutter of soft green muslin.

CHAPTER ✦ TWENTY-ONE

And so you see, Lord Youngblood"—Lord Ashley, champion of the common man, swept a hand across the rooftops of the slums of London—"there is much work to be done."

David could hardly believe he stood here, in the bell tower of St. Paul's Cathedral. He hadn't entered the cathedral for years, but he hadn't forgotten the grandeur of the building designed by Christopher Wren. The dazzling colors in the ceiling alone could steal the very breath from a man's lungs. And the exquisite architecture fashioned a yearning in his soul to do better, to follow God in the spirit of gentleness, goodness, and truth.

He stood with Lord Anthony Ashley, Viscount March having excused himself due to his fear of heights, Lord Aaron Campbell hardly able to climb the stairs with his arthritis.

The seventh earl of Shaftesbury turned to face his companion. "Why are we here? In your own words, Youngblood. I've heard what the others have to say on the matter."

"I'm looking for a purpose, I suppose." David pointed out of the window. "Out there." He placed his hand on his heart. "In here, perhaps, as well."

"And how do you know you are the man to accomplish anything?" Ashley's round eyes bonged a melancholy deeper than the lowest toned bell in the church tower. David had heard that Ashley, given to bouts of depression, didn't exactly have a belfry full of warm comrades. He could well believe it. The man, so direct as to be alarming, made David feel as though he had stepped into a cricket match in progress, the air rife with competition.

"Anything I might accomplish wouldn't be done from my own strength. I know I'm *not* the man to accomplish anything worthwhile, my lord. It's only through God's strength."

"I see." Ashley set his hand on the window ledge. "And how do you tap into God's strength, my lord?"

"Chiefly by prayer, a study of the Scriptures, although I must admit I'm very much lacking in the knowledge of the Scriptures."

"Good works as well?" He crossed his arms and examined David more closely.

"That's why I'm here, Lord Ashley."

The venerable man who had crusaded against oppression for years nodded. "As I said, there's much work to be done. Will you be taking your seat in the Lords?"

"I hope to."

"Good." No smile appeared, no inclusionary nods. "I have a question. A personal one."

David couldn't imagine what it could be, for this man seemed cut from a cloth that included not one thread of talebearing. "Please."

"Your mouth—"

David breathed in deeply. Dear God, not here too?

"Has it made you a better man?"

Not the question he expected. "In the long run, yes."

"Has it given you an understanding of what it is like to be disadvantaged?"

"At times."

"Have you accepted yourself the way God made you?"

David had to think a moment. "Some days I succeed in forgetting about it."

"That is all?"

"That is as close to the truth of my soul as I can come, my lord."

He laid a hand on David's shoulder, and the melancholy eyes glimmered with a trace of warmth. Just a trace. "Then you are an honest man, David Youngblood, and it will be a pleasure to work with you."

"Thank you for granting me the privilege of meeting with you, my lord. You have changed England for the better. Would I could do the same in my time."

Ashley sighed, looking all of his sixty-nine years. "My heart is anything but pure, though, Lord Youngblood. I've trusted no one. And they all seem to hate me despite what I've done."

"Of course they do!" David said, remembering the tales he'd already heard regarding Ashley's paranoia. "People have hated me all of my life because I remind them of their own imperfections. The life you've led, the causes you've championed, have shone a bright light on indifference, apathy, and ignorance. No one wants to admit they possess any of those qualities."

"So you're telling me we're two of a kind?" His stern eyes dropped their lids halfway.

"Is that so hard to believe?"

He shook a weary head, hands fidgeting with discomfort. "I suppose not. God can use anybody. I've proved that in my lifetime. Campbell down there has proved the same thing. When I think of his first day in the House of Lords . . . it was a disaster!"

"And so God will use me and he will continue to use you, and we will work together for the good of those who so desperately need help."

Ashley smiled briefly. "You remind me of a young lad I met many years ago. His name was Curtis Jones, and he went to work on one of the ships that used to congest the Admiralty yard." A faraway look thinned his irises to reveal the heart of the man who was speaking. "He had the same facial condition as yourself, but he was determined to be the best sailor he could be. A group of boys, 150 of them, actually, came to a dinner at my home on the night before they embarked."

He told David of the orphans sitting all over the house and on the lawn, plates in their laps, smiles on their lips as they ate probably the most wonderful meal of their miserable lives. How life on an old ship and the hope of a good future, learning seamanship, getting out of the orphanage for good, had transformed them for the better from the day they'd heard the news they'd been chosen.

And there Curtis Jones, mouth full of peas and onions, vowed to be the best sailor that ever tugged on a rope, saying that God would show him what to do. "Will God show you what to do, Lord Youngblood?" Ashley asked, finishing up his story. "Does he work in you to do his good pleasure?"

"Yes, he does."

"Then let us dive from these lofty heights into the dirty pool of humanity who know not that their sins can be taken away. Let us show them the love of Christ by doing all we can to make their lives better."

That was something David knew he could do.

On the carriage ride back to March's house in Lambeth, the viscount made good on his promise of days before, and David, helped along greatly by Aaron Campbell, told about the sacrifice the Lamb of God had made for Gerald Raines.

Lord Ashley's commitment had provided the perfect excuse.

Wooten hovered at the doorway of the kitchen. "Lady Charlotte Door, my lady."

Camille, seated at the worktable in the kitchen chopping cabbage, looked up in surprise. "Aren't you supposed to be gone now, Wooten? You were given the day off."

"Yes, ma'am. We were just about to leave."

She brushed the ribbons of cabbage from her fingers and pushed them into a neat little pile. "Tell her I'll be right there, and then you and your wife should hurry out before his lordship gets back."

"She's in the drawing room, ma'am."

The kitchen clock struck four. The others had left to go riding in Richmond Park with Monica and Gerald Raines, giving Camille some quiet time in the kitchen. So much for that. She would buck convention, however, and have Charlotte come below stairs for her visit. A little slumming would do her good.

Up the narrow staircase she trotted, keeping her apron tied around her waist. She entered the drawing room. "Lady Charlotte! This is a surprise!"

"Thank you for receiving me out of the blue, Camille." Lady Charlotte Door sat on the cream sofa, pulling a small, hinged box out of her tiny, drawstring bag. A snuffbox. "I had to do something a little different, a bit out of the norm, or I thought I'd scream. I only have an hour, though." She pinched out a bit of snuff and sniffed it up her nose. *Pfch*. "There. Much better. I do believe I have a cold coming on."

Likely excuse. "Well, I'm right in the middle of cooking our supper, but if you'd—"

"Cooking? My dear!" She gasped. "You mean you don't have a cook?"

Camille laughed. "But of course I do. He's an arrogant, ghastly fellow. We gave him the night off. My family is crying out for some chicken in a pot and homemade baguette."

Lady Charlotte laid a hand, fingers stacked with rings, up to the side of her face. "Good heavens! You mean you like to cook?"

"I love it. Come down into the kitchen with me. The staff is gone"—she hurried to assure her—"and I'll make you a cup of tea."

"I'd rather have a drink."

"Well, look over there in the cabinet if you insist. Grab whatever it is you'd like and follow me down." Perhaps Lady Charlotte really did have a drinking problem? *C'est dommage!*

Lady Charlotte chuckled. "You're not disappointing me, Cammy darling. You really are unconventional." She opened the door to a cherrywood cabinet in the corner and yanked out a bottle of blackberry brandy and a small snifter. Holding the items by their bellies, she stood up straight. "Let's go then. I'm armed for anything now."

Camille eyed Lady Charlotte's gown as they clicked into the entry hall. Surprisingly, she had dressed in a most normal manner that day. The exquisitely cut saffron-colored outfit headlined an intricately embroidered bodice. Dreadfully English, though. Those bows and that lace! "Speaking of convention, you're looking very proper today. A far cry from yesterday." She pointed toward the staircase. "Down there."

Lady Charlotte laid her hand on the iron banister with a groan. "I hate Wednesdays! They're my normal day. The day I act the proper baroness. We rode in Hyde Park this morning, had an early lunch with some very stuffy people at their home on Piccadilly, then walked around Vauxhall Gardens. I'm about to go have tea only God knows where because Cyprian hasn't thought to inform me yet. Oh, how I hate all this muss and bother!"

They made it safely down the steep, narrow staircase and into the cheerful kitchen. Camille loved this spot. Brick floors glimmered with wax. Whitewashed walls shone. Copper pots dangled from a rack over the giant worktable, and at the end of the room, near the windows, a long trestle table already held the place settings for tomorrow's breakfast for the servants.

"Sounds like a busy day and one I don't envy you." Camille pulled another chair over to the worktable and motioned to Lady Charlotte, who had already uncorked the brandy. She poured it into the snifter, the glugging sound all too familiar to Camille.

"I'm going to need this!" She gulped down a quarter of the contents with a grimace. She spoke deep and husky, her throat opened wide by the potent liquor. "I've still got hours to go before I can get home. I didn't even get my sunbath today."

Not about to comment on that, Camille said, "What do you have left?"

She swallowed her voice back to normal. "Oh, this is the worst of it! A *conversationale* at Lady Wexley's." Her heavy emphasis on the word told Camille it must be every inch as boring as it sounded. "And then, to Almack's. I'm surprised I wasn't blackballed from that place years ago."

Even Camille had heard of the club where the ton would gather, the women showing off their daughters as though it were some marriage market. "They must be unaware of your nude sunbaths."

Lady Charlotte let out a hoot! "Oh, I like you, Cammy. I really do. Now"—she threw back some more brandy—"tell me the rumors I'm hearing are true! The ton is abuzz with it."

Camille didn't bother to ask. "Every one of them is true."

"So you've heard them?" The final sip slid to its demise within Charlotte's gullet.

"Not a one. But there's no sense in denying anything."

Lady Charlotte poured some more and lifted her glass in a toast. "Mum's the word?"

"If that means that I plan to remain in silence, yes."

"Oh, sorry, dearest. I forgot you probably don't know all of our dotty expressions."

Camille set a pot of water on the hot stove and began peeling potatoes while Charlotte continued to drink. "So what's happening after Almack's?"

"Nothing. We go home then. Or at least I do. Cyprian will find some amusement to keep Bertie occupied until all hours, I dare say. I wish you could come to Almack's with me. But I'm sure the patroness will blackball you and David."

She said it so matter-of-factly, it took away a bit of the sting. "Oh?"

"Yes. Even the duke of Wellington has been turned away for showing up late. It's all part of the tradition."

"And what do you think the general consensus is regarding my husband? Are we fools to even stay in London? Should he try and fill his seat in the Lords?"

Charlotte leaned forward. "You won't be welcomed at court, I can tell you that. Victoria is a self-righteous prig who knows nothing about living a real life. She's been so overprotected all of her life she has no real idea what temptation is, and how hard it is to be good." She sniffed. "Mmm. Something smells good. Bread baking. What kind? Baguettes, did you say?"

"*Oui*, just baguettes. They're due out of the oven soon. I'll slice you up some. But go on. You were talking about Queen Victoria and how she won't welcome us at court." To be honest, the news came as a complete relief. "And from what I heard, she may have taken a bit of a shine to her Mister John Brown." Camille raised her brows knowingly.

Lady Charlotte waved a hand. "Pah! She's just a weakling who needs a man by her side for support—not sex. Although she did have many children by the Prince Consort, I still can't see her as the type that needs that sort of activity. Not like us!"

Camille smiled. "You see right through me. Or you think you do."

"We are very much alike, Cammy dear. Women of base needs, sensual appetites."

"Cammy" knew that was true, but she wasn't about to talk about it to Charlotte Door. "You seem to know a lot about the queen."

"I'm one of her ladies-in-waiting." She rubbed her index finger around the rim of her glass. "I really have them fooled, don't I?" A well-lubricated chuckle slipped from her throat.

Camille continued peeling the potatoes. "You certainly do. How did you manage to become a lady-in-waiting?"

Lady Charlotte's expression assumed a theatrical confidence. "Cyprian suggested it to Bertie and it went on from there. But you see"—her voice dropped, took on an edge—"I can give the queen something no one else can."

I know what that is! Her own words were a singsong in her mind. "Are you willing to share?"

"I can bring her husband's ghost back from the grave."

"What?"

"It is true. I learned the gift from my Ayah in India."

"We held fake séances in Paris all the time. It was good sport. Nothing more, Lady Charlotte."

She sat up straight. "Oh no! It's real, I assure you. I've seen the Prince Consort's specter myself."

Just then a windup timer clinked on top of the oven. The bread was done. *Dieu merci!* Camille jumped up from her seat. What was it that David always said? You can't scheme a schemer? Not sure what that meant literally, she did know that it meant, "Don't lie to a liar and expect to get away with it." She sliced up the bread and set a plate of butter between them. "Tell me about Absinthe Pencraig. You two have been friends for a long time, yes?"

"Yes. Truth be told"—Charlotte let out a sigh—"although we may appear so different, Abby is the best friend I've ever had. She understands me and she accepts me for who I am, underneath all of my glitter and mystery. There isn't a thing about me since I left India that Abby doesn't know."

Interesting. "One can always use such a friend." Camille took a piece of bread and liberally spread it with butter.

"Do you have a friend like that, Cammy?"

Camille nodded, biting into the bread. "Two actually. David and God."

Charlotte burst out in laughter. "God? Oh, darling, you really are a character. I never know what to expect from you."

Camille realized that she could say the same about Charlotte.

But Charlotte quickly sobered. Or her voice did, at least. "I wish I could say the same about Cyprian."

"From what I've heard, you two are very much in love." Georginia had filled her in on that little tidbit.

"Sometimes passion prevails where friendship cannot. It's a complicated tale, Camille, and one that I will not bore you with today."

Her eyes, shuttered from all expression, made it quite clear to Camille that the topic would most likely never be discussed at all.

CHAPTER ✧ TWENTY-TWO

I'd like you to meet my dear, dear, *dear* friend Elspeth Youngblood."

The deep, smoky voice that spoke those words belonged to Sir Keir Faraday. Elspeth gazed up at the middle-aged scientist, proud to be introduced by such a man, feeling adoration. Now this was something worth worshiping! His black hair, windblown from the carriage ride out to Oxford, contrasted with his flushed cheeks. Who cared if he was a good four inches shorter than she was! His large personality more than made up for it. Talk about a study in economy. There was more vibrancy, kindness, and intelligence packed into this man than anyone she had ever met, including the taller set!

An all-day ride and he'd chosen to sit next to her. In fact, he'd moved her best friend Natanya Morris to the seat across saying, "Not today, Nattie. Elspeth's all mine for the journey." Then his deep-set eyes had wrinkled up pleasingly above his smile. She found his weathered skin intriguing, and she ached to rub her fingertips along the sloping line of his jaw.

And what a splendid drive it had been. He had talked to her, looked her in the eye, taken her hand, even leaned forward at something particularly witty she had said, what it was she couldn't now remember, for when he had come closer his lips had found the spot just between her left eye and her left temple. They had lingered there just slightly, but with a warm softness that presupposed an intimacy that she had not prior known he had felt.

When he pulled back, he reached out a hand and ran it tenderly over her hair. "You're a lovely girl, Ellie."

She felt like a girl around him at times. Heavens, but he was old enough to be her father. And yet, just being with him made her feel so womanly. She'd never thought much about loving a man until Sir Keir Faraday came into her life. The first time they'd met, at a small party given by a mutual friend two years before, he'd asked her all manner of questions about her facial condition, fascinated with her responses, looking her comfortably in the eyes. "I like your spirit, Miss Marquardt," he'd said. "You are a woman like none I've ever met before."

No one had called her a woman before that night.

Natanya had warned her away from him in the carriage on the way home from the party. "He's got quite a reputation, Ellie. The deflowering sort of reputation."

Elspeth had giggled at that time, but thought nothing of a rumor sounding positively medieval. And the more she got to know this man who looked her in the eyes, and made her feel important and normal, the more she realized such talk was nothing but gossip. She would stare back at him, examining the fine lines around his hazel-colored eyes. He wasn't most women's idea of handsome, for his nose was too large and his chin a bit too strong, but Elspeth lay awake at night thinking of him.

He'd haunted her dreams for two years.

And now they stood at the door to Parrish House, greeting their host, an eccentric old man named Chisholm Gulliver, a man with more money than time, and more brains than sense.

After the necessary formalities were dispensed he cried, "Come in, then! Come in from the chill!" His high, cottony voice made Elspeth involuntarily clear her own throat. "The pleasure is mine!" he said, as if the scraping of her larynx necessitated a reply.

He led them to a large room overlooking the small courtyard garden at the back of the house. The narrow stone home, a towering, four-story affair with little grounds to keep up, needed a good redecorating. Elspeth looked out through the large windows. A rusted velocipede, almost completely shrouded by grass and weeds, leaned against the crumbling brick wall at the back of the garden. Elspeth smiled.

"What do you find so amusing?" Keir stood directly behind her and she felt his breath on the tip of her ear. His hands came up to rest on her shoulders. More warmth. Keir was always so warm.

"I was looking at that velocipede outside." She pointed, keeping her face to the window. "We had one back when I was a child. Aunt Miranda used to ride it around. And she taught us to ride as well."

"You can ride one of those things?" His voice held no small measure of astonishment. "Really."

"Yes, really. Just because my face looks like this does not—"

"Stop!" he commanded. "You know how such talk upsets me, Ellie. The fact that *anyone* can ride one of those shows a keen development of coordination."

Elspeth waited to hear a discourse on how habitat affects development, et cetera, et cetera, et cetera. Not that she normally didn't like to hear Keir go on about such things; she loved it. She loved hearing his deep voice and watching his lips round out his words. But right now, things seemed too lovely and natural to be coolly shaded by scientific cloud cover.

"Sir Keir Faraday, you old cad! I never thought I'd ever see *you* again!"

Thank heavens, an interruption. They turned in tandem at the sound of a loud American accent. New England if Elspeth heard correctly. "What on earth are you *doing* here? I can't tell you how relieved I am to find you after all of this time. I was telling Mother that it seemed as if you just up and disappeared!"

Elspeth beheld quite possibly the ugliest woman she'd ever seen in her life. "And believe me I use that term sparingly!" she said later that night as she and Natanya readied themselves for bed.

Natanya, a plump girl with sparse brown hair and a face widened by the twenty extra pounds she had been, according to her mother, lugging about since puberty, fumbled at her updo. "I know who you mean. I've never seen her before. I can't imagine where along the way Keir picked her up."

"I don't know, but she was most annoying. Draping herself all over him like melted cheese on toast."

Elspeth shuddered at the memory of the horrible woman named Lestina Smothers. An apropos name if there ever was one. Not that Keir really seemed to mind her, surprisingly enough. Without explanation, he had excused himself from Elspeth and followed that giant rump, led by an enormous belly, right out of the room.

It took him hours to reappear, until supper, actually, when he had been extremely quiet, but not inattentive. The well-insulated Miss Smothers had disappeared, thank goodness.

Natanya turned her back toward Elspeth. "I hate to ask you to play ladies' maid, but would you please unhook my gown?"

Elspeth didn't mind in the slightest. Natanya hailed from a family with a servant for every task, rendering her quite incapable of the normal little functions of most people's everyday lives. She busied her hands on the buttons that followed each other all the way down Natanya's back. "He's asked me to meet him alone tonight. At 12:30."

Natanya breathed in sharply. "Where?"

"Down in the games room."

"What do you think this is about?"

Elspeth felt her stomach go sick with fear, not the fear of what might come, but the fear of what might not. "He said it's time we take our friendship a step further."

"Meaning?" Natanya turned and shot Elspeth a look that her friend had seen on many occasions. She crossed her arms.

Elspeth felt a girlish giggle arise from her throat without warning. "He's been so pleasant lately, and a new quality has come into our relationship, a . . . an . . . intimacy. I can't explain it."

"And you will meet him, then?"

"Oh, yes."

Natanya held her friend by the upper arms, gently yet firmly. "Be careful, Elspeth. Remember his reputation."

She didn't like the tone of Natanya's voice. "Oh, come now. All that talk is rumor!"

"You know nothing about the world."

"And you do?" She pulled away from her friend's grasp. "Why the warning?"

"I don't think I have to explain it more than that, Ellie."

Elspeth began to brush her hair. "I don't think he wishes to take our relationship a step further *that* way."

"He's a man, isn't he?"

"Well, yes, but that doesn't mean he's a cad."

"Lestina Smothers seemed to think so." Natanya stepped out of her gown and picked a hanger out of the wardrobe. "And just because a man finds you desirable doesn't mean he's a cad."

"But Aunt Miranda always told me—"

"Aunt Miranda, Aunt Miranda. Ellie, there is more than one valid opinion on matters. Your aunt isn't the final arbiter of moral matters."

"I know, but she's made such a success of her life, with that birthmark and all."

"Oh, pooh! You don't know what you're talking about." She slid the hanger into the armholes of the dress. It fell back onto the floor.

Elspeth picked it up. "Yes, I do. The only person that understands me more than Aunt Miranda is my father."

"Who disappeared for years."

The cruelty of Natanya's words cut through her heart. But then the girl had always gone to any length to make her point. Elspeth had been putting up with it since boarding school days.

"You don't make sense, Natanya. You tell me to be careful, then you tell me my aunt's morals are old fashioned and I should do what I want. Which is it?"

"All I'm saying is be careful."

Elspeth secured the dress on the hanger. "Oh, please, Nats, I've never even kissed a man and you're talking about sleeping with one? I have no idea when it comes to these matters."

"That's what scares me." Natanya hung the dress into the wardrobe. "But believe me, Elspeth, you're one of the smartest women I know." She paused. "I don't know why I'm worried. You know your biology. You'll do fine."

An hour later, Natanya snored like a weary woodpecker while Elspeth watched the minute hand of the small clock on the bed-side table travel excruciatingly slow. Midnight clunked its way into the darkness and she counted every *clonk* the old timepiece burped into existence. Thirty minutes to meet her fate.

Should I go?

What does he want?

Elspeth could only hope he wanted to love her. Eighteen years old now, a woman by everyone's standards, including, finally, her own, she dreamed of being held in a pair of loving arms. Of course, she did.

Sir Keir. He was the one. She had given her heart to him, but should she let him know?

He waited for her in the darkened room. A lone candle propped in a holder on the mantel illuminated dimly the thread-bare tapestry that hung above it—satyrs and nymphs cavorting in a circle. *Oh dear*, Elspeth thought.

"Ellie." He extended his hand as she neared him.

Even his voice caressed her. The way he said her name filled her with a quake so potent he might have run a smooth hand up her naked back.

"I'm glad you came."

Elspeth felt uncomfortable, her body singing with anticipation. "I confess I came merely out of curiosity."

"Always playing the smart girl, dearest."

He stood by the garden doors, a sharp silhouette against the moon glow whispering through the frosted panes. Pushing off against them he came toward her. Small, his movements that of a lynx, or maybe a Siamese. Slowly, soundlessly, his head moved forward slightly. With firm purpose.

"I try to use whatever advantages I *do* have to the maximum, Sir Keir."

Standing in front of her now he placed a hand on the intersection of shoulder and neck. He squeezed her lightly, the warm pressure of his fingers delightful. Elspeth closed her eyes and sighed.

"Are you weary, Ellie?"

"Not really."

"Does this please you?"

She nodded.

"I'm glad."

"Is this why you called me here? To give my shoulder a massage?"

He chuckled. "No, but I must admit it's a nice activity. You seem so untouchable, Ellie. At times I wonder how a man like me will ever get through to you."

How could you not? Elspeth turned away from him, thinking she must be misunderstanding his meaning. "I thought we've always communicated quite well, Keir. I thought I understood perfectly what you've always said to me. At least that's what you've told me."

"You do. I've never met a woman before who understands the things I say."

"Does this please you?" she parroted his earlier question with a laugh.

"More than I could say."

"And is that what you brought me here tonight to say?"

He turned her to face him and she stared at his visage in the moonlight, relieved her own face was veiled in shadow. "That and one more thing." His fingertips slid over her cheek, and leaning forward he followed their movement with his lips. She turned her face before they could reach her mouth. "No, Sir Keir."

"No?" He pulled back. "You will not allow me to kiss your mouth?"

She froze. How could she? She'd never be able to bear the shame. "There are plenty of other places made for kisses, sir."

"I'd like to explore each one." His whisper, soft and sensuous, made his meaning so clear Elspeth felt her skin begin to hum.

She felt his lips on the curve of her neck. "What else did you want to tell me?"

"I wanted to tell you that I love you, Ellie. I've loved you for a very long time now."

"I find that hard to believe."

"No man has loved you before?" His voice trembled, and his caresses continued, gentle fingers stroking the sensitive skin of her neck.

"No." She closed her eyes, lost in his touch, her heart exploding with happiness. The world spun and his words barely infiltrated the red-hot mist.

"Ahh," he said. "Yes, that's good, Ellie. That's very, very good."

David sat in the dining room, papers from Lord Ashley spread before him, old acts passed years before, stepping stones to where they were now. All well and good, he thought, as the grandfather clock in the hall emitted a beautiful, haunting chime, turned down low for the dark hours, but the fact of the matter was, the clock had bonged four times and Elspeth had yet to sneak across the threshold. He shook his head, wondering how in the world he'd found himself in such a predicament. An unruly daughter!

He remembered all of those conversations with Mrs. Wooten. All of those head shakes accompanied by a wagging finger, tear-filled eyes, and the words, "You're going to end up reapin' what you're sowin', Master David."

When he was quite little he always thought she meant "sewing" and it made little sense. But once his parents had sent him to live up at Greywalls, once he'd seen the plowing of the fields, the sowing of barley and oats, and then that first fresh blush of pale green through the fertile soil, he'd understood. Barley sowed, barley reaped. He remembered the dawning in his mind, and often during his misspent youth he thought of that day the simple truth had taken root in his own mind. But it was too late by then. The weeds of his parents' indifference and his own anger and hate had all but choked completely the seeds sown by Mrs. Wooten. And in his bed, late at night, after a day of drinking and fornicating and causing all manner of social ruckus, he truly believed he'd kill himself by his own lifestyle before he'd have to reap the seeds he'd scattered.

Camille came in several minutes later with sleepy eyes and a cup of tea. "Here, *chéri*," she said. "I thought you might need something for your vigil." She set the tea down in front of him. "It's already fixed. I'm afraid I didn't trust myself to carry a tea tray up the steps again. If it's not sweet enough, let me know, I'll go back down and get the sugar."

David took a sip. "Not sweet enough" didn't begin to describe it. He couldn't imagine how many spoons of sugar she'd shoveled into the cup. She must be as preoccupied as he! "A perfect cup of tea for sitting up all night," he declared. That wasn't a lie, was it?

"So she's not back yet?"

"No."

Camille tied her robe more tightly around her ample waist. "Some girls have a stormy sea to navigate. I was that type, you know."

He knew. "You'd better get back upstairs, *chérie*. When she gets home, you're the last person she'll want to be hanging around the entry hall."

"I don't know how much longer I can stand her little comments, David. They're not overtly bad, it's just"—she waved her hands—"she knows how to couch things."

"She's much too intelligent for her own good."

"Like her father. The day I understand you Youngbloods is the day—"

"—your torture really begins," David finished with a laugh.

A draft across the room told them the front door had been quietly opened.

"Elspeth!" he barked. "In the dining room! Now!"

"David," Camille whispered, "don't attack. I promise you she won't want to be attacked right now."

"How would you know what I want?" Elspeth said, displaying a very well-honed set of ears. She walked over to her father. "Isn't this the pretty little picture? Doting parents waiting up for the wayward child."

"Elspeth, you may not talk to your mother like that."

"Mother?" Elspeth laughed. "Oh, really, Dad. You can't expect me to think of her like that. She's only ten years older than I am." She turned to Camille. "Run along now, Camille. I'm obviously in trouble and, quite frankly, I deem it none of your business."

David watched as Camille paled and turned toward the doorway. "No, darling. This is your house too."

Elspeth crossed her arms. "Oh, isn't that sweet."

"It's all right, David. I'm only getting in the way. I'll see you upstairs in a few minutes."

Elspeth flinched at the words. David knew why. It didn't matter what his daughter would ever say to his wife, it was Camille's arms which cradled him when all was said and done. Elspeth obviously realized this.

"Sit down, Bethie," he said.

Elspeth plopped in the chair. He could smell the alcohol on her breath.

"All right, you know what I'm going to ask, so just go ahead and tell me. And for the record, I can smell the booze on your breath, so don't even try to get out of that one."

She breathed in through her wide, flat nose. "I went to the theatre with Natanya. Sir Keir Faraday was there. Well, one thing led to another, and we ended up in his apartment."

"That was where you were drinking."

She nodded. "We were playing a Japanese drinking game. The one where you tell two stories and the others have to guess which one is the true story. If you guess wrong—"

"I know, I know. I've played them all."

"Natanya is a terrible player. We waited for her to sober up a bit before coming home."

"I see."

She unwound her throw from her shoulders. "I'm sure you do, Dad."

"You're not going out of this house for the next three days, Elspeth."

"What!" She jumped to her feet. "You can't do that to me. I'm nineteen years old!"

"With no prospects in any area. My goodness, Elspeth, you've got a good brain in that head of yours. And you seem to be doing all you can to waste it."

"What would you have me do? Be a governess?"

"Or a teacher. Something other than this life you pretend is so intelligent and . . . scientific, for want of a better word."

She flattened the palms of her hands on the surface of the table and leaned forward. "I won't stay here in the house for the next three days, Dad."

"Then you'll find another house to sneak into." It broke his heart to say it. But, blast it, she'd cornered him! Nobody had ever told him what to do in situations like this. Camille would probably know, but he wasn't about to bring her back in on things.

With a huff and a muffled yell of frustration, Elspeth turned and ran up the steps. "You didn't mention *wife*, Dad!" she yelled. "You didn't mention that as a possibility for me someday. Why is that?"

⌒

Elspeth slammed her body down on the bed. She knew she was being difficult and she knew the blame did not fall at Camille's feet. The truth was, her father owed Camille a debt too. The rumors had been flying around London the past week. And if they were correct, it was her father who had sullied Camille to begin with. She sat up.

"Get hold of yourself, Elspeth!" she chided, pulling pins out of her hair. Camille seemed like a nice enough person, really. And Lily was perfectly delightful. Of course, she wasn't her father's daughter, but the child couldn't choose the parent, right? She knew that herself, from bitter experience.

Three days here at the house. Being held a prisoner.

Humiliating.

Well, Elspeth thought, if Mohammed won't come to the mountain . . .

She sprang off the bed, walked over to her writing table, and pulled out a sheet of paper. They didn't say Sir Keir couldn't come here. She scratched a quick note inviting him to dinner that very night.

But to make sure the plan went along without a hitch, she'd have to show some remorse. In fact, she realized just then that Camille would be the perfect ally!

She felt guilty about the grand lie she'd told down there. Japanese drinking games indeed. She'd thought about it all the way home from the tryst at Keir's. No simple lie would do for her father, no! But he'd fallen for that one.

⁓

"Sir Keir will be here in thirty minutes, Elspeth," Camille said, utterly aware of what her stepdaughter was doing. "Would you like for me to help you with your toilette?"

Elspeth nodded, putting a final, perfect white rosebud into the arrangement for the dining room table. "That would be fine. You have a way with the female appearance."

"I think with just a bit of cosmetics around your eyes, Sir Keir will be smitten."

"Who's to say he isn't already?" Elspeth said sharply.

Camille bit her tongue. "Of course. I'm sorry to have offended you."

How difficult this child had been today! Hot one minute, cold the next. Camille thought she much preferred the old Elspeth. At least she knew where she stood with that one!

The meal with Sir Keir began with the obligatory round of questions from David. Camille sat back, sipping her wine with amusement, watching the emotions ebb and flow on Elspeth's face.

"So, what part of the country are you from, Sir Keir?" David asked as a servant set a tureen of terrapin soup before him and a stack of shallow bowls. Camille thought her husband looked striking in a black suit and amethyst colored tie. And she loved the way he had taken to serving the soup himself at supper.

He cleared his throat. "Up north, Cumbria."

"Lovely country," David said.

"I wholeheartedly agree. My mother loved it there. Never left, but still, I couldn't wait to get to London to live. That's where my father spent most of his time. That was years ago, of course. After Oxford." He looked down, playing with his peas.

"Oh, you're an Oxford man as well? Queen's, perhaps?"

"Christ's Church."

"Ahh, 'the House.' Very good."

And so as the evening wore on, Camille learned much about Sir Keir, who was more than willing to talk about himself. He was forty-two, "a physician by training, not fortitude, unfortunately," but knighted for his achievements in biological research, "the discipline I followed due to an inability to stomach people's physical ills." An only child, he grew up with a sickly mother, tending to her needs, and an absent father who, though untitled, had a "considerable, though tied-up, inheritance." Judging by his short stature and odd upbringing, Camille could see the man lacked a certain confidence. He wasn't anything like David, who exuded a likeable arrogance. He couldn't look people in the eye. Except for Elspeth. Camille didn't care at all for the way he treated Elspeth, telling her, "Don't forget to eat up your peas" or "Have you read chapter eight yet of that book I lent you?"

Elspeth obviously thought nothing was amiss. Clearly, her feelings clouded her vision.

Later that night, after the house was quiet and David snored softly next to her, she heard Elspeth sneak out. And Camille prayed, knowing far too well the path on which the girl trod.

CHAPTER ❖ TWENTY-THREE

Camille glanced sideways at the woman beside her. She remembered informing David she wouldn't step out into society, wouldn't make much of a public fuss. For Lily's sake. *So why did I agree to an afternoon of shopping with Lady Daria Christopher?*

She'd come to call only a week ago, insisting they do something together "as girls, darling." She'd talked about Tobin and Miranda and seemed as familiar with the Youngbloods and their foibles as David did. She knew all about Camille's past and waved it away with a "What's done is done. Today is when I met you." Lady Daria Christopher was at one and the same time an innocent and worldly wise.

"We choose to see what we wish to see, dear. And if anyone ever tells you differently, they're delusional!" She trilled a laugh as they strolled down Bond Street.

David had told her about some of Lady Daria's many costumes he had witnessed. The jungle getup with palm leaves and coconuts on her hat, the time she'd shown up at a party looking like a porcelain doll. And could she ever be a convincing Queen of Clubs!

Lady Daria, wearing a magenta gown trimmed with tiny silver bells, tucked her arm through Camille's and talked about "the parade we're in." They jingled as they walked, the soft sound of Daria's bells surprisingly soothing.

Camille had already noticed it seemed more like an event than mere shopping. Young, marriageable women escorted by their mothers or some chaperone, cocked their heads proudly, bent on "being seen." More than once she had been glared at while some hawkish matron yanked some precious, innocent young birdling out of her sullied path. *I should just go home right now.*

"At one time, during Beau Brummel's day, women weren't even allowed on the street here past noon!" Daria raged. "What cheek! At least things are getting better for us."

Camille rolled her eyes. "We have a long way to go." Lady Daria would be a perfect addition to the tea biddies.

"Let's go in here!" Daria pulled her into a milliner's shop and Camille gasped. How she loved felt and feathers, sparkling folderols and braided trim. She breathed in the smell of leather, fabric, and freshly woven straw.

No one minded the front of the store. "Mavis!" she cried. "It is I, Lady Christopher! Oh, look!" She pointed to a wide-brimmed hat trimmed with turkey feathers. "Isn't that darling, darling?"

Camille thought her eyes had never been plagued by anything uglier in her entire life. To say turkey feathers trimmed the hat was pure understatement. The hat *was* turkey feathers. A veritable haystack of turkey feathers.

A young brunette with eyes the size and color of hazelnuts emerged from the back of the shop, her mouth half opened by a wide smile. Her clothing, black and simple, looked very smart, actually, for an Englishwoman. She held out both hands. "Lady Daria! Hallo!"

Camille noticed the way the woman's eyes rested briefly on Daria's purse.

"Dee Dee! I'd like you to meet my new friend, Lady Camille Youngblood. Camille, Dee Dee is the finest milliner in London. She'll even let you design your own hats!"

The smile on the milliner's face faded. And she nodded politely. Her voice dropped several notes. "May I speak with you in private, Lady Christopher?"

"Oh, certainly!" Daria obviously had no clue as to what Dee Dee had in store. And certainly it was more than hats! Camille could see this one coming from the moment the woman had entered the room.

Dee Dee the milliner pulled Daria over to a comfortable area clustered with several chairs, placed there, presumably, for bored husbands and lovers who had been coerced by their women to accompany them on a shopping spree. The young woman, now perched on the edge of a chair, spoke softly, yet her expressions, her movements created an ardent display. Daria grew redder as the conversation progressed. Her easy posture stiffened in the comfortable chair, and her fingers gripped the arms more tightly as the conversation ensued.

No, not a conversation really, for that implied a two-way communication. Dee Dee the milliner did all of the talking, eyes now grown to the size of walnuts, hands waving in the air like young branches in a spring breeze.

Even now Dee Dee had to rein herself in several times to keep from pointing at Camille. Daria finally shot up out of her chair and held up a hand. "Silence! I've quite heard enough! I'm through with this shop, Dee Dee. If my friends aren't good enough for you, well, then my money certainly isn't either! Really!"

Dee Dee paled. "But my lady, I didn't mean to imply . . . you must understand that I am a businesswoman. If they see her in here . . . well"—she straightened up her frame to a standing position—"I could lose my shop!"

"You just might anyway when word gets around what you've done to me."

"But Lady—"

"I don't know why I shop here in London anyway, fashions are so much better in Paris!"

Dee Dee the milliner tried to steady herself, her shaking hands finding the back of a chair. "Ma'am, please."

But Daria, obviously a slave to momentum, could not be deterred. "Did you know this street is near a burial pit from the time of the plague? Well, I can believe it now! It still stinks around here!"

Camille discreetly left after that remark. She couldn't bear it if Daria stormed over, took her arm, and said something like, "Come, Camille, we'll take our business elsewhere" or "The hats were ugly anyway" or "You're too good for this place, you know."

Because none of that was true.

She emerged into the street, hailed a hackney cab, and spit out her address. Daria would understand. Camille stepped up into the vehicle, grateful when the cabby slammed the small door behind her.

Camille scurried up the front steps and into the entrance hall. She was weary and in no mood for anything but food.

"Well, well," Elspeth called from the parlor. "Back from your jaunt so soon? I guess hobnobbing with the gentry wasn't all it was cracked up to be!"

It was just the remark Camille didn't need to hear. She walked over to the doorway of the parlor. Elspeth looked up, placing a book on the tea table. "Look here, Elspeth. Make up your mind if you want to be nice, or childish and ridiculous. Then stick to one! I've had a terrible morning and I can't bear your insults."

She pushed her shoulder off the door frame.

Wooten came into the hall. "I just heard you arrive, my lady. May I take your wrap?"

"Please, Wooten. And have something sweet sent up to the dining room with some tea."

"The dining room, my lady?"

"Yes. I'm serious about this little snack."

He bowed. "Of course, my lady."

Camille sighed. "I don't know why I ever came to this country," she muttered. With a sad shake of her head, she walked into the dining room.

Elspeth stood to her feet and looked at herself in the mirror that hung between the front windows. Of course, she'd never liked what she saw there. Fate had been cruel. But when had she decided it was fine for her to be cruel as well?

She looked across the hall and into the dining room where Camille sat, head bowed, back facing her. This woman had done nothing to her. Why couldn't she keep from saying unkind things? *This isn't like me.*

Before she could convince herself it would be all right to do otherwise, she quickly made her way to the seat next to Camille. "I'm sorry," she said simply.

Camille turned to face her. Elspeth was surprised to see her dry-eyed. "It's been a terrible day."

"Would you like to talk about it? Or would you like to wait for my father to come home?"

Camille shook her head. "Your father wouldn't understand."

"He can be like that."

It was a simple statement, but suddenly, Elspeth realized that she stood on common ground with this woman. Why Camille was choosing to trust the Youngbloods was difficult to understand. She obviously could learn something about maturity and grace from this beautiful creature her father had married.

She listened while Camille told the story and something strange happened within her. An ire ignited deep within. This wasn't just any Camille talking. This was Camille *Youngblood!* How dare that Dee Dee woman behave as such to a Youngblood? How dare she!

Mrs. Wooten delivered an entire cake and two delicate plates. Elspeth served while Camille continued to tell the story, considerably slowed down now that she stuffed in cake by large forkfuls. Elspeth had never before seen Camille in such a vulnerable light as the woman talked about blackballing at Almack's and how they'd never be accepted. Her heart went out to her.

Elspeth leaned forward and patted her stepmother's hand, decision made for good. She would love this woman. After all, they had a very long future together. "You must not think very highly of English society so far." She took a bite of her own cake.

"If it wasn't for people like Gerald Raines and Aaron Campbell, I'd just move to Greywalls!" Camille leaned forward and sliced off her third piece of cake. She probed her fork into the moist yellow innards of the cake, twisting off a bite. "It's hard to believe such horrible people are called the *beau monde*."

"'Good world,'" Elspeth echoed in English. "I suppose that's different from nice world."

"Yes. Good as in good food, good clothing, good wine."

"Good horses, or horseflesh as they say."

Camille took another large bite. "Good breeding. Good ankles." She giggled.

Elspeth pounced on the sudden turn to the better. "Good teeth. Oh, that's right. It's the English we're talking about! Couldn't possibly be good teeth!"

Camille pointed her fork in Elspeth's direction. "As we say in France, '*Amour, amour, quand tu nous tiens. On peut bien dire Adieu prudence.*'"

Elspeth translated, thanks to Sylvie Wallace's French lessons during her time up at Greywalls. "'Love, love, when you take hold, we can say farewell to caution.'"

"With your father, that about sums up my life! Look where it's taken me."

"He found a real gem in you, Camille." She meant every word of it. Now.

"Well, I may be a gem but I'm certainly not a flawless one."

"Who is?"

"Who can ever hope to be?" Camille said, finishing up the last bite of her cake. "Mmm. Delicious."

Wooten cleared his throat at the doorway. "My lady, Lady Daria Christopher is here to see you."

Camille stood up and brushed away the crumbs that had managed to work their way beneath her napkin. "Send her right in, Wooten."

"Darling!" Daria rushed in, arms extended. "I'm so sorry! How dreadful it must have been for you!"

Elspeth watched in fascination as profuse apologies gushed out of the woman's mouth like water from a street pump. With each movement of her head her perfume wafted about them in thicker strands. Not at all oppressive. Just very Daria.

Much to Elspeth's relief, Camille finally held up her hands and said, "That's enough, my lady, all this isn't really necessary."

And as quick as that Daria stopped and noticed the cake. "Oh, that looks marvelous!"

"It is." Camille swept a graceful hand toward the table and pulled out a chair. "Have a piece."

"Only if you'll have one with me."

Elspeth knew her stepmother lacked any capability of refusing another piece just then.

Daria consumed the entire piece of cake in four bites. "Darling Elspeth! I've not seen you for weeks!" She let her fork fall with a clang onto her plate.

"I know, Lady Daria. And whose fault is that?"

"Valentinia's to be precise."

Lady Daria had become quite a doting grandmother and had just recently returned from helping to care for her daughter on the birth of her fourth child.

"And how is the fair Esmeralda?" Elspeth asked.

"That baby is even more beautiful than the last one. I keep telling Valentinia and Hamish that they must keep having them if they get better and better. But she's doing fine now. In fact, I think she was rather relieved to see me go. Said something ridiculous about peace and quiet. Another piece of cake, dear."

Elspeth picked up the cake knife. "Anything else of note you think I should know?" She loved to hear Daria's stories. The woman's crazy escapades had made her famous. If she wasn't shaping her topiaries to look like MPs, she was planning trips to Roman dig sites all over England. Not that she knew a thing about archaeology, mind you.

"I heard from Lord Hayden Walsh the other day." She dangled the words in front of Elspeth like nine pieces of Turkish taffy.

Only Elspeth didn't much care for taffy. Poor Daria was going to be frightfully disappointed when she realized that Elspeth would never agree to meet this man whom Daria had picked out for her years ago. The fellow was *blind*, for heaven's sake! He lived in a lonely house on the English Channel down near Plymouth. He played a harp! Elspeth hated harp music. Plunk, plunk. Bringgg.

Horrible.

"And how was our Lord Hayden? Still bent on never setting foot in London?" She leaned toward her stepmother. "He calls it the abscess on the Thames."

"Who is this Walsh man?" Camille asked, lifting her cup to her mouth.

"Just someone with whom Lady Daria has been trying to set me up with for years. I haven't told her about Sir Keir."

Daria's eyes ignited with interest. She set down her cup. "Sir Keir? Does this mean you have a beau?"

Well, *lover* described it better these days. But that kind of detail deserved a respectful silence. "Of sorts. We enjoy each other's company."

"Do I know him?"

"I doubt it. He's a scientist."

"Ah, that explains it then. Would I approve?"

"Probably not," Elspeth said.

"Is he the man for you?"

"I'm not sure yet." Best not to commit to anything.

"So there's still hope for Hayden?"

"Oh, Lady Daria, you can be maddening!"

Daria laughed. "Once I get an idea in my head, I find it hard to let go."

"Well, you can let go of this one." Elspeth arose to leave the two ladies to their own brand of conversation. "I have no intention of betrothing myself to a blind lord from the south."

"Blind?" Camille asked, then turning to Lady Daria, she laid a hand on her arm. "You can't mean it."

"Why not? Lord Hayden Walsh is the nicest man I've ever met. Who cares if he is blind?"

Lady Daria certainly wouldn't, Elspeth admitted. The woman loved everybody. Except, apparently, Dee Dee the milliner.

⁓

David watched in horror as the royal carriage stopped just ahead of them.

"You've been summoned by the queen!" the driver called.

They'd been out walking, praying, and searching for guidance. In fact, he could hardly believe he and Camille had made it well outside the city limits. His back definitely felt improved these days. Eventually, he might be able to do away with the cane.

"Don't bother to even tip your hat at the queen?" the coachman called down.

David pulled off his hat and bowed. "Forgive me. My wife and I were deep in conversation."

A voice sounded from inside the vehicle as a footman opened the door. "Come closer please, we wish to speak with you." Queen Victoria, queen of all that mattered to David just then, peered out. Her round face caught the afternoon sun on its aging surface. Her sad eyes pulled at David's softened heart.

He took Camille's arm.

"Leave your wife there, Lord Youngblood." Definitely a command.

David gently unwound Camille's arm from around his and cast her a silent look of apology, regret constricting his heart.

"It's all right," she whispered. "I understand."

He walked forward, dread filling his stomach like ice-cold porridge. "Yes, your majesty." He bowed as low as his back would allow.

"We are aware of your foibles, your escapades, your disdain for all things proper. We are aware of the disappointment your parents felt at your behavior. And would that we could, we would disinherit you, rather than have you rewarded for your unruliness, your sauciness, your disregard for decency."

David could deny nothing.

"Do you have anything to say to this, Lord Youngblood?"

"No, your majesty."

"You've heard, no doubt, that you will not be welcomed at court, such that it is these days." She took out a lacy handkerchief and held it up to her nose.

"Yes, your majesty."

"You've abided by that, which speaks well of you. And we're most relieved. We simply wanted to tell you that your banishment from court remains. We wanted to tell you face to face."

"Thank you, your majesty."

Queen Victoria cleared her throat, her several chins vibrating. "Standards must be upheld, you understand. We simply cannot encourage lewd behavior, past or present, no matter how much the person has appeared to change."

This didn't surprise David. He bowed again. "Yes, your majesty."

"Very well." She nodded to her footman, who shut the door, hopped onto the back, and banged on the coach twice. It rolled forward toward Kensington.

David couldn't move until it faded from sight. He turned to face Camille. The sick feeling remained. It had been one thing to know they weren't welcomed at court, but for the queen herself to stop the coach and—

"David?"

Camille. What was she thinking?

"It's all right, *chéri*," she said, holding out her hand.

"But she just told us we were unwelcome here. Officially."

Camille shook her head, the sun glistening on her blond hair. "She has a job to do, David. Just like us."

David didn't agree, not yet, anyway. "All of those sins she listed, *chérie*, could be applied to half the people at court."

"We were just stupid enough to exhibit it before the world."

"At least we weren't hypocritical about it."

She put her arm through his, and he turned them around to start back home. "You know, David, I used to feel the same way about such things. But I changed my mind about that after Lily was born."

He knew he was in for some simple wisdom, Camille style. "How so?"

"It's about shame, David. We did what we did without shame. You can understand what that means? You can call people hypocrites who sin in private and refuse to traipse their transgressions before everyone, but they have a sense of shame you and I did not."

There was something to what she said, he had to admit. But he didn't feel at all magnanimous at that moment.

"Can you really blame her, David?"

"I suppose not," he managed to get out. "But where does forgiveness come in? What about grace and mercy?"

"If those qualities were so easily exhibited in humans, maybe we'd be a little less needy of God."

He chuckled, putting his arm around her and pulling her to his side. "Where did you get all these wonderful thoughts?"

"Oh, I'm not as brainless as I seem. I just don't know the proper terminology!"

"You do the Youngblood name proud." He kissed her cheek. "And believe me, *chérie*, it needed some help."

They laughed together, Victoria's carriage far behind them now. Nothing had changed, really. The path before them remained the same. But they felt different somehow. "We've been banished officially, David," Camille said. "How does that make you feel?"

"Well, if I analyze it, I'm relieved, really."

"Me too. Who wants to go to that stuffy old court anyway?"

"Not me, *chérie*. I'd much rather spend my time with you."

"And if I analyze that, I'd say you are one highly intelligent man."

CHAPTER ❖ TWENTY-FOUR

The young man preached a message so moving, so powerful, so filled with the grace of God, that Camille found herself weeping, right there in the rescue mission. David put an arm around her.

"He will accept you right where you are, no matter what you've done. He'll accept you today, this minute. If he waited until we cleaned ourselves up, well, he'd have a very long wait!" Reverend Phillip Williams looked each member of the congregation in the eye. Each drunk. Each prostitute. Each earl. Each countess. "The ground is level at the foot of the cross," he said. "Jesus has paid for your sins. In full. Forever. The past is wiped away."

Of course, Camille knew this, in her head. But the words of this young man barraged her heart. She looked from side to side. So many people nodded, and Williams continued. "Come today, won't you?"

A young woman sat at the piano, and she began to play a soft tune. Camille didn't know what it was, but other people, dressed respectably, sang softly. Camille closed her eyes and prayed a prayer of thankfulness. Did she understand this redemption of which this man spoke? Most assuredly. For she knew herself to be the chief of sinners.

Afterward, as the mission served a hot meal to those who needed it, the Youngbloods left. The carriage rolled toward home. "Now *that*," Camille said, "is what church should be."

"Pastor Williams was telling me they need a hand down there during some of the evenings now that Miranda and Tobin have moved back to Greywalls until their house is finished. Maybe you and I could go down there together. Would you like that?"

"It's a wonderful idea! Finally, a place where I won't be looked down upon."

David nodded thoughtfully. "I could say the same."

"And I doubt that the queen will go there!"

He laughed. "I did like that Williams fellow. Powerful speaker."

"Yet gentle," Camille agreed. "Sort of comical looking, though, with all that curly brown hair sticking out from his head at all angles!"

"I guess he's got more to worry about than his hair, *chérie*," David drawled.

They arrived home to find Elspeth and Sir Keir sitting together in the living room, heads close together, mouths murmuring.

"I just don't like him, David," Camille whispered that night in the bedchamber, having endured another uncomfortable meal in the man's presence. "I don't trust him with Elspeth."

"Neither do I. Not that I'm supposed to. After all, I am the girl's father."

They changed into their nightclothes.

She began to brush her hair. "I feel like she's settling for him. Like she's worried he's her only chance at love."

David agreed, yanking his shirt up and over his head. "The sad truth is, *chérie*, he just might be."

"I don't have a good feeling about this, David. Maybe I'm wrong, hopefully I am, but I think this relationship is an intimate one . . . physically speaking."

"You really think so?" David asked. "I was hoping—"

"You're her father, *chéri*. You're not supposed to see such things, and if you do, you're supposed to hope against hope for a little while at least that you're overreacting."

He nodded. "But you're not going to let me do that."

"I can't. For I, more than anyone, know how much is at stake. And I know once your innocence is gone, it's gone forever no matter how wide you smile, how bright your eyes."

"I don't know how much good it will do for me to talk to her," he said, shaking his head, then catching his reflection in the mirror. He turned away.

"And I don't have the right to," Camille sighed. "Oh!" she blew out in frustration, "I wish someone had told me about such situations long ago! But honestly, David, I never once thought my bad choices would ever affect anyone else."

"No one ever does, *chérie*."

"Well, we can pray, David. And maybe, God will open up a way for me to talk to her, to warn her."

David, now dressed in his nightshirt, pulled down the counterpane and sat on the bed. "But she's a Youngblood, Camille. We don't take kindly to warnings. Just severe bashings over the head."

"All too true, David. I'm afraid you are exactly right."

Nobody could say anything, really. In fact, nobody even tried to prove David Youngblood deserved to be banned from the House of Lords. Alan Richelieu had confessed to the murders back in France, and the earl of Cannock had been cleared of all charges. A rumor that he had been doing "missions work" in South America had even begun circulating a few weeks earlier due to a conversation at Pratt's, his old gentleman's club. He'd gone in on a whim, remembering Dormerthwaite was a member and wondering how the older gentleman had been getting on since they met at the Pencraig's party.

There had been a general buzzing when he made his way into the kitchen on a cool October evening, limping on his cane.

Dormerthwaite called him over and introduced him to the gentlemen at the table. Apparently, they were all friends of Tobin. Lord Percy St. Dennis he recognized immediately. Recently married to Viscount March's sister Monica, he and his bride had insisted the Youngbloods come to the wedding. Camille politely refused, and Monica had understood.

A bespectacled Hamish Smirke had seated himself next to Percy. The popular playwright and husband of Valentinia Christopher was a wispy sort of fellow who, by the way he gulped at his liquor, David could see, gave drink a place of prominence. Introductions made, Dormerthwaite took the conversation they'd had at Pencraig's a step further. "What exactly were you doing in South America anyway, my lord?"

The gears of David's mind picked up their speed. He thought about what his main purpose on Devil's Island had turned out to be. "Missions work, actually."

Opposite him, all six eyebrows jumped almost high enough to encounter the hairlines above them.

Dormerthwaite held up his hands. "Bless me, but I never thought I'd see the like!"

And now here he was three weeks later being escorted into the House of Lords for his ceremony of introduction. Yesterday, at the state opening of parliament in the chamber of the House of Lords, the queen had already twittered her speech before all the MPs and peers of the realm, clutching her orb and supporting the heavy crown for which the occasion called.

Today, however, was another matter entirely. Time to step to the fore, to begin to change the Youngblood reputation for the good. Blast, though, but the wig itched! Wearing this horsehair topper was one tradition he could do without!

He stood outside the door to the House, breathing in deeply, hoping that the past two months since they had arrived in London had been used wisely on his part. Hoping that even though the queen had turned her back on the earl of Cannock, the peers of the realm might extend him a chance to prove himself. Certainly Lord Ashley's recommendation would help.

Nevertheless, there he waited for the door to open and the procession to begin. Another man waited to be presented that day as well. A life peerage had been issued by the queen to a man from Northumbria, a new seat that would only last as long as he lived. This man, Lord Phillip Hatcher, stood behind David, clearing a very dry throat and muttering to himself. Chin up, eyes forward, purposeful step. And all of that.

In front of David stood a royal herald known as the Garter King of Arms, and ready to lead the procession awaited Black Rod. Even as child, David had been intrigued by this quirky position in the government fully known as the Gentleman Usher of the Black Rod. In this case Sir Joseph Pitts held the honor, a man who had risen high into an illustrious military career during his younger days. A slender fellow with yellow-gray hair that curled beneath his chin, Pitts strung his posture more tautly than a Celtic harp. He held his chin high and his black rod with a firm grasp. The knee pants he wore were a bit over the top as far as David was concerned, but then he'd never been one for ceremony and costumes and the ridiculous like upon which so many Englishmen thrived.

On either side of David stood two peers. Lord Aaron Campbell and the duke of Beaufort, who, much to his own surprise one night at Pratt's, had volunteered to escort him. "It will be good to have another Pratt's man about the Lords," he'd said with a "Ha, Haaaah!" and a slap on the back.

"You ready for this, old boy?" Campbell whispered.

"There's no going back now," David said.

Beaufort laughed. "Of course there is. You are free to do as you wish, Youngblood."

"As I said"—he firmed up his jaw—"there's no going back."

His stormy gray eyes met Campbell's clear aqua eyes. Campbell nodded. He knew some things a man did not by choice but by the need for redemption.

Inside the chamber the conversation buzzed, but when the door opened, it ceased almost immediately. David breathed in deeply again. This was it. Ten years ago he couldn't have foreseen this day. Wouldn't have wanted to!

He stared down at his feet, tightened his hold onto his cane, and followed the procession down the aisle that vertically dissected the chamber. His empty stomach churned in nervous waves beneath his full parliamentary robes, and he wanted to examine the attendees sitting on the front rows of the seats he passed between. But he couldn't. He had a part to play. He must be pompous, serious, responsible, and sure. What had that Lord Hatcher been saying about chins and eyes? The royal herald's hair, a frizzy, iron gray mass, served as good a place as any to set his eyes, and the fact that some parts of it curled more tightly than others made it more interesting than it might have been.

The Lord Chancellor was presented with Lord Hatcher's letter from the queen. And then the time for the oath began. David said the words with conviction and no second thoughts. Later that day, when Camille asked what he said, he could barely remember. "I promised to uphold lots of things, *chérie*," he drawled.

She hit him on the arm.

After taking the oath, he and Phillip Hatcher signed the roll of the lords, then moved to their party's bench. Hatcher went to the Liberal party's bench and David, still not willing to vote anything other than his conscience, still unwilling to commit himself to a party line, walked over to the cross benchers.

The men of both sections doffed their hats to the Lord Chancellor three times.

Almost over, now. He hadn't tripped. He'd resisted the urge to display some disrespectful gesture to the people who had always despised him. He'd managed not to give way to even the slightest of grins that they would now have to put up with him on a regular basis.

As he made his way over to the Lord Chancellor, a murmur of approval rose from the assembled Lords. He shook the man's hand, returned to his seat, and sat down.

David Youngblood was a member of the House of Lords.

"So then what happened next, Dad?" Elspeth sat forward in her seat and set her fork down on her plate.

The celebration at Mivert's sparkled with fine china and cut crystal. Camille, excited about the success of the day, said what any woman worthy of her gender would say. "Let's celebrate with a night on the town. The whole family!"

And that is what they did. "Yes, darling. Tell us." Camille felt the heat of excitement in her face. Her wild David, a member of the House of Lords! It was worth stepping out into the eye of the public for such an occasion. Not that many people had bothered to acknowledge their presence. And her relationship with Elspeth seemed to have finally turned the corner for good.

"Not much else was exciting, I'm afraid. Speeches, agendas, very businesslike happenings. You all would have hated it."

"He's lying, you know. You would have loved every minute of it!"

Camille looked up to see the owner of the unfamiliar voice.

"Campbell!" David arose and shook the man's hand. "Darling, this is Lord Aaron Campbell."

Camille examined the striking man, still astonishingly handsome though clearly not young. *Juste ciel.* She held out her hand. "My lord. It's a pleasure. I've heard so many wonderful things spoken of you."

He took it, bowed over it, and bestowed a small kiss on its back. "Lady Camille. The pleasure is indeed mine." Their eyes met, and he clearly conveyed his familiarity with the Youngbloods, where they had come from, what they had been through. "I'm looking forward to a long, fruitful association with your husband."

"As am I," Camille said.

Aaron Campbell let out a great laugh and turned to David. "I like this woman, I do. But you failed to tell me how beautiful she is." He looked again at Camille. "My own wife is quite fetching as well. Perhaps you've heard of her. Maria Rosetti, the opera singer."

What news! An opera singer. How nice to know David couldn't claim to be the only peer with a less-than-typical wife.

"Maria was the soprano in Tobin and Miranda's first opera," David said.

"*Fields of Gold*!" Aaron nodded. "She loved singing in it. So, are you here celebrating your husband's day of triumph?"

"We're trying to. But David insists on downplaying it."

Campbell slapped David's shoulder. "Good man!"

Camille watched the two men together, relishing in the camaraderie between them. David introduced Elspeth and Lily next, and before much more could be said, Campbell moved on with a polite apology. "Many deals to be made tonight, friend. I'll see you tomorrow in Westminster."

All three of them watched as he began to circulate the room. Though his arthritis slowed him down, his vibrancy flowed from him like wine. Camille knew that man had charmed his share of women in his time!

David turned back to her. "Quite a man, isn't he?"

"Almost as wonderful as you, *mon cher*."

He smiled into Camille's eyes, and she felt her heart leap like she supposed other married women's hearts did when their husbands have just accomplished something wonderful. She would see to it they'd have business of their own to take care of once everyone else fell asleep! Power held a terribly alluring, terribly exciting quality. She wanted to be as close to him as possible.

But her hopes for a night of loving David proved to be short-lived. By the time they returned home after seeing a play, exhaustion landed so heavily upon him, he plodded up the steps and began snoring like a two-handled saw before Camille had even said prayers with Lily.

She leaned down, kissed his cheek, and tucked the covers around his bare, bony shoulders. He looked so vulnerable at times like this. She'd always loved him the most tenderly when sleep smoothed away his edges, and that hadn't changed. "Sleep then, *mon cher*. God be with you."

Camille, however, didn't feel at all sleepy. It had been too exciting of a day to just lie down and succumb to the arms of Morpheus. Though she hadn't been in the Lords to see David's induction ceremony, she'd had a sort of ceremony of her own with the tea biddies. For the past two months they had begun building strong relationships where they could. David with Campbell, March and their cronies, the men at Pratt's, a few of Pencraig's inner circle, Camille with Absinthe's group. So far, however, they had not managed to get David and Cyprian together in the same room. But that would soon change.

Charlotte Door had invited them over for dinner that very day!

Camille still relished in the prospect, for life had taken a dull turn. She still enjoyed being a mother, but Lily, now engaged during the day with a tutor, had better things to do than traipse around London with her mother. And the cook had finally told her in no uncertain terms to "be gone" from his kitchen. She hadn't told David yet. He'd be furious over Joyce's actions.

So, tea on Tuesdays, work at the mission on Thursday and Friday nights, and the occasional invitation to Monica's and Georginia's houses, left lots of room on her social calendar.

Too much room compared to the old days.

Camille knew Joyce would be snoring in his room up in the attic, dreaming of butcher knives and sieves, and so she stepped quickly down to the kitchen to throw some scraps into a pot and make a good soup. Ah yes, a good soup always made everything better. Mr. Joyce wasn't going to like it one bit when he came down in the morning, but just then, Camille didn't care. Even when living the life of a kept woman, she kept her feet on the ground with her cooking.

Life had become . . . . not complicated, really . . . just different. And a strange different that she had never before experienced. Some "differents" had enough "sames" in them to keep one comfortable. But that clearly did not apply here. David had become a better man, a good man—that was different! Lily was learning to read and write and do Latin things—that was different. Having a grown daughter in Elspeth—that was *extremely* different.

If Camille didn't know better, she'd say the young lady was in love.

This "Sir Keir Faraday" came around at least twice a week now. Oh dear, what times *these* were. *Ciel*, she thought she'd die of boredom sitting there while all those large brains effused about matters she not only didn't understand, but didn't even think she *cared* to understand.

She did know one thing, though. This man had a controlling effect on Elspeth she didn't like. And something sexual played a definite role in their little drama, she was sure of it now. Camille would recognize that look in his eyes even if she hadn't spent the latter part of her youth fostering such an expression. *If there's one thing I know, it's men!*

Sir Keir, while attentive and kind, seemed to "call all the shots," as David said. And Elspeth just sat there, parroting his opinions as if she didn't already have a wonderful mind of her own. Camille pulled out a big pot and thunked it on the stove with a resonant clang. She turned up the gas and threw in a large spoonful of lard. Next she sought out an onion from the bin in the cooler recesses of the pantry.

She emerged to find herself no longer in solitude. David stood there at the stove, swirling the lard around with a large wooden spoon.

She set the onion down on the worktable. "Couldn't sleep for long, eh?"

He turned with a smile. "I missed your snoring."

"I don't snore."

"Oh, yes, you do. A soft, high-pitched whistley thing that seems to emanate from your right nostril, if I'm not mistaken."

She would have thrown the onion at him, but didn't want to waste good food. "Enough of that. Fetch me some carrots, would you? And some potatoes."

"As you wish, my lady." He bowed and went into the pantry. "I might even splurge and pull out a turnip or two."

Juste ciel, how she loved him just then!

They worked side by side, chopping the root vegetables as the smell of the onions caramelizing infiltrated the dim room, bullying away the "middle-of-the-night" lonely feel that had predominated when Camille had entered. David turned the gas lamps higher, put the kettle on the hob, and readied a pot for tea.

Much to Camille's delight, a nice ham and a plump stewed chicken rested within the ice box. "I've no idea what Joyce has planned for these items, but they'd go nicely in my soup."

"Use them!"

"But what if he gets angry?"

David took her by the shoulders. "*You* are the lady of this house, *chérie*. And I am the master. If you want to use up some leftovers, well, then I guess it's clearly your right."

"I just don't want to upset the staff." She'd always gotten along so well with her staff in France. But these English servants loved everything so formal!

"Has the cook been giving you problems?"

She said nothing. And that said everything.

"I wondered why you weren't making me your soup anymore!" David rubbed her upper arm. "I'll speak to Mrs. Wooten about it. Does she know the cook has been giving you problems?"

Camille shook her head.

"Leave everything to me, *chérie*. And for goodness' sake, use that ham! I've got a hankering for it myself."

Camille stood on tiptoe and kissed his mouth. "All right." She leaned back into the ice box and looked around. "Oh, look! Here are some *haricot vert*! And"—she stood up and turned around with a plate in her hand—"fresh mushrooms!"

"Put them in, girlie! Mivert's was nice, but let's really celebrate the day!" The tea kettle began to scream.

She slid the contents of the plate into the pot. "It isn't every day you become a member of the House of Lords!"

He poured the hot water into the dumpy, plain brown pot used by the staff. "I don't know why we wasted time at Mivert's tonight when you, my dear, can cook a finer meal than any hotel in London."

She put her hands on her hips and cocked her head. "From what I've tasted of the food over here, *mon cher*, I'd say that's not much of a compliment at all!"

As they sat together in the kitchen, drinking tea and eating soup, Camille was warmed by the thought that this was indeed what living was all about!

Elspeth heard her parents laughing in the kitchen as she quietly shut the door to the service entrance behind her. What a grand sound to hear, this sound she'd matured inside of, due to Uncle Tobin and Aunt Miranda's wonderful sense of humor.

But for now, Keir waited.

She hurried around to the street, walking with a crisp gait, stiffened by urgency. It was almost one A.M.

The familiar fire entered her belly as she thought of him, thought of the way his eyes caressed her, followed by his hands. She knew what they were doing was wrong somehow, although according to him, why should it be? Simply acting upon natural instincts, they lived the way nature had dictated long ago, nobly shunning the societal strictures man had placed upon himself millennia before.

"We're above all that, Ellie," he said the first time he'd taken her up to his rented room. "We can love without fear or guilt."

Easier to say than to do, however.

Something inside her rankled, but she felt powerless to resist the way he forced her to meet his gaze, the way he demanded not only a physical intimacy, but an emotional intimacy. He demanded trust, promising never to abuse it, saying he loved her at all costs, for all time.

Elspeth knew she could deny him nothing.

A week later David pulled Camille into his arms. She needed a little encouragement right now. They were about to leave for supper at the Door's home. For one of the first times since David had known her, Camille nervously fretted about her appearance. "The dress is beautiful. The jewels are striking, and you"—he lingered a kiss on her mouth—"are a magnificent creature, Lady Youngblood."

Every word he had spoken was true and she knew it. Camille had always known such things, he reasoned, but for some reason, it didn't seem to be making her feel better. With her body clad in a bloodred gown, a deeply hued masterpiece of satin and silk brocade, the blond of Camille's hair was even more brilliant. She wore it in a simple style, pulled back tightly in a Spanish fashion, the chignon at the back held in place by two stunning ebony combs.

"Are you sure this isn't too much?"

"No. You look creative yet not overdone. The Cannock rubies have never looked better." He leaned down and rested his mouth on the smooth, perfect skin above her breast, the cool of the fiery gems brushing against his cheek. It had been a set Camille had immediately adored, this set that his own mother had despised.

She smiled at him, the earrings bobbing back and forth as she leaned forward and returned his kiss, deepening it, expressing a need he couldn't quite understand, but one he could try and fill. Oh, her mouth, her soft lips, the way her eyes would tear up at moments like this. He held her to him more tightly, his hands traveling down the length of her back. "Oh, *chérie*," he murmured against her mouth. "*Chérie*."

She pulled away, green eyes glowing with a perfect passion. "I love you, David. I've always loved you, just for times like this. Moments of peace within the storm."

He laughed. *Her memory must be terrible or she's overly forgiving. Peace within the storm, indeed.* "Years ago, I *was* the storm!"

She kissed him again as the hall clock bonged.

"Are you ready to begin what we set out to do on Devil's Island?" he asked. So crucial in many ways, tonight truly began the process.

She pulled from his embrace and grabbed her small evening bag from off of the bed. Her eyes met his, so green and unwavering. "I'm ready whenever you are, David."

"Ah, that's my girl." He swept an arm toward the door. "After you, *chérie*."

As she passed by him, he couldn't help but give her rump a little whack. Their laughter echoed around them as they made their way down the steps.

CHAPTER ❖ TWENTY-FIVE

If this wasn't some sort of absurd theatre play, then Camille was still an innocent! Two identical African servants, dressed up in suits of gold with knee pants and lavender sashes, met them at the doorway. Be-turbaned and be-slippered in jeweled gold, they kept their wide, smooth faces guarded yet polite as they took David's and Camille's cloaks. And then, in a lithe parade of glittering exoticism, they led the Youngbloods into the drawing room to await the Doors.

With perfectly synchronized bows, they backed out of the room, shutting the double doors behind them.

"*Pour l'amour du ciel!*" Camille spun a slow circle, her mouth dropping. "I've been around in my time, David, you know that. But I've never seen anything like this!"

The look on his face spoke of a certain humor, or perhaps a certain nausea. The air, thick with the smell of burning incense, a heady, musky smell more odor than aroma, was actually taste-able. Exotic flowers bloomed on the table that sat before the sofa as well as on either side of the mantel. Candles hungrily consumed their wicks on every available plane. "I swear, if the Doors walk in wearing perfume of some kind, I'll pass out." David held his nose.

"I've never smelled so many fragrances at one time."

David rubbed a finger along a spiky sort of plant squatting on an old harpsichord. Its blooms reminded him of two pork pasties joined at the back and sprouting hair along the edges. It began to close on his finger. He jumped back with a yell. "What in the name of heaven *is* this thing?"

Camille thought it had to be one of the most disarmingly ugly plants she'd ever seen. "You don't know? They didn't have this sort of thing in French Guiana?"

"No, they did not!" He tapped his foot, agitated. David hated to be embarrassed.

She laughed and turned to him, placing a kiss on a delicious spot of neck below his earlobe. "Oh, darling. Don't get all out of sorts. Besides, there's too much to see in this room. It's a fantastic place. Look at that plant over there! It must be twelve feet tall! And look at all those white beans on it! What do you think it could be?"

"If I knew that, Camille, I should be a botanist. And I'm not a botanist."

"As if the smell isn't enough, there's the sound to contend with," Camille said. Clocks ticked all around her, and once she got past the smell of the place, she realized the noise wasn't just irritating, it was obnoxious. Skeleton clocks and glass-domed clocks lurked on tables. Larger mantel-style clocks huddled on shelves around the room. Tavern clocks hung on the walls, and three ornate grandfather clocks stood like ornery sentries daring anybody to be late.

"You're here!" Lady Charlotte's voice echoed on the rafters.

Camille and David immediately turned to face her. "Charlotte!" Camille greeted her. "What an unusual room."

"I'm so glad you're here." Lady Charlotte walked smoothly over to a chair near the fireplace, floated almost, and sat down. "Cyprian's a collector, as you can see. In this room it's clocks. In the dining room there are shelves and shelves of model boats. Even in my salon his collection of snuffboxes is on display." She breathed a deep sigh. "What we must accept in our men, eh,

Camille? Dinner will be ready shortly. And my lord"—she held out a hand to David who took it and kissed it politely—"it's a pleasure to finally meet you. Have a seat on the couch. Do you like squid?"

Camille, thankful to have been blessed with the ability to hide her feelings, wanted to roll her eyes. Instead she smiled and sat down, David following suit. "I'm sure squid will be lovely."

"And it's fixed with a wonderful curry my aunt brought back a few months ago from India. Are you used to spicy foods?"

Camille shook her head. So did David. "But Camille and I love to try new things, don't we, *chérie*?"

"Yes." Her smile felt wide and shallow, and lipless, yes, as though her mouth had curled in on itself at the thought of such cuisine.

Lady Charlotte fingered the sapphire blue satin of her gown. Although the air had turned too cold for a sari, the low-cut gown was no less exotic. Golden scarabs and graceful silver snakes looped upon the surface of the sheer silken overfabric of the plain bodice. The satin skirt had been embroidered with the same motif, only larger. Once again she'd piled her jet hair in a braided coronet atop her head, and around her neck five strands of heavy silver and gold beads, curiously carved, reached almost to her jaw.

When Cyprian Door walked in, Camille gulped down a gale of laughter. The man wore a Nehru jacket, a purple Nehru jacket with a belted crimson sash, the ends of which trailed down to his knees! His hair, falling in loose curls above his ears, glinted a striking shade of gold shot through with auburn. It was too dim for Camille to tell what color eyes the man had, but they were extremely light. Probably blue. His garb, so much at odds with his English physical characteristics, interested Camille. Perhaps they harmonized with the brain beneath the surface.

"Lord and Lady Youngblood!" His voice, warm and easy, failed to reflect the stiff material of his jacket, thank goodness. He crossed the room and shook David's hand, then gathered Camille's outstretched one between his palms.

"It's indeed a pleasure," he murmured, raising her hand to his lips. His eyes held a genuine friendliness.

He let go of her hand, then waved an arm, dismissing the room. "I'm sorry the twins put you in here. It's a quite ghastly room. Two minutes in here and you'll stink for a week and quite possibly lose an arm to one of those plants. But"—he sat down on the arm of his wife's chair and took her hand in his—"it's a small price to pay for having the most unique woman in England by one's side." He raised it to his mouth.

"One of the most unique," David said.

Cyprian smiled. "Ah, yes. Lady Camille isn't the average wife of a peer either, or so Charlotte tells me."

Charlotte smiled up at him. She really loves the man! Camille couldn't believe it.

David nodded to Charlotte. "I do appreciate the way you've taken Camille under your wing."

"Oh, none of that!" Charlotte waved away his remark with a fluid gesture. "Camille is a delight. We have an amusing time together, more amusing than most, I would say, and therefore, it is she who extends me the favor."

One of "the twins" announced dinner. David looked at Camille and swallowed hard. Taking her hand they followed their host and hostess into the dining room.

Squid. *Zut alors!*

"Do you have some place in which we can hide our squid when they're not looking?" Camille whispered.

David patted his coat pocket.

"But you'll ruin it."

"Just think of it as a necessary sacrifice, *chérie.*"

Seated in an intimate fashion at the middle of the long table, David and Camille sat directly across from their host and hostess.

"By the way," David asked. "What is that terribly tall plant back in the parlor?"

"Oh, that thing"—Charlotte waved an elegant hand—"is just a castor plant."

"Those beans it grows?" Camille asked.

"Are its seeds actually," Cyprian supplied, reaching for his water. "But don't touch them, they are highly poisonous."

It took all of Camille's self-control not to look at David as a plate of food the likes of which she had never seen before was set in front of her. She picked up her fork and prayed for a strong stomach.

~

The meal had been every bit as awful as they had expected. David recognized almost nothing except rice. Unfortunately, he hadn't been able to spirit away so much as one piece of the squid that lay on his plate like an empty slug. He drank an overabundance of water and had to keep himself from drinking too much wine. Anything to drown out that taste.

Cyprian lifted his glass to his lips. "Good to have you in the Lords, now, David. I was surprised to see you with the crossbenchers, though. There are a few things I'd like to discuss with you soon, if you don't mind."

"No doubt," David said, examining the unique black walls of the dining room. It was amazing how the artwork came to life on such a backdrop. With gilded frames on each painting, and polished furniture upholding silver vessels, it was truly a stunning room. Fires roared in hooded stone fireplaces at either end. And yes, model boats littered the room as well.

"We could use your help. I'm not sure where you stand on the issues, but I did hear you've been round March's camp quite frequently, and that you and Aaron Campbell are in cahoots."

"You've heard correctly, then."

"Ah, well, then. Good. What say we meet tomorrow? You belong to any of the clubs?"

"Pratt's, the Beefsteak."

Cyprian's eyes lit up. "Yes, the Beefsteak it is, then. Two o'clock?"

"Perfect."

Encouraging news, indeed.

The conversation shifted to a variety of topics, not the least of which was women's rights. Both men admitted they liked the idea in theory, but it would take some getting used to. When Camille asked what the opposition believed, Cyprian suggested they repair to a salon off the dining room, and there they talked in comfort. He was certainly well-spoken and never once blasted his opposition personally. David respected that.

The Youngbloods climbed into their carriage at eleven thirty that evening. David opened the windows and let the cold air come flowing through. Tucking several lap robes around himself and his wife, he pulled Camille closer to his side as she put on her gloves. "I've never really heard the conservative party's views before tonight," she said.

"He certainly knows his opposition, does he not, *chérie*?"

She waved a hand. "*Ciel, oui!* But I can't say that if I wasn't born to such status that I wouldn't fight to keep all the privileges it holds completely intact. Actually, I find it hard to believe you've aligned yourselves with the liberal party."

"I've aligned myself with no party," he reminded her.

"Well, for all practical purposes, then. Anyway, what is our next step? You seemed to get on well with Lord Door."

"I did rather. For all of the intrigue, he is a fascinating fellow. All of that military experience, his collections, and, blast it, Camille, but I found myself enjoying his company."

Camille crossed her arms. "And his propensity to murder his own family?"

David closed his eyes. From Becket's description of the crime, it didn't seem to be something Cyprian was capable of committing. "What did you think of him, *chérie*? Do you think he did it? Really? And what about those poisonous castor beans on display?"

Camille drummed her fingers on her forearm. "I don't know. He seems more of the harmless type to me. Still, people can fool you."

"I know."

"What about Charlotte? She seems rather capable of anything, doesn't she?"

"Charlotte? Oh, really, Camille, she may be ambitious, but Cyprian's the man in charge in that relationship."

"I don't know. I have to admit I liked Cyprian too." Camille looked out of the window. Her voice flowed thin and pensive. "I don't understand this, really." She sighed.

"What?"

"I was prepared to hate Cyprian Door."

"I was too."

"But I don't. He was quite a charming fellow. Very nice. I can read people well, David. He wasn't acting a part." She turned to him and he noted the crease of her brow. "You don't think Becket Door was lying, do you?"

"No. But maybe he just didn't know the entire truth. Maybe he was making assumptions."

"What do you mean?"

"Lady Charlotte, *chérie*. Now there's a person playing a part."

Camille nodded, shutting the curtain in front of her coach window. "I agree with you wholeheartedly. I suppose we must determine whether or not she's acting in a comedy or a tragedy."

"Do you think she might have done it? She's certainly in love with her husband. Crazily so."

"I thought so too. But why kill her in-laws when all she wanted was their son?"

He squeezed her hand. "I think that's where you come in. Charlotte is the key to finding out about all of this."

"That's what I'm afraid of."

"I'm not asking you to parade yourself or Lily around town, *chérie*."

"I know. Actually, I'm perfectly intrigued now. Even if you decided to abandon this mission, I would still wish to find out what makes Lady Charlotte Door tick."

He laughed out loud, remembering that ghastly, noisy room full of clocks. "No pun intended?"

Camille shuddered. "Definitely not!"

Throwing the covers aside impatiently, Camille slid out of bed. David snored so loudly she knew there was no hope of getting any sleep. She peeped in on Lily, remembering the wonderful time they'd had together while she readied herself for dinner at the Doors. She had allowed Lily a bit of lipstick and rouge, had even piled the child's hair up on her head. What a lovely thing!

She stifled a yawn as she slowly descended the staircase. On her way toward the kitchen stairs, she peeped into her husband's study. Elspeth, wrapped up in a blanket or two, lay on the thick Persian rug before an enthusiastic blaze in the fireplace. Two bed pillows supported her head.

Well, better this than eating food she didn't need! If she gained another pound she'd just stop eating altogether! As if that was a possibility.

She hadn't seen Elspeth for at least three days and wanted to get the latest bit regarding Sir Keir. Camille tried not to speak too loudly. She didn't want to startle her stepdaughter. "It looks so inviting here I might have to break my rule and actually try to read a book!"

Elspeth sat up and pointed to the blaze. "Or you could just come and mindlessly watch the fire." She held up the small volume in her hand. "This is actually just a prop."

"You don't mind if I join you?"

"Of course not. Sit here on the rug or the sofa, whichever suits your fancy."

Camille chose the sofa, easing herself onto the dark green leather, then kicking off her slippers and sliding her feet beneath her. A soft woolen blanket, woven in one of those boring clan patterns, had been neatly draped over the back of the couch. She yanked it down and spread it all around her, cupping the top and pulling it up to her neck. "This is nice."

Elspeth leaned back against the couch. "I've been spending my winter evenings this way for years. A fire is automatically lit in here now at nine o'clock."

"You're not going out to meet Sir Keir tonight?"

"No. I haven't been with Keir for several days now." The sudden drop in her voice spoke volumes.

"How far has this gone, Elspeth?"

Elspeth wouldn't say a word.

That obviously didn't work. She changed the subject. No use in alienating the child up front. "Is he away on a lecture?"

Elspeth nodded then grabbed the single braid that was pinned between her back and the sofa and brought it around to the front of her nightgown. She played with the tufted end, rubbing it against the palm of her hand, beneath her chin, on her cheek. "He's at Oxford for a few days."

Camille reached out and laid a gentle hand on the girl's shoulder. "Would you like to talk about whatever it is that's bothering you?"

Elspeth turned her head toward her stepmother. "It's not that I don't want to share things with you, Camille. It's just that I don't see how you would understand. I feel more alone than I've ever felt in my life."

"Has Sir Keir ended things?"

Her eyes filled with tears. "No," she whispered. "But I'm so confused. Things aren't right anymore. All the things Keir said used to make so much sense, but now I don't know."

"You mean about who we are. And all those scientific things?"

She nodded. "Do I believe those things just because I want his approval? Or do I really believe them? His words cast such doubt over beliefs I used to hold so strongly—in fact, wiped them away for a time—that I wonder if I ever really believed them at all? I'm so bewildered."

Camille could barely understand what the child was getting at, let alone offer helpful words of advice. Sometimes she felt so stupid and thick around these Youngbloods. But she knew this. Elspeth Youngblood needed to come back to God. "I'm afraid I'm not much good with answers, Bethie. I've made so many mistakes and yet there was God, who accepted me as I was . . . as I am."

"But you're so beautiful. Why wouldn't he accept you?"

"Since when has God looked on anything but our hearts?" Camille slid a hand over Elspeth's hair. "I was as evil as one could get. Beautiful outwardly, yes. But inside was another matter, *chérie*. Inside I was no better than a Paris sewer. Yet he lifted me out. I don't know how he turned me to him, or even why. But I know this, Bethie. I know that he did."

"But how can you be so sure?" Her tone floundered within an inherent agony.

"To think too much beyond the simple truths of God is hard for a woman like me. I'm not an intelligent creature like you are. I am a woman of baser needs and simple thoughts. I only know what he's done for me. It's like it says in that beautiful song your Aunt Miranda hums. 'I once was lost, but now I'm found.'"

Elspeth finished, her words barely audible. "'Was blind, but now I see.' Is it that I've become blinded by my own desires? My own need to be accepted, and having once been accepted to keep that acceptance?"

Camille shook her head. She'd never met anybody this deeply introspective. "All I can tell you is what the Savior did for me. I can't argue psychology or philosophy or even theology. He pulled me from the quicksand I had willingly jumped into. This I know."

As Camille spoke, Elspeth's face broke down bit by bit until she sprang up off the floor and onto the sofa, sobbing in her stepmother's arms.

⁓

Absinthe Pencraig assessed herself in the mirror as she did every year on her birthday. Forty years old today and still surviving to take inventory. Four portraits, miniatures executed by her own hand years ago, lay on her dressing table.

Mother. Mary Elizabeth O'Shea. Nose and brow.

Father. Patrick Joseph O'Shea. Mouth and chin.

Sister. Katherine Niamh O'Shea. Eyes. They all had shared the same eyes, Katherine, Joe Jr., and Absinthe. Granny's eyes. But Absinthe wasn't called Absinthe then, she was called Bridget.

The final portrait was of her Uncle Kenny. Hair just like hers. Dead like the rest of them. And she had been left to carry on.

"Curse the day you were born Alexandrina Victoria, queen of just-too-blasted-much."

Absinthe's study filled with the diluted morning light of winter. Tomorrow Christmas Day would come barreling in as usual. But for now, she remembered from whence she had come. On Christmas Eve she slid her past from out of her pocket and looked it in the eye, remembering those she had loved, those whom Queen Victoria had killed. Thirty-five years ago the queen had refused to allow enough of England's bounty to be sent for sustenance to Ireland, the land of Absinthe's birth. If the monarch had pulled a trigger and blown off their heads it would have been more merciful than allowing starvation to claim their lives.

Only Absinthe had survived, taken to England by her mother's brother, Lord Devlin Hamilton of Cumbria. Lord Devlin had adopted her, had been kind enough, she supposed, but didn't know what to do with a child. She'd taught herself all she could in the lonely expanses of the library, day after day, huddled under a tent of bedspreads in winter. In summer she'd take books out to the formal rose garden where a kind young Scottish man named Fergus MacDougal taught her the ways of the earth.

She smiled at her reflection. Absinthe had been Fergus's favorite liqueur made from his favorite plant.

Wormwood.

He'd been her first lover. On her sixteenth birthday. And she loved him. She still did, really. But he couldn't begin to help her fulfill her purpose in life.

Blessing the day the dashing Sir Merlin Pencraig came to visit her uncle, blessing the day Uncle Devlin betrothed them, blessing Merlin's successful election into Parliament, Absinthe Pencraig tenderly set the miniatures in the satin-lined drawer of her dressing table.

If anybody knew her plans, they'd have thought her crazy. But Absinthe knew she was far from crazy. And she knew exactly what she was doing.

"How dare you ask me that?" Elspeth sat down in the rickety straight chair in the corner.

"You don't understand, Elspeth! I love you!" Sir Keir turned away from her, thrusting his fingers into his hair and scraping backward. His shirt, loose from his britches, hung open down the front. He turned back around, agitated.

Elspeth didn't know what to say. She'd just been given news that should have had her yelling at him and not the other way around. But she sat mute with folded hands, squeezing her fingers against the protruding tendons that ran from wrist to knuckles. She sat watching his chest heave with his frantic breathing, glad she'd dressed before he'd even awakened and told her the horrible news. She'd never noticed how the skin of his chest drooped slightly.

He ranted in his rented room, a smallish, attic chamber with only a bed, a desk, and a chair. All sorts of fungi and viruses and who knew what else grew in petri dishes on the desk and the sills of the two small windows. His coal bill was horrible, he'd told her. "Don't leave me, Ellie."

"You're marrying that large girl, Sir Keir." It was all she could think to say, all that really mattered just then. "Of course," she went on, "she wasn't really fat as normal fatness goes when I met her in Oxford, was she? There was a horribly good reason for that belly."

He rushed over to the chair on which she sat, skidded down to both knees, and took her hands in his. "Oh, Ellie. I've never loved her. You must know that."

"You slept with her! Has all of this been so casual for you? Is what we've shared together at all important to you?" She pointed to the bed, trying to close her mind against the memories that flooded inside it, memories created in the dark of night, memories that were more touch than sight. "Or were you just doing what came naturally?"

"You can't believe that. We were expressing our love, Ellie. I do love you. You've got to believe me."

"Then what was it you were doing with her?"

"It was before we met. Before I knew what making love meant. Don't you understand? With Lestina it was a base act, and yes, if you will, just doing what came naturally. It was different with you, Ellie. It always was."

She felt as if she had not put on her clothes at all, felt naked and exposed. Natanya had been right about him all along. She saw that now. "I can't believe that."

"You must. Loving you has made me believe again that life is about more than impulses or urges."

The man's desperation angered her. "You've stolen my innocence, sir! I was warned about your game, but I refused to listen. What more do you want from me?"

"Nothing." He waved his hands. "Everything. Just take me, Ellie. I give myself to you. I give myself wholeheartedly and completely."

"You don't have that luxury. You've got other responsibilities now." She looked away from his face. It was a sad face. A pitiful face. Old and lonely. "I should go. You've got a lot to do before the wedding."

He squeezed her hands. "You can't leave me! What will I do without you? I had no idea this would happen when I . . . when we . . . Oh Ellie, you must believe me. I never meant for this to happen. I thought we'd marry. Soon. I thought we'd be together forever. We can still be together forever."

"But you're marrying that woman."

"I'll tell her no!"

"You can't. The damage is done. How you could even ask me to be your mistress is mystifying."

"Forgive me, Ellie! I'm so desperate. I thought we could still be together."

"I'm sure Lestina's father, whoever he is, would have had something to say about that."

He scrambled to his feet, turning this way then that, a moving portrait of tension, lithe for a man his age. "I know. We'll run away together." He ran to his closet and dragged out a trunk. "Yes, that's it. We'll go to Italy. Or America! Yes, that's it, exactly! We'll go there. Get married and begin a brand new life!"

She closed her eyes against the prospect. It would be wonderful to do just as he proposed. A brand new life.

Remembering her own childhood, what it was like to be born illicit, Elspeth stood to her feet. "A brand new life? One brand new life is enough, and you've got to be responsible to it now. Oh, Kier! How could you do this to me? Do you realize what you've done? Have you any idea?"

This was it! She'd expended it all on him, and there could be no turning back.

"Good-bye." She reached for her small purse.

"No, Elspeth! Please don't go! I love you!" He stood in front of the door now, barring her exit. "Please, Ellie. It's Christmas Eve. Stay with me. I'll take care of you." His voice, soft and shaky, might have been enough had the circumstances not been so dire.

She swept her hand in a small, floppy sweep across the bare room. "How can you take care of me when you cannot take care of yourself? Let me go."

He stood still, his eyes darting back and forth within her gaze, searching for some hesitance on her part. She firmed up her chin and closed her eyes. She couldn't look into his lovely face, couldn't remember the nights they'd shared, the way he had accepted her completely. "Now. Please."

Hearing his sigh, she heard him step sideways. She had known he would. Eyes still closed, Elspeth turned the knob and stepped out into the corridor. "You're much too old for this sort of behavior," she said. "I'll go on. But where will you be a year from now?"

"Missing you, Ellie," he said.

Elspeth had to control the laughter that suddenly bubbled into her throat. So who was more pathetic?

CHAPTER ✦ TWENTY-SIX

Camille never knew Christmases could be like this!

She gazed around her at the group gathered in the library of Greywalls. Everyone had flocked to Scotland for Christmas. Tobin and Miranda and their gaggle. The Smythe brigade. Everyone but Elspeth who adamantly refused to leave London, stating she didn't want Sir Keir to spend Christmas alone.

"Oh, *cheri*." She turned to David and laid a hand on his thigh, watching as Lily hopped her dance between each of her three gifts, not sure which one to open first. "Other than the day Lily was born and the day I was reunited with you, I think this is one of the most wonderful days of my life."

He raised her hand to his mouth and kissed it. "And why is that, Lady Youngblood?"

"Look around you. And I am part of it all." She fingered the beautiful pendant he had given her.

"Do you like your gift?"

"*Juste ciel!* How could I not like it!" She lifted up the cameo suspended on the golden chain. It must have cost him a fortune to have the image of Lily carved into the ivory. "It's the most wonderful gift I've ever been given."

"You deserve it. You're a wonderful mother."

They looked deeply into each other's eyes, the room suddenly disappearing.

Lily's screech yanked them out of their trance. She held up a necklace, hopping from one foot to the other. "Look, *Maman*! Look!" Running over to her mother, she flew into her lap.

Camille took the necklace. "Oh, David." Tears nipped the corners of her eyes.

Another cameo rested on a bed of purple velvet, this one bearing the image of Camille.

"May I put it on you, Lily?" David asked.

"Oh, yes, please!" She jumped from her mother's lap to his.

"You see," he explained, his deft fingers easily working the clasp. "You can always keep your mother next to your heart, and she can always keep you next to hers!"

Camille felt her heart burst with the love she was feeling just then.

David ran a hand over Lily's blond curls, Camille watching the exchange in fascination. "Go on then, you've got two more presents to open. You'd better do it before one of your cousins decides to."

And cousins abounded! Lily ran to the remaining two presents, squealing and hopping at a cherubic baby doll and a new purple wool coat. She held it up and shouted, "Wouldn't the countess de Boyce love *this*?"

A gasp sounded from the doorway.

Camille felt her blood run cold as she saw Sylvie Wallace standing there, wrapped in a cape, arms full of presents. She stared in horror at David. "What is this?" she breathed, eyes turning to Miranda.

Miranda jumped up and ran over to her sister-in-law. "Sylvie, I'm sorry."

"You didn't tell me he'd be here." The Frenchwoman had gone beyond white to gray.

This woman David had loved beyond all reason.

"I didn't know if you'd come." Miranda took the presents and handed them to Adele, who rushed over to help at the first sign of trouble. "Come in the sitting room and let me explain."

Camille grabbed David's arm. "Go to her, *chéri*. This conversation is long overdue."

David nodded and stood up. He leaned forward and kissed Camille. "Bless you, darling," he whispered, and followed the women out of the room.

David breathed in deeply and uttered one of the fastest, most heartfelt prayers for strength he had ever prayed. Surviving Devil's Island, taking his seat in the Lords, bearing the queen's scorn seemed like nothing compared to this moment.

He stood in the corridor, listening to Miranda's soft voice, hearing words like "forgiveness" and "redemption" and "change," and phrases like "time to put this to rest" and "you need to do this, Sylvie."

Without warning, Matthew Wallace rounded the corner, fire in his indigo eyes. "What's the meaning of this, Youngblood?" he asked, controlling the volume of his speech.

"Miranda didn't tell you I'd be here, did she?" David asked softly. He couldn't blame the man before him. Not at all. He just hoped Matthew Wallace would keep his fists in his pockets!

"No, she failed to let go of that little detail."

"Matthew." David bowed his head for a moment, begging God for the words to say. "Say the word. I'll go quietly upstairs to my chamber if you think that I shouldn't ask for Sylvie's forgiveness today. She's your wife." He laid a hand on the man's shoulder. "She loves you." His smile felt sad and skewed as he admitted to Matthew Wallace that the better man had indeed won.

Matthew's eyes rounded, and he rocked back on his heels. "I ..." He shook his head. "You ..." He breathed in deeply and raked a hand though his dark curls. "David Youngblood? Is that *really* you?"

"What's left of me, yes."

"So Miranda was right about you. You really did come to know the Savior all those years ago?"

"I cannot deny it. Nor would I wish to." David remembered the day he had surrendered his soul to the Master. "I had no idea your sister had this scheme cooked up for today, Matthew. Truly."

"And on Christmas too!" His ire showed through. "Mira." He shook his head.

David could understand his feelings. After all he'd put these two through, Matthew deserved to feel this way. "So what will it be? May I talk to her?"

Matthew regarded him frankly. "And your feelings for my wife? What are they now?"

"I'm a married man, Matthew. Camille and I are extremely happy together. We're two of a kind."

"But do you still love Sylvie?"

David had been avoiding that question himself. He'd been crazy about Sylvie, crazy enough to commit murder in order to take her for himself. But now, face to face with the issue, he knew the truth. "I love my wife more than any woman I've ever known," he said to Matthew. "And that, Mr. Wallace, is the truth as even God himself knows it."

Matthew nodded. "All right then. If Sylvie will talk to you, I will not stand in your way."

David laughed. "It's a good thing! Because these days, I don't believe I'd be able to force my way by. Matthew?" he asked, seizing on the opportunity before him, his voice going serious. "I need to ask your forgiveness too. I made your life a hell for a long time. I'm sorry. I'm truly sorry."

Matthew hesitated, and David could almost see the memories racing across the backs of his eyes. And then a visible forcing of will strained Matthew's features. "Before God, because his Word commands it, and because he has forgiven me"—he reached out a hand and placed it on David's shoulder—"I forgive you."

What else could be said but, "Thank you."

Miranda stepped into the corridor. "She wants to talk to you first, Mate," she said to her brother. Matthew entered the sitting room and shut the door behind him.

David turned to Miranda. "Will she let me talk to her?"

"Yes. She just wanted to make sure Matthew didn't mind."

"Matthew and I have made our peace," David told her.

"That's good, David. That's very good."

David looked at Miranda, gratitude overflowing in his heart. This woman had given him the Lord, and now she was giving him what he most desperately needed, the forgiveness of the people he had wronged so greatly. "Thank God for you, Mira," he whispered. "You've always known exactly what I need."

She embraced him quickly, kissed his cheek. "They both want to kill me right now! But you know me, David. A peacemaker to the end—even if it does cause a ruckus at first." And she left to rejoin the loud festivities in the great hall. Before she disappeared around the corner, she turned. "You're a good man, David Youngblood."

By far the greatest compliment he had ever received.

Swallowing, David stepped into the room. Other than those who had lost their lives because of him, he had most greatly wronged this woman sitting on the sofa, hands folded in her lap.

Matthew left, casting a warning glance at David as he shut the door behind him.

Sylvie was still a young woman, only twenty-eight years old. But marriage to Matthew for the past eight of them had seasoned her kindly. No longer the angular creature she'd once been, she had rounded out nicely since the birth of three children. Laugh lines accentuated the loveliness of brown eyes grown softer with time.

He had to begin this.

"Sylvie," he said, walking over to where she sat.

She put out a hand, and he bowed over it, kissing its back politely, in the manner he had done more times in his life than he could count. He kept her hand in his. Their eyes met, and when hers filled with tears, remorse overcame him so heavily he dropped to his knees beside the sofa. "Sylvie, Sylvie," he muttered, his face crushed in his remaining hand. "Oh, dear God, Sylvie, how can you ever forgive me?"

He heard her sob, and felt the tumultuous racking of her body as she lost control. At a loss, suddenly, he didn't know whether to rise and comfort her, or to stay where he was. But when she let go of his hand, leaned forward, and put her arms around his shoulders, he knew what to do.

Beside her on the couch instantly, he cried with her. "I'm sorry," he said over and over, remembering the night he'd killed her parents, remembering drunken Armand, too inebriated to really know what was going on, remembering the fear on Collette's face when he grabbed her, remembering the smell of their blood, the breeze through the open door. "I'm so sorry."

"Oh, David!" She buried her face in her fists as they grabbed his lapels. "How could you do it?"

"I don't know, Sylvie. I look back now . . . at that man . . ." The monster who shot two people in the head still lived as long as he walked in his shoes. It was a thought he tried not to think about, but at times he could only lift his eyes to heaven and beg for a steady stream of divine mercy.

Sylvie looked up, her face beautiful and wet with tears. "I forgive you. David, I've always loved you. Not as you wished me to love you, but—"

"Shh," he said. "That's all over now. It wasn't good what I felt for you, Sylvie. It wasn't proper. If it led me to do the things I did, it wasn't even sane. When God turned me around, I turned my back on those feelings. I had to."

"*Un amour défini est un amour fini?*" she asked.

A love defined is a love that is over.

"That sums it up, Sylvie. It was a crazy love, a diseased love. Once I knew that . . ."

"So you really do love Camille?" Her tone spread with wonder and even a little relief.

He smiled, pulling back from the embrace. "Camille is my soul, Sylvie. I don't know if you can understand it. But we are two parts of one whole. No one will ever understand me the way Camille does, no one will ever accept me the way Camille does."

She nodded.

The air cleared. Forgiveness was given. Forgiveness was received.

"But there's something else I need to know," Sylvie said, leaning back on the sofa. "Whatever became of Claude Mirreault?"

"You mean you never found out?"

"I was afraid to."

"He's dead."

Her eyes widened. "And you're sure of this?"

"Yes. You are safe."

"What about that man of his, that Didier fellow?"

"He died before Claude. Shot himself in the woods the night Mirreault was taken to the Bastille." David took her hand. "It's all over, Sylvie. You've been safe for a very long time."

"How did Mirreault die?"

David breathed in deeply. "Guillotine. Not long ago, actually. He could only buy his life for so long."

"Too quick a death for him, I'd say," she shot out.

"I agree."

"And you? Where were you for all those years?"

"You don't know?"

"No. Miranda and Tobin would tell no one. Only Elspeth, and you know Elspeth can keep a secret better than anyone I know."

She certainly spoke the truth there.

"I was on Devil's Island, Sylvie."

Her mouth opened in horror, and her eyes closed, tears spilling out once again. "For seven years?"

"Yes."

"*Si j'avais su!*" Her whisper was intensely rendered.

"It wouldn't have mattered if you had known, Sylvie. I needed to go there. It was less than I deserved. We both know that."

255 ◈

"It's true. And I thought that you getting your punishment would make me feel better, David. I just never pictured someplace like Devil's Island. *Horrible!*"

"It was. But"—he dropped her hand and spread his arms wide—"you see that I survived."

She smiled. "You will always survive, David Youngblood. It's your way."

"Yes, Sylvie. It's my way. So my secret is safe with you? If this is found out it will not only destroy me, but it will destroy Camille."

"I could extract my own vengeance upon you now, David." Her eyes were serious. "And I would be justified."

He froze. It was true. "I am in your hands." That was true as well.

"But there is Elspeth to consider and I have forgiven you." Her features relaxed. "If you survived Devil's Island, then apparently, God has plans for you and his justice has been served."

"If it makes you feel any better, Sylvie, there were nights on Devil's Island when I wished I was dead."

"I believe you, *mon ami.*"

Her words filled his heart with joy. "And that is what we are once again? Friends?"

"Oh, yes. I feel as if a part of me has finally come back from the dead."

"As do I."

She took his hand. "Merry Christmas, David." She kissed his cheek.

"Yes, it is rather merry, isn't it?" He pulled away and looked into her sweet face. "Should we go and celebrate it with the ones who have learned to put up with us all these years?"

She laughed. "That, *mon cher*, is the best idea I've heard in a long, long, time!"

Arm in arm they sauntered out of the room, slowly down the corridor, and into the library. All the adults in the room froze when they entered. And then, seeing the looks on their faces, proceeded to whoop up a holler of relief so energetic the children became silent with wonder.

His eyes sought Camille's, and when she opened her arms to him, he rushed forward into her embrace.

CHAPTER ✦ TWENTY-SEVEN

The next day dawned with the silver light of falling snow. David wound his way down to the kitchen early hoping for first dibs on a bowl of Pamela MacDowell's oatmeal. With lots of cream. And butter. And sugar. His lost weight had been taking its time on its return journey. But his back felt good enough again to leave his cane behind. What better Christmas present could there be?

"Yon snow's just a day late!"

The voice that spoke cracked on the last word. It came out of a darkened corner of the kitchen. But David Youngblood knew that voice anywhere.

"Angus!"

The lad stepped forward. Lad? Well, actually, David calculated, he should be thirteen by now. "My lord."

Yes, the voice was changing, to be sure. Puberty had begun ransacking spindle-legged Angus. "Look at you! You're getting so tall!"

He could hardly believe it. The youngster who had fed him during his months in hiding stood just a few inches shorter than David himself. His red hair, thick and curled, had been pulled back in a ponytail.

The familiar freckles danced into a new pattern as the lad's face spread into a grin. "Nah, m'lord. Just growin' a wheen. It's the way."

"I'm glad to see you, Angus."

"Been too many years. Greywa's is glad yer back hame."

"Where have you been the past few days?"

"School."

"Really?"

"Aye. In Aberdeen. Lady Miranda sends me off." He shrugged.

"I like the sound of that. Someone will need to run Greywalls someday."

Pamela MacDowell, the castle cook and Angus's mother, entered the room with a bustling gait. "Och, m'lord! If I had known ye were goin' ta be up sae early, I woulda had the pot bubblin' sooner! Whit will ye be havin' yon mornin'?"

"Oatmeal."

"Aye, comin' up, then."

They chatted about castle matters as she worked. Angus declared he'd take David on a ride over the lands as soon as David wished to go. "Mr. Wooten has done a fine job settin' things ta right aboot the place. The harvest this year was grand!"

"So I saw in the books."

"Still, ye need ta be seein' it fer yersel'."

Well, he was the Lord of the Manor now, wasn't he? "There's much I need to know."

"Well, I'm the man ta tell ye!"

"Sit yersel' doon, m'lord," Pamela said, excitement quivering in her voice. "I'll fix a lovely wee cuppa for ye while yer waitin' for yer porridge."

Tea sounded lovely, indeed. "I'll agree to that proposition, Pamela, but only because of the company that goes with it!"

She waved a hand. "Och, go oan wi' ye, yer lordship! We're just simple folk, ken?"

"Just what I need at this point," he said, pulling out a chair, happy to be home. Life in London couldn't compare to this. "No' e'en a wheen," as Angus would say.

James MacDowell arrived next, and David thought that there could be no finer way to start the day than eating breakfast with the MacDowells.

One fun activity bled into another that day. Lily never stopped hopping except to sit at the table, and, much to Camille's surprise, Sylvie Wallace spent almost the entire day talking with her in the sitting room. She found she rather liked the woman David had loved too much for his own good.

Before the day he came to his senses, and married me.

Of course, they talked about children, about being a wife, about running households. And all in fluid, rapid French. A relief in itself.

As Frenchwomen, after all, they had much in common. Every so often their husbands would saunter by. "Don't interrupt!" Camille raised her hand to David as the light of day faded over the horizon and darkness began to settle in. "We're having much too much fun to have it spoiled by the likes of you."

Sylvie nodded. "*Oui. Nous avons d'autres chats à fouetter.*"

Matthew Wallace's brows knit as he translated. "You have other cats to flog? What's that supposed to mean? Sylvie, you come up with the strangest sayings."

David cleared his throat. "It means they have 'other fish to fry.'"

"Oh, good then." Matthew waved a hand. "We were busy anyway, and were only trying to be gentlemen, thank you very much."

Sylvie took her husband's hand. "And what were you two doing?"

David answered. "My theological training is sorely lacking, as you must know. Matthew here has been kind enough to start pulling volumes off of the library shelves."

Camille felt her heart leap. "Truly? But this is wonderful!" She clasped her hands together. "You'll take them back to London? You'll tell me what is in them?"

"Of course, *ma femme.*" David's tone dropped intimately. "I'll read them to you word for word if you'd like."

"Oh, no! I need you to tell me what they mean!" Camille nodded and turned to Sylvie. "I cannot read, you know. Especially English!"

Sylvie leaned forward, placing a hand on Camille's knee. "Would you like for me to teach you?"

Afraid she didn't possess what it took to learn, she declared the schoolroom was no longer her cup of tea.

"Well, Matthew, shall we?" David cocked his head in the direction of the library.

"Lead the way, my lord. We're just getting started!"

Sylvie turned to Camille, tears in her eyes, tongue returning to her native French. "I never thought I'd see this day."

Camille nodded. "David hungers for God. He just needs someone to show him the way."

"A task for which my husband was born, Camille."

The clock on the mantel chimed seven times.

Camille listened as the final tone died. "Sometimes I find God very hard to comprehend. How he can take something so ugly and make it so beautiful. I am not so very different, eh? Until the Savior touched me, everything I touched turned to rot."

Sylvie sighed. "It is the way of the earth. Only God's love is capable of truly redeeming anything."

"I'm so thankful he provided a way of escape for me," Camille whispered.

"I understand all too well about escaping, Camille."

Camille laughed. "For two women who don't have much in common, we have an *awful* lot in common!"

A loud cheer erupted from the great hall where Angus and Miranda had the children gathered for a game of blind man's bluff. Tobin, busy composing in the library, had been holed up all day with nothing to eat but tea and roast beef sandwiches with horseradish.

Camille stood to her feet, ready to join in if they were having that much fun. "Come, Sylvie. Let us see what the children are doing. It's almost time for their tea anyway."

But when they entered the hall, they realized the cheer did not hail for the winner of a game but a new arrival to the castle. There stood an exhausted but smiling Elspeth. "I'm so glad to be home," she said, falling with relief into Miranda's arms.

Angus watched from across the room. Camille could spot, even from such a distance, young eyes swollen with love and pain.

Elspeth slogged her way up to her room. It was still the same as it had been before they'd moved permanently to London four years before. Aunt Miranda had allowed her to pick out new furniture, new draperies, and a new counterpane, in whatever color she wanted. Elspeth had chosen green. Green and blue. The most restful combination she could imagine. And she'd been so exhausted the past week! Never before had she felt so weary and tired.

The familiar bed felt more soothing than a caress from her father as she lay down. Folding her hands across her stomach, she fell into a deep, penetrating sleep.

New Year's Day had come and gone, the Youngbloods had returned to London, and Elspeth still haunted Greywalls like some fabled ghost in Northanger Abbey. Her father had tried his best to bring her out of the doldrums. Camille as well. Questions ran rife. But she could only offer the fact that she and Keir no longer sought one another's company and that the announcement of his betrothal to another woman would soon be appearing in the *Times*.

She had blatantly refused to answer any of her father's questions, knowing that Camille in her wisdom would convince him she needed time to heal. Camille understood the pitfalls of being a woman, of living by the heart. Yes, Camille understood it all.

Her stepmother's advocacy would be a necessity when she went back to London. But she didn't want to think about that now. Elspeth wanted only to get on the moor and walk off her troubles. How lovely *that* would be, to just pick up one's feet and walk away from it all. Unfortunately one always took one's self along for the trip.

And so she bundled up in her warmest wool underthings, her heaviest gown and cloak and some extra pairs of stockings. Pulling up her hood, she then slid on a pair of red woolen mittens Aunt Miranda had knitted her for Christmas. They brought on a rare smile. Aunt Miranda could have afforded to buy her a pair of maroon gloves in any one of the Bond Street shops, but she took the time to knit some for her niece. Time had always been worth more to Elspeth than money. Sir Keir had understood such ways, she thought as she found herself on the open moor more than a mile from the castle.

Oh, Kier! How could you have done this to me?

She fell to her knees, the agony of it too great to bear, the implications now too devastating to ignore. Sobs jolted through her, and she rested her tortured face in her hands. The dormant heather cradled her knees and she cried. It felt good to let go, to give birth to the deformed spirit that had been maturing inside of her, that thing more of an aberration than her facial defect. It felt good to get it out, to push it away from her, this violent stepchild, this monster. She had needed to do this for so long, to cry out to God.

She was finished with this. Finished with the lies she had been fed, lies that felt good but left her with nowhere to turn when there was no place to go, no one to trust when everyone else had gone. Lies that left her a creature of ragged, deafening solitude.

"Look at this! Look at this!" Piercing the heavens with her gaze, she placed her hands beside her deformed face, framing her mouth with her fingers. God didn't care. He didn't protect her from those who would prey upon her. He didn't protect her from Keir, and he didn't protect her from loneliness. He didn't protect her even from herself. "What kind of Father are you?"

No clouds parted, no beam of sun shone down on her face. No voice saying *you are my beloved child* resonated around her or inside of her. Silence assaulted her on all sides, and her tears gushed from her eyes with greater force as she curled her torso down to meet her knees, falling over sideways into a fetal position. The heat of her skin melted the snow beneath her cheek.

Her insides ached with desolation, deep sobs pummeling her throat and stomach, watering her cheeks. But finally the tears abated and she lay breathing quietly, eyes swollen and sore. And a voice spoke.

"I've been waitin' for ye ta come hame, Bethie. I came oot ta find ye. Ta bring ye back where ye belong."

Does God have a Scottish accent? she thought, sitting up. Opening her eyes, she saw Angus standing before her. He sat down on his haunches and extended a hand. "Come on back where it's warm."

A shard of warmth penetrated her frozen heart. She smiled. "Angus. I'm so glad you're here."

The young man's eyes grew round. "Ye mean it?"

"Of course. Why wouldn't I?"

"Because I get on yer nerves, tha's why!" He screwed up his mouth and rolled his eyes, a sparkle lighting up their brown irises. "I ken I'm a bit bothersome, the way I'm always mytherin' o'er ye, Miss Elspeth. Bu' yer the best friend I ever had, an' I miss ye, an' when yer finally here, I find I canna get enough o' yer company."

No guessing with Angus.

"Yer so fine ta me, Miss Elspeth." He sat down, finally, his proclamations finished.

The love in Angus's eyes was so penetrating, so unmistakable, it hit her with a force. God was in this person. "We were friends for many years, Angus."

"Aye. Until London."

Regret filled her. "Yes, until then."

"When ye got too big fer yer britches!"

"Angus!"

"Sorry, miss. It's hard fer me no' ta speak my mind."

She laughed, then sobered. "I'm not the same girl I was then."

"No. Yer a lady noo." He reached into his pocket and pulled out a knife and a small carving he was working on.

"Still working with wood, I see?" she asked.

"Och, aye. It keeps me and ma Da close."

Like Tom Jones did for me.

"I'm not the lady you think I am, Angus." The time for confession had approached. She had to tell someone. Angus would understand. Well, maybe not exactly, but his love for her was strong enough to weather almost any storm.

"I dinna ken how tha' can be, Miss Elspeth. Other than how sad ye are noo. So sad."

"I've got a good reason to be."

He held up a hand. "Unrequited love?"

"Ooh, you're the man with the big words now, aren't you?"

He shrugged. "Book learnin' and maybees a little o' life doin' some teachin' in there as weel."

"What would you know of unrequited love at your age?" she asked.

He merely pointed at Elspeth, saying nothing.

"Oh." Elspeth dropped her eyes. "Of course. That was callous of me."

"I've got used to it."

"Angus!"

"Sorry. Ye were tellin' aboot bein' so sad. Are ye in love? No' tha' I really want ta hear the word 'yes' bu' I'm man enough ta handle it."

True enough. She twisted her hands together in her lap, wondering where to begin. "I don't know how to start."

"Ye know wha' they always say, Miss Elspeth."

She nodded and told him about the night she and Keir first met. Angus listened, carving ferociously when Elspeth revealed the more intimate moments of her liaison. Not going into any detail, of course, lest the poor lad faint clean away! Almost finished, she said, "And now—"

"Yer expectin' a bairn," he finished up.

His words forced her chin up violently. "How did you know?"

"Yer no' eatin' so muckle as a bite, Maw says. An' I heard the chambermaid whisperin' tha' ye've been losin' yer stomach on a regular basis. An' noo after wha' ye've just said, weel, just doin' ma sums on tha' one." His red face and heavy breathing related his discomfort. "Aw gosh, Miss Elspeth. I'm so sorry."

Now that she spilled the news Elspeth didn't know what to do. "I'd better go."

Obviously, the thought of leaving suited Angus for he said, "Aw right, then. I've got ta leave for school onyways. I'll walk ye back."

They returned to Greywalls in silence, Elspeth feeling as if she'd lost her last friend on earth. What would happen next, then?

She had to return to London. She had to tell her father.

They entered the castle. As Elspeth sought the stairs, Angus laid a hand on her arm. "No matter what ye've done, Miss Elspeth, I'll always love ye."

Tears formed in Elspeth's eyes again. "Thank you, Angus," she said, barely able to form the words.

She ran up the steps and began to pack.

CHAPTER ❖ TWENTY-EIGHT

David took one of the cigars that Cyprian Door proffered. The humidor, of a glossy burled oak, freed the full aroma of Cuban tobacco as he opened the lid. David would have almost killed for such on Devil's Island—had he thought about such small luxuries. He had been too busy worrying about matters such as food, a rip in his uniform, or finding a private place to relieve himself.

Over and done now, right?

Here in Cyprian Door's study, they discussed politics, strategy, and fishing. Cyprian Door loved to fish! How bad could a man be who loved to fish?

"When I see the potential of even my own dear wife, the keen intelligence she possesses, how can I not fight for her right to vote for the school board?"

David clipped off the end of his cigar. "How does Bertie feel about such matters?"

Cyprian puffed at his cigar to get it going. "Right now I don't think he wishes to be grievous to his mother, the queen."

"A good son, then?"

"Yes, very good."

David lit the cigar. "Why are you his friend, Door? Really."

Cyprian blew out a stream of smoke. "An honest question, Youngblood. I like that. Most people believe I am setting myself up for the future. Garnering power into my political storehouses, if you will."

"Lesser men and greater men alike would do so." David pulled in on his cigar.

Cyprian's study quickly filled with a smoky haze. The baron of Dividen waved away the smoke and opened up the French doors leading into the gardens. "It's cold outside, but Charlotte hates the smell of these things."

David stepped out into the January chill. They'd been back from Greywalls for three days now, and he'd spent every afternoon with Cyprian. He found he rather liked the man, but vowed to remain true to his mission despite Door's genial ways.

"In answer to your question, David, yes, I became friends with Bertie purely out of political motives. But you know"—he pointed his cigar at David—"after spending some time with the man, I've found I actually like him. There you have it."

"Must be nice to be in the inner circle of the prince of Wales. I'm sure his dear mama won't ever let the likes of me near him."

"That's true, unfortunately. But there's more to our system than the monarchy. Thank God."

"True enough."

A stiff breeze tumbled across the lawn and the men pulled in deeply on their cigars to keep them lit, the resulting clouds of smoke quickly blown away.

"I for one am glad you're here, Youngblood. You'll certainly make the Lords more amusing, and Charlotte has taken a real liking to Camille. Which is saying something for your wife."

"Glad to hear it."

"Yes, well, Charlotte needs good friends. Very much so."

David wanted to ask him to explain, but Cyprian Door had turned his back and, throwing his barely smoked cigar into a stone planter, walked back into the study.

And so began a friendship. The next day found them by the cold waters of the Tyburn with their fishing rods, bringing home a string of perch. Their wives had been lounging in the conservatory at the side of the house, Camille having refused, in no uncertain terms, to while away the day among hungry plants and cacophonous hours and half hours. A game of Chinese checkers sat on a game table between the ladies, and Charlotte clearly had the advantage. Ah well, Camille not much of a strategist, would, perhaps, put her other skills to good use on the fish.

"Here we are!" Cyprian shouted as they entered the room.

"Oh, dear. The conquering heroes back from the hunt," Charlotte drawled, turning up her pretty nose at the men's catch. But Camille reacted quite in the opposite manner. She jumped off of her chair with a loud "Bravo, gentlemen! *Fantastique!*"

David, proud of his wife just then, smiled as she grabbed the knotted string and kissed him lingeringly on the mouth. Mmmm. She was a sport, and there was nothing he liked better than a sport.

She held up the catch. "Point me to the kitchen, Charlotte, dear."

The baroness's mouth opened. "You're not seriously going to cook those, are you?"

Camille closed her eyes. "With butter, some shallots, and wine!"

"I'll come taste it first just to make sure it isn't bad fish," Cyprian volunteered.

"And I suppose I should do the same." David followed suit with a laugh.

Charlotte obviously knew the die had been cast. Her laugh harmonized with David's. "Oh, all right, then. Down to the kitchens! My chef won't like it one bit, being usurped like this and all."

"That's all right," David said. "Camille is used to battling cooks for space in their kitchen."

Cyprian pulled his wife into an embrace. "We'll make it a party! A kitchen party, Charlotte, dear. Who's heard of the like? I've got a lovely merlot down in the cellar that will be perfect for the occasion!"

"Bring up at least two bottles," Charlotte commanded. "I'm going to need as much as I can get." She extricated herself from his arms. "Kitchen party, indeed!"

Much later, when the time to say good-bye arrived, Cyprian pulled David briefly aside. "Thanks for the day, Youngblood. I don't think I've had such a one since I came back to England years ago."

"Well, we all need to relax and have a little fun every once in a while. But what about the prince of Wales, surely you have fun with him?"

"Oh, yes. But not relaxing. This has been just the ticket for me. I bless the day you returned from your travels." His sincere expression, so boyish and clear, embarrassed David.

"We all need good friends, Door. It's as simple as that."

"I agree. Well"—Cyprian held out his hand, his discomfort at baring a tiny portion of his heart apparent—"Godspeed, then."

"Godspeed."

David slammed the door of the coach and settled himself on the seat. "I just don't think it's Cyprian, *chérie*."

Camille thrust her hand into the crook of his arm. "Charlotte seems capable of it to me, though. Is there any way you can ask Cyprian about what happened that night?"

"Not yet. But soon. I have to gain his trust, which might mean baring some of my own transgressions."

"Not too many, though." As if she needed that!

"No. Just enough. The good thing about it is, *ma femme*, that there is no official record of any of my deeds that anyone can use to prove anything."

"The scandal alone would be enough, *mon mari*."

"Most likely you are right."

"Perhaps, with all of our dirty laundry"—she laid a hand on his knee—"we should leave the vengeance up to God on this matter."

"Perhaps God is using me to exact his vengeance, my love."

Camille didn't know what to say to that. These Youngbloods, blast them. Always one step ahead of her. So she pleaded with him, "Don't rush things then, David. At least promise me that. Perhaps you are God's whip, but only move when you feel his hand unmistakably compelling you to strike."

He leaned forward and kissed her. "If there was one thing I became proficient at on Devil's Island, it was waiting. I've made it an art."

Her passion for him ignited just then. She loved the survivor in him more than almost anything else. "I can think of other arts at which you are more than proficient." She pulled her lips into a pout.

"Are you trying to tempt me, *chérie*?"

"I don't know. Am I?"

He banged the roof of the coach, yelling for the driver to take the long way home. "We'll just have to find out," he drawled, grinning wickedly and pulling her into his arms.

David patted the sofa. "Have a seat, Bethie. I'm glad you came back to London."

Elspeth smiled a faded grin as she walked into the study. "My heart is here."

"Sometimes I don't know where my heart is. I love Greywalls, but I go crazy in all that quiet after too long."

She sighed and he took her hand.

"Is there something you want to tell me, Bethie? You seem troubled."

She nodded. "I don't know how else to say it. Sir Keir and I . . ." She fumbled for words.

"Has he asked you to marry him?"

"No, Dad. I'm pregnant."

Her words hung between them. The roar of the fire seemed to silence itself, and David stared at his daughter, feeling shock, then pain, then a grief so full, he couldn't contain his emotions.

"Please don't cry, Dad. Please."

David heard the words, but he couldn't see Elspeth for the tears in his eyes. "It's my fault, Bethie." His voice sounded hoarse and he tried to clear his throat, but couldn't. Filled with physical emotion, it constricted against his will. Tightening, opening, tightening again.

"I don't know what to do, Dad." Her palms ground against each other. "I didn't know where else to turn. Not really."

He succeeded in pressing back his tears and pulled her closely against him. "Oh, Bethie. I don't know what to do either. But whatever it is, we'll do it together."

She sagged against him, tears now soaking through his shirt.

"I mean it," he continued. "You won't go through this alone."

"Thank you," she whispered.

Help me to help her, he prayed. *Show me what to do, Lord.*

She looked up at him, staying within the snug circle of his arms. And he ran a tender hand along her hair, feeling its soft thickness beneath his fingers. Despite her recent apocalypse, his heart swelled with pride and relief. She had come to him during her time of trouble. A parent couldn't ask for much more than that.

He held her face in his hands and looked penetratingly into her eyes. "I cannot judge you. You do understand that, don't you? I deserted you, my greatest treasure, when you needed me the most."

But Elspeth shook her head. "You don't understand, Dad. It's all a mistake, just a big mistake. *I'm* just a big mistake. If you had been the young man you should have been, I would not exist. My deformity attests to the fact that I'm one of nature's mistakes. And though I do believe God exists, and I do, Dad, I cannot understand my life. I cannot understand how we keep finding ourselves making the same mistakes over and over. I shouldn't be here. I'm a direct result of sin. How do you think it feels to live with that? And now, I've carried on the Youngblood tradition! This child inside of me is just another mistake of a headstrong, idiotic family who cannot say no to their wants and desires!"

David let her anger soak into him; he tried to bear it for her. "You're not a mistake, Bethie."

"I can't believe that, Dad. I simply can't."

He took hold of her chin and gently lifted her face to meet his gaze. "I'm going to try and explain it to you the best way I know how. Knowing how God has always had his hand on me has given me a small measure of peace when I look back over my life and see the havoc I've wreaked. But the simple truth is this, Elspeth. God created a world that is ordered and governed by the natural laws he has set in place. When we break one of those laws, havoc results. But the beauty of it all is summed up in one word. Grace."

He heard her echo the word softly.

"It's by his grace that God will take our own transgressions and turn them around for our good. So that even what we view as a mistake, what is categorized as sin, in the end brings glory to him. And in that way, there are no mistakes with God."

"But I've done such awful things. I've turned my back on him so many times. I'm ugly and unworthy. How can he use anything I've done to bring glory to him?"

David thought for a moment. "It takes an even greater genius to take that which is ugly and fashion it into something beautiful. That's what God does to us. He sculpts our fallen selves with his chisel of grace, not through any great measure of our own, but because his Son died for us, because Jesus loves us."

Elspeth buried her face into his chest. "Oh, Father!" she wailed. "Oh, Father!" Her heart was splitting in two, and David realized she wasn't crying out to him at all.

⌒

"Twenty-nine years old and I already get to be a grandmother. Just think of it, David. A sweet little baby to warm up the house. Those soft cheeks to kiss."

Camille tried to cheer David up. Not that it did much good. He had been moping around the house, shaking his head and muttering things for three days now.

"Nappies to change, spit-up to wipe."

"Well . . ." She sighed, scooting her rear end off the edge of his desk where she'd been perched in a slightly provocative manner. "I'm going to go now since you're refusing to engage in any worthwhile conversation."

"Give the tea biddies my regards," he said dully.

Then he grabbed her wrist and looked into her eyes, imploring. "I just need a bit of time on this one, *ma femme*."

"I know."

"I don't know what to do. I don't know where to turn. Elspeth doesn't want to stay in London. She doesn't want to go to Greywalls. I don't know where to send her. Who would keep it a secret?"

Camille thought for a moment. And the answer struck her. "Who in London knows virtually everybody in England, the discreet and the indiscreet, and would want only what is best for Elspeth?"

David looked puzzled. "The last thing I need right now is a guessing game, *chérie*."

Not a bit put out, Camille pouted. "Come now, darling. It's no game. The answer is obvious. Lady Daria Christopher!"

"Blast it, but you are right, Camille!"

"I'll send for her right away. Let the tea biddies soak!"

His brows drew together. "But weren't you meeting at Charlotte Door's today?"

She nodded.

He placed his hand over hers. "I think you should go, *chérie*."

"But—"

"No, Camille. Leave Elspeth to me. I'll get in touch with Daria myself."

Well, he's perked up, Camille thought as she shrugged into her heavy winter coat and headed out. It made her feel good to provide the man with a little direction every once in a while.

Absinthe Pencraig leaned forward and patted Charlotte Door's knee. "You're such a dear to have the tea here this week, darling Charlotte."

"Better here than among the paint fumes at your house, Abby. I simply abhor the smell of paint."

Sitting in the conservatory at the Door home, Absinthe looked about her. She positively loathed this home. So many odd things, living and dead, cursed these rooms. The conservatory, a glass-domed affair stuck to the west side of the house, had been nicely warmed by afternoon sun and a coal stove in the corner, however.

Georginia gracefully added more sugar to her tea, the charm from her golden bracelet picking up some icing from the delicate tea cakes Camille Youngblood had brought, thank you God, for Charlotte's chef had provided some absolutely heinous treats. "I abhor the smell of paint as well. But do tell me, Abby, what you are having painted, and why?"

Absinthe laughed. She knew Georginia's news at the next gathering on her agenda would contain her plans. No thank you. So she lied. "I'm having my bedroom done in a marvelous shade of eggplant."

"Eggplant!" the aging dancer gasped.

"Yes. It will soon be all the rage. And in the dining room ... parrot green!" She held her shoulders back, trying to look proud, smug, you name it, as long as it was convincing.

Camille raised a hand to her mouth, obviously onto Absinthe's charade. Monica Raines did much the same. Charlotte, naturally, seemed to be more worried about the ropes of pearls tangling on her chest.

"Parrot green!" Georginia echoed. "I've never heard of the like!"

Camille sat up straight. "Well, you know Abby, dear. Always one for decorating. Her study is fabulous, you know." The Frenchwoman winked.

By golly, but she liked Camille!

Monica filled her plate for the third time that afternoon. "I'm simply starving these days, you know. But there are days too that I just don't feel as if I could keep down one bite."

Camille and Georginia, both mothers, exchanged knowing glances but said nothing.

And so the afternoon dragged on for Absinthe. It just wasn't the same, gathering here in this depressing house with this depressing food. Georginia was still going on about pigment with Charlotte, and Camille and Monica were talking about newborn babies. How boring. As Georginia detailed what rooms in her mansion were in dreadful need of repainting, a man walking by with a wheelbarrow full of sticks and leaves stole Absinthe's attention.

And he looked almost exactly like Prince Albert.

Aha!

"And how are your séances with the queen going, Charlotte?" she slipped in when Georginia took a breath.

"She's been calling me in more than ever. At first I was glad about it"—she shook her head—"but now, well, I'm not so sure. I'm dreadfully weary of the drive to Kensington. She cannot sleep these days."

"How often do you go?" Georginia asked.

"At least three times a week. It's becoming an exhausting endeavor"—she flipped her hand forward in a little wave—"but I can't exactly say no to the queen, can I?"

Heavens, not that! Absinthe's mind started to zip along at its usual lightning pace. The plan was really coming into focus now. "I have a suggestion, dear. I've an old sleep remedy from my great-grandmother."

"Don't we all?" laughed Monica, Camille nodding as well.

"Yes, but this one really works. I'll drop it by here the next time I come out. Put it in the queen's wine right before you start our nonsense—"

"It isn't nonsense!" Charlotte said with just a bit too much conviction.

Absinthe felt herself beginning to snap in two under a weight of great annoyance. She breathed in deeply and smiled a broad, placatory grin. "Do you wish to get some sleep or not, Charlotte?"

"Well, yes, of course."

"Then just do as I say."

Charlotte rubbed her eyes. "Yes, I do. I'll arrange it. It would be a good thing."

"And this remedy will do the trick, mark my words."

Oh, would it!

⌣

Camille felt a bone-deep exhaustion. She'd fallen asleep on the way home from the tea, thinking that Absinthe had been overzealous in her concern for the queen. *Ciel!*

All she wanted now was a very long, very hot bath, the kind that sunk through her skin, straight to her very weary heart. Last week at the mission had been rough. Another child deserted on the doorstone. Of course, Reverend Williams didn't know what to do with these foundlings. And they prayed and wept over the boy child, no more than three months old, and took him down the street to the foundling home. The East End Home for Foundling Boys wasn't nearly so caring a place as the mission.

"Why can't we open up an orphanage?" Camille asked the young missionary.

"We can, my lady. Or rather, I should say *you* can. We'd be behind you one hundred percent if you'd like to raise the money and take charge of the project. In fact, it's something we've been wanting to do for a long time."

Well, Camille thought now, stepping out of the carriage with the help of a young groom, *that's what I get for complaining about not having enough to do!* And, naturally, David had been all for the idea, so she didn't have that excuse for backing out. Oh, these Youngbloods were infectious with their zest for life and their ability to dive headlong into a raging river without giving so much as a thought if there were rocks waiting beneath the current.

Each step up, as she slowly made her way toward the front door, was aching and slow. At least Lily would be there to add some verve and take away a bit of this lethargy. My, but she'd been so warm inside of the coach with the heated footrest Absinthe supplied, not to mention the hot potatoes a kindly servant had shoved into her coat pockets.

Wooten opened up the door as soon as her foot touched the landing. "My lady," he said with a bow. "I'm glad to see you are home safe and sound."

She picked off her gloves. "Thank you, Wooten. I'm exhausted. Could you have one of the maids draw me a bath, please? Very hot."

Wooten cleared his throat. "Uh, madam . . . I'm sorry to have to say so, but you have a visitor."

Zut alors! "Who is it?"

"It's a Racine de Boyce."

That would do for a quick burst of wakefulness! "Is she in the parlor?"

"Actually, no. She's in the study with Miss Lily. There was already a fire in there," he explained. "Of course, if you'd rather—"

"Oh, no, Wooten. The study is fine." Her hands began to shake as she hurried back to her husband's study. She'd been quite successful at shoving thoughts of Racine de Boyce aside. Now she wished she'd thought more about what she would say if she ever saw the countess again.

Lily's childish laughter bounced into the hallway. A good sign!

Camille stood in the doorway and watched them as they played a game of Chinese checkers together at the games table. Although it didn't look as if they were really playing the game. It looked more as if they were making pictures on the board with their marbles.

Best to get it over with. Camille cleared her throat.

Dowager Countess Racine de Boyce looked up. An expression of profound pain alighted in her eyes momentarily before she stood slowly to her feet. She relied more heavily upon her cane now, Camille noticed.

"Countess."

"My dear," Racine said with a sheepish smile. "How wonderful it is to see you. I've come to ask for your forgiveness."

Camille ran across the room, gathering the old woman into her arms. "Oh, Countess." She breathed in the familiar scent of the woman's perfume. "I'm so glad you've come. And please"—she closed her eyes against the tears that formed—"there's nothing to forgive."

"Oh, but there is!" Racine pulled back and took Camille's hands in her own. "I'm commanded as a Christian to forgive—many times over. But I failed to do so."

"Yes, but considering the circumstances—"

"Our Lord didn't name any circumstances that do not apply, did he?"

Camille squeezed her hands lightly. "No, but I still don't understand how you can begin to forgive me. Not after all I've done."

The countess dropped Camille's hands and hobbled over to the sofa. She sat down with a groan. "I've had several months to think about all of this, my dear. Our parting didn't occur just yesterday. Do sit down."

Camille obeyed and Lily climbed up between them, guaranteeing that the past would not be dredged up in great detail. Camille wasn't about to send her away!

The countess continued. "When I realized that, yes, I had indeed forgiven you, I took the first available boat over here."

"Isn't it wonderful, *Maman*?" Lily clapped. "I love surprises!"

Camille stroked her daughter's hair. "If it is a surprise like this, I do believe there is no better kind."

Racine's eyes became serious. "Life is too short to keep oneself away from love. I love you, Camille. I love you *and* Lily."

"We love you," Camille said, leaning forward. "I can't tell you what a weight has been taken off of my heart."

"I understand, *ma chère*, believe me."

"You'll stay with us?" Lily asked.

"For two nights." The countess held up two fingers. "And then, I'm going to Scotland to visit my granddaughter, Eve."

"Eve de Boyce?" Lily's eyes grew round. "Why, she's my cousin. Well, sort of."

The countess's eyes met Camille's and they laughed together. "Never forget," the countess said, "family is the most important thing of all."

That night, after dinner, David escorted Racine de Boyce into his study. "Have a seat, Countess, won't you? Can I get you a blanket?"

"Yes, David. That will be nice."

David looked on the woman with tenderness. Something he *never* expected to feel. This woman had hated him during the days of his youth, had hated the dark influence he'd had on her son, Rene. And yet, she'd been one of the few dedicated Christians he'd known. He remembered how he had despised her, thinking her the greatest hypocrite he'd ever known.

But God's grace had been sufficient. Was still sufficient. He'd already made his apologies regarding the debauched life to which he'd introduced her son, and she'd accepted it, making apologies of her own, telling him that surely a little love from her might have gone a long way back then!

He shook open a tartan blanket and let it settle gracefully onto her lap. "Camille is putting Lily to bed. Would you like a little company, or perhaps some peace and quiet?"

"Sit with me, David. We've got a lot of time to make up for."

David pulled a leather wing chair close to the couch and sat down.

The countess tucked the blanket in on either side of her thighs. "I feel as if a heinous chapter of my life has finally been resolved."

David agreed. "As do I."

"Some of us need more drastic circumstances to teach us the simple lessons of life."

"I know that firsthand."

She smiled. "I still am astounded that God got hold of you."

"None is more astounded than I."

"Your soul came at a terrible price to me," she said, and David thought of the mess of years before, the mess surrounding this woman's weak son.

"I know that too."

"Well, it seems to me that you aren't wasting your life anymore."

"No, my lady."

Her eyes filled with tears. "A life for a life, then?"

David looked down at his hands. "I hope not."

She took a hankie out of her pocket and wiped her eyes. "Rene would have done nothing of import with his life. I'm honest enough to realize that."

"Oh, my lady, you can't say—"

"Yes, I can, David. So you use your life for greatness, won't you? At least redeem his death with your own life. Make a life that did the things that God calls us to do."

He reached out and took her gnarled hand in between his own. "I can only do the best I've got with what I've been given."

"Then you will do just fine. Sit beside me, David. I'm still cold."

David did as she requested, putting his arm around her and drawing her slight frame close to his side. "I do believe I am safe in saying that this is a moment neither of us could have ever foreseen!"

"You speak correctly, dear boy. If only I had taken my Christian duties seriously back then. Perhaps I might have sowed a few seeds of goodness."

"Oh, you sowed many good seeds, Countess. You showed Camille the Savior, and in that you were instrumental in giving me the life I couldn't fathom, but knew, deep down inside, was possible."

"Thank you, David. You are gracious."

"No, Countess. God is gracious."

Her eyes shone into his and he leaned forward to kiss her temple. The skin felt soft and moved beneath his lips. Yes, God was gracious, indeed.

CHAPTER ❖ TWENTY-NINE

Absinthe Pencraig perched on the carriage seat as though sharp rocks sat beneath her derriere. The back of the man's head was visible now as he walked down the right side of the road going west of Harrow. She strained her body forward, neck reaching toward him, as though somehow such an action might cause the carriage to get to him more quickly.

The meeting had been arranged during tea at Charlotte's.

Prince Albert indeed! Absinthe in no wise believed Lady Door's protestations that her séances had feet in reality; however, this scheme bordered on the ridiculous. The gardener! Prince Albert the gardener! Oh, that was rich!

Well, she reasoned, *if he is willing to take a risk and fool the queen for Charlotte, he should be more than willing to help out the likes of me.*

Things were turning out to be, as Camille Youngblood would say, *extraordinaire*!

"My suggestion is simple," Lady Daria said after hearing Elspeth's confession. "Elspeth"—she had taken her hand—"you must leave London at once. The disgrace would be unbearable for you, my dear."

Elspeth nodded. She didn't need to add her transgressions to the already lengthy Youngblood list of faults. "Where can I go?"

Lady Daria cleared her throat. "I know you've heard me speak of Lord Hayden Walsh for years."

Oh dear, not Lord Hayden the Blind again. Elspeth looked down at her hands. "Yes."

"He's a man now, dearest. Twenty-three years old."

"But didn't you say he was a recluse?" Elspeth asked.

"Precisely, my dear. He lives south of Plymouth, right on the coast. On Penlee Point. You should go there for your confinement. Most gorgeous man I've ever seen."

"As delightful as the young man sounds, Daria," David spoke up, "you really think this is necessary?"

"Yes. Don't you see the beauty of it, David? Elspeth will have the utmost privacy. And I can assure you, Hayden is a delightful young man. Yes, he's reclusive, but he's intelligent and appealing and a man of varied interests."

"How can I trust him to do right by my daughter? Is he a man of solid morals?"

"Of course! I can vouch for that personally. Nothing untoward will happen to Elspeth."

David turned to his daughter. "Is this what you want?"

Elspeth didn't hesitate. "It has to be, Dad. I've got to get away."

David took her hand. "I can certainly understand that feeling." He turned to Lady Daria. "Would you find out if he would be agreeable to this?"

"I'll send a message right away. In the meantime, Elspeth, you go on with your life as normal. It will cause less suspicion."

And Elspeth had done exactly that for the next two weeks. Waiting for the letter from Lord Hayden Walsh, she sought to spend as much time with her family as she could, getting to know her stepmother far better, and coming to appreciate the woman's simple wisdom. Her nonjudgmental ways covered Elspeth's aching heart like a silken robe. And Lily! Well, Lily, bless her soul, unaware of anything, gave her great joy. Elspeth stayed with her stepsister for most of those days, helping up in the schoolroom, taking her for walks in the frigid January air, making chocolate and drinking it together before the fire.

Their time was soon drawing to a close.

Camille fell into her new mission with more velocity than a cannonball dropped from the top of the Tower Bridge. As much as the Bond Street ladies had jumped out of her way when she walked among them as an equal, they were just as willing to receive her now that she seemed to "know her place."

Yes, a reformed prostitute should be busy paying her debt to society, not buying the latest in hats!

Daria had been more than a help. She'd literally sat down and made a listing of all the women who would most likely open up their pocketbooks for such a worthy cause. And so, in the two weeks in which they awaited the response of Lord Hayden Walsh, the dining room table was cluttered with stationery, ink pens, and lists of things to do.

"I think it's a wonderful way to introduce yourself to society, darling," Daria said as she addressed an invitation to a charity tea, given at her home, for the Grace Home. "And what a perfectly wonderful name you chose. Who's Grace anyway, dear? One of the women at the mission?" She handed the parcel to Camille.

Camille, unable to write, of course, dropped a blob of silver wax onto the back of the envelope, sealing it with an imprint of the Youngblood coat of arms. Daria was indispensable to her now. She could have never done this on her own.

Elspeth jumped in with an explanation. "God's grace, Lady Daria."

"Of course!" Daria Christopher clapped her hands with delight. "How quaint!"

After Daria had left for the day, and the sun was just about done with London, the great clock in the hall chimed. "How would you like to help out at the mission tonight, Elspeth?" Camille asked.

Elspeth agreed it would be a fine thing. And so after supper Camille, David, and Elspeth piled into the carriage. Lily sprang up next to Elspeth, her little boots clicking on the carriage floor.

Reverend Williams was delighted to see them. He handed them all a hymn sheet, and the service began. Now this, thought Camille, is what living with the Lord should be! Not that churches like Westminster Abbey didn't have their place. It just failed to speak to her where she was, where she saw herself to be. A denizen of the gutter dressed in lovely clothes.

But God had found her. And in him she had been elevated to royalty. She was a daughter of the King of heaven. And she had a job to do. Now if they could just settle this little matter of Charlotte and Cyprian Door! Then she could really get down to work!

After the service, she told Williams about the tea. "It will be in a month. We're expecting a good response."

"It sounds wonderful, Lady Camille." His youthful features spread wide with pleasure, and he raked a hand through his brown hair as he said softly, "You are an answer to a prayer I prayed a year ago."

"I feel so honored," Camille said.

"It *is* an honor to be used by God, my lady."

"It certainly is."

"We need an orphanage so badly. One where these children are loved, not just fed, clothed, and sheltered."

"And shown the love of God!" Elspeth said, coming in late on the conversation. "A child needs to be taught that from the beginning. It saves them a lot of grief in the end."

"But that's the beauty of God's grace," said Williams, smiling. "It transcends age, race, class, and circumstance."

They all agreed.

"Have you heard anything more about that little baby boy left a few weeks ago?" Camille asked.

Williams nodded. "I've been checking on him. He seems healthy enough, but . . ."

"Such a shame," Camille said.

"You've got a job to do, my lady," the young minister said. "But from what I've seen so far, you're the woman to do it!"

"Hear, hear," David said, placing a possessive, encouraging hand on her back.

Later that night, a light tapping at the door wakened Camille. Elspeth stood there. "Are you awake?"

"Uh, yes. Yes."

"Would you mind talking with me? I could use a little company right now."

Camille shook the sleep from her brain, grabbed her robe, and put her arm through Elspeth's. "Let's go down to the kitchen, Bethie."

Elspeth stoked up the fire and put a kettle on the hob. "Camille, tell me your story. Tell me of God's grace in your life."

And Camille, while throwing together a marvelous soup, testified to Elspeth of God's love and assured her that all would be well if she trusted God to guide.

Elspeth pulled a note out of the pocket of her robe. "Lord Hayden Walsh wrote to me today. He said he'd be delighted to have me at St. Stephen's Hall." Her face crumbled, and Camille immediately took her into her arms.

"I'm frightened," Elspeth said. "I'm frightened of being a mother so soon. I'm frightened of leaving here. I'm frightened of what I should find at Lord Hayden's."

"Then stay here!" Camille said forcefully. "Stay with those who love you the most."

"I can't! Don't you see? For the first time in my life I have to do what's right for everybody. Not just for me. I've got to go." Elspeth pulled away, sobs wracking her body, and she ran out of the kitchen.

Camille stirred the soup. She'd give anything for Elspeth to stay. But unfortunately, the girl was right. She should bear the child in secret and give them all at least a sporting chance.

On to Penlee Point Elspeth had to go. They left the house early for Victoria Station on a misty morning, just she and her dad. He held her hand but said nothing. Just what Elspeth needed.

Daria arrived at the station with little time to spare.

It would take all day to get to Plymouth by train, settle into a hired coach, and arrive at St. Stephen's Hall. And then, Lord Hayden Walsh would welcome them.

Or so he had assured Lady Daria.

But Elspeth had to wonder why any single gentleman would want a pregnant, deformed girl staying at his house. He should either be canonized or sent straight to an asylum!

~

"I'm simply exhausted, Lady Daria." Elspeth raised a hand to her puffy eyes, feeling the grainy stretch of tired skin as she rubbed. Her stomach had soured even further with exhaustion.

Daria nodded in sympathy. "The first three months are the worst, dear."

The coach swayed back and forth, much like the train car, only with jolts and bumps thrown in to make it more nauseating. More than once since they ventured out of Plymouth did the driver, more than irritated, have to stop and let Elspeth out. But when Lady Daria pointed out that he'd have to do the clean-up if they didn't pull over, he kept his mouth shut. And her comment about "pushy servants" did little to set the man's temperament to rights.

"Only a quarter of an hour more, darling."

"It's so dark tonight."

Daria looked out of the window. "No moon that I can see."

It had been like this all day. Nothing but trivialities spoken between the women. Elspeth wanted to scream at the inane topics. Truthfully, though, the silence in between the conversations disheartened her even more.

"Now, dear, I'll stay with you tomorrow, to see you settled in. But then I must be getting home to London."

Elspeth would have felt the same had the pendulum been swinging the other way. "All right. I brought plenty of books to read."

"And Lord Hayden has an extensive library as well. Overlooks the channel, lots of large windows to let in the light and the view."

Ah, good news, that.

"A bright spot in which to grow a baby," Daria said, and Elspeth wished she had kept that particular comment to herself. No mind now, the carriage had stopped. She disembarked, the grave feeling that her fate was in all wise sealed guiding her foot as it touched the pebbled drive.

A great wind tumbled off of the Channel, and her curls flagellated her cheeks.

"A storm is comin'!" the driver hollered. "Can we please hurry?"

The women, pushed forward by the breeze, walked quickly to the front door of St. Stephen's Hall. All was dark inside.

David sat on the floor with his back against the sofa and stared blankly at the blaze in the fireplace. Elspeth's fire. His focus relaxed, softening the view of the blaze.

Camille had, in her usual fashion, laid a pillow on his lap and proceeded to make herself comfortable on the floor beside him. She took out her hairpins and eased her head onto the pillow, looking up at David with large, sad eyes. "She'll be all right."

"I hope so."

"*Chéri*, I know she will."

The house felt like an empty suitcase with silken lining. "I don't know what I would do right now if I didn't have you, Camille."

"It's one of the advantages of marriage. Feeling safe at harbor. Being loved."

"Yes." He thrust his hand into his wife's hair and kneaded the nape of her neck, taking comfort from the familiar bow of her skull, the silkiness of her hair, the way she smelled. "I just can't bear to think of her all the way down there. All alone. So remote."

Camille curved a hand up to rest on his shoulder. "Perhaps that's what she needs. Some time alone. Perhaps she's finding her own safe haven, *mon chere*."

"But she's pregnant, Camille. What future does she have? Really?"

"Don't forget I found myself in much the same state, *chéri*. And it turned my life around."

A valid point, David knew. But like any father before him, he yearned to turn back the clock, to somehow do better to protect his daughter from such drastic lessons.

Speaking of lessons . . . "I'd sure like to teach Sir Keir a lesson or two."

Camille's brows drew together. "We've already discussed this, David. And you promised Elspeth you wouldn't let him know of the baby's existence."

"I know. Wish I hadn't." He grumbled, feeling a bit of the numbness going away. Clearly, he could only give Elspeth over to God, completely and with all the faith he could muster.

⁓

The darkness masked most of St. Stephen's Hall. But nevertheless, Elspeth craned her neck, leaning back to examine the roofline of the large home. Nothing in size compared to Greywalls or Blackthorne, the doorway nevertheless boasted an artistic impressiveness. She could just make out a large, domed cupola embedded in the center of the roof. A weather vane that looked like it could be a fish riding on top of a chicken pointed southwest in the stiff wind.

Daria had already rung the bell, and they stood there waiting, shivering in their socks. "I do hope someone answers soon," Daria said in a voice vibrating with chill.

"It's all dark inside."

They waited a minute more, Elspeth wondering if they should go to the inn they had passed twenty minutes earlier and bed down for the night. Maybe that would be better anyway.

Yes, prolonging the inevitable might not be a grand idea, but sometimes it felt better for one's inevitable to be around the corner and not staring one in the face. And maybe Lord Hayden had changed his mind. Then what would happen?

Greywalls, she supposed. Never to set foot in the light of day until the babe was born and . . . then what? What would happen to the child?

A grating groan scuffed the air as the door began to open.

So much for procrastination.

"Come in, please," a voice said from out of the darkness. A raspy voice, unaccustomed to much use obviously. Much like the front door, Elspeth supposed. "Lady Daria, is that you?"

Daria stepped boldly forward and laid a hand on the man's shoulder. "Yes, Lord Hayden."

"And Elspeth? She is with you?"

"Yes, she is."

He stepped forward into the breeze, a large silhouette against the dim illumination of the English Channel. Elspeth felt dwarfed in the presence of this man with the hoarse voice. Pulling a candle out of his pocket, he handed Daria a box of matches. "Come in, and light your way. I'll show you to your rooms."

They did his bidding, following him as he slowly made his way into the belly of the house and up a curving staircase. Elspeth noticed he wore only stockings, feet seemingly every bit as sensitive as the fingers that felt along the wall every so often, touching picture frames, each frame carved differently.

Lady Daria chattered, seemingly oblivious to the fact that he failed to reply to all of her questions.

"Here," he said, stopping short. "Your rooms. Across the hall from one another. Miss Elspeth, your room is this one, by the Botticelli. Lady Daria, as usual, you have the room by the sleeping madonna."

Elspeth heard the smile in his voice, but refused to turn and examine him. She couldn't yet. If the rest of him matched his size and his voice, she was in for another showing of Rigoletto for the next seven months. *Except it won't be one beast, but two.*

Involuntarily her hand covered her mouth.

"Bless you, Hayden." Lady Daria leaned up and kissed his cheek.

"Good night, then." He turned. "Glad you've come," his voice echoed as he retreated.

Elspeth turned and watched him fade down the hallway. Yes, extremely tall, his stature had the best of Dad and Uncle Tobin. The light of Lady Daria's candle caught at the light blond streaks in his ash hair. Hmm. From the sound of his voice she'd expected black hair.

Daria led Elspeth into her room. "Well, he's certainly not one for words," Elspeth remarked.

"No, he lives here alone, except for a few servants."

"What of his parents?"

"Dead. For years now."

"He seems able to navigate the house without mishap. Does he go out?"

Lady Daria shook her head. "I don't know, Bethie. I suppose you'll be finding out all of these things." She took a candle down from the mantel, dipping her own to light it. "You might just as well go to sleep in your shivvies. I doubt if that horrible man will be heaving the trunks up the steps tonight! And who knows where the servants are."

With a kiss and a good night, she left with a weary sigh.

Elspeth lit the rest of the candles in the room. It was brighter now, and more cheerful. A sweet room in all actuality. Lemon yellow walls. And they were freshly painted. The smell of lemon infused the air. Lemon and . . . gardenias! Where did they come from at this time of the year?

She swiveled in a complete circle to capture the entire view. A fire burned in the grate, warming the room. A large doll sat in a small chair to the right of the blaze. And a music box rested on the surface of the dresser. Three vases of gardenias perfumed the room. The smell, so peaceful and lovely, curled its way to a place in Elspeth's heart that needed such care.

And then her eyes came to rest on her bed pillow. A single rose lay there—a white rose, tied with a yellow satin ribbon.

How did Lord Hayden Walsh know that yellow was her favorite color? That gardenias were her favorite flower, with roses close behind?

Elspeth smiled a very real smile, took off her gown, and laid it over the chair as exhaustion overtook her. The sleep she quickly fell into was sweet and fresh, a gift from God and Lord Hayden Walsh.

CHAPTER ❖ THIRTY

Lady Daria breezed in just as the sun began to rise.

"I've decided to just go back now. Why bother with all the mess of unpacking for one day? And I don't have my maid, and I really do think it would be for the best. Valentinia and Hamish will be leaving for France on holiday, and I'd hate to miss one more day with my grandchildren than I have to—"

She babbled on and on, and Elspeth knew that to try and stop her midstream might prove dangerous. Damming up Lady Daria's river of expression was akin to dropping a brick wall in front of a charging brigade.

Frankly, Elspeth could do with a little solitude. "It's all right, Lady Daria. I shall be fine."

She rushed over to the bed and sat down beside Elspeth. "I was so worried you'd be upset."

"Of course not. I'm nineteen years old and perfectly able to take care of myself. Lord Hayden didn't seem to be a bad fellow. And if he gets to be too much, it will be easy to avoid him."

"Don't be cruel to him, Bethie," Lady Daria warned. "He may be blind, but his other senses are working far better than yours or mine will. He'll be able to find you no matter where you go."

"How so?"

Lady Daria pointed around to all the flowers. "After a night in this room, darling, he'll be able to follow your scent anywhere."

And here Elspeth thought his actions had been a reflection of his temperament. "Then I shall get rid of the flowers right away!"

"It's his home, Bethie, and he's graciously received you for your confinement. The least you can do is honor him by allowing him knowledge of your whereabouts."

"I thought I'd have some privacy, though."

"Oh, believe me. Hayden is a very private person. He'll respect yours utterly. Probably too much."

Elspeth tapped her chin. "So I guess what you're saying is not to judge Lord Hayden Walsh too quickly."

"Precisely. I've found with men it's best to just let them unfold their wings on their own." She reached down and picked up her small valise. "They're not mysterious beings at all. It's a matter of patience and acceptance when it comes to dealing with them."

Elspeth sat up and put her arms around Lady Daria. "Thank you. Thank you for bringing me here. I think I'll be just fine. I've got this lovely room—"

"Yes! It's perfectly delightful, isn't it? Hayden wrote me and asked me to write down a list of your favorite things. It appears as if he's taken it to heart."

"Taken it to heart, indeed. I'd say he's got it memorized forward and backward!"

Elspeth looked around the room. The sun shone, its light gilding the molding around two very long windows on either side of the bed. "Look, over there is a bowl of walnuts and a nut-cracker. On the table is a copy of *Tom Jones* and the Bible."

"Now that's quite a mix," Daria laughed.

"And look, there on the dresser is my favorite perfume."

Daria's eyes became serious. "Be kind to him, Elspeth."

"Why wouldn't I?" This turn of conversation seemed awfully abrupt, even for Daria.

"Because some of us tend to despise the people that are the most giving. We feel we've got some sort of upper hand and take advantage of their kindness. I know about such things from experience."

Elspeth took her hand. "Are you speaking of Uncle Tobin?"

Lady Daria nodded, her eyes filling with tears. "I really did love him. But I waited too long. I thought he'd always be there for me. And then, when I was truly ready, his heart had been captured by another."

"But you always acted so relieved that Aunt Miranda came along!"

She took a hankie from her pocket and wiped her eyes, the tears ending as quickly as they had begun. "How could I not? I do have my pride, dear, and I could see this was the love he had been waiting for all of his life. This was the love he needed. I freed him out of my love for him. I could do nothing else and truly want only the best for him."

What a revelation. "I never knew. No one did."

Lady Daria smiled, patted Elspeth's hand, and placed it back on the quilt. "And no one ever shall. You'll keep this between us?"

"Absolutely." Elspeth hugged her again. "You've always been so good to me, Lady Daria. Now go home. You've got a good life in London, and you don't need to be dillydallying here with me on the coast of nowhere!"

Daria laughed. "You are a gem, Bethie. Perhaps this is the setting where you will shine most brightly."

Elspeth doubted that, but she said, "We shall have to wait and see. Shall I get dressed and see you off?"

"Oh, heaven's no! That blackguard driver has already pulled round." She kissed Elspeth one last time. "I'm off then. Make sure to write me, darling."

"Oh, I will. I'll have lots of time to do things like that!"

"I'll put your father's mind at ease, dear."

And Daria was gone, leaving behind a larger hole than she'd taken up. It was always like that.

Elspeth, relieved to see her trunks sitting outside her door, quickly dragged them in and began to unpack. Not having a maid to tend to her would be a bit bothersome, but ensuring her privacy was well worth the extra effort. In fact, Lady Daria had assured Elspeth that Lord Hayden kept the staff to a minimum at St. Stephen's. Just a cook, a housekeeper, and a gardener. There were no horses to be taken care of, and a solicitor in London handled all of Lord Hayden's business concerns, "So life couldn't be more simple," Daria had said.

It took an hour or so, but by the time the small clock on the wall near the door chimed nine o'clock, Elspeth had unpacked, washed, and changed. She carefully arranged her hair in the latest style and dabbed on some of the gardenia perfume left for her. If Lord Hayden wished to know her whereabouts, so be it. She'd not go sneaking about ever again. That only got one into trouble!

Cyprian Door's invitation to take luncheon at the Brooks's club had been a godsend. David looked at the mound of paperwork on his desk. He needed a good escape. From many matters.

Shouts floated into his study. From the kitchen.

Oh, dear. He let out a sigh and hurried down the steps in time to see his wife stomp a very angry foot. Her pointed finger shook at the cook. "*Minute, papillon! C'est plus fort que moi!* I must cook! I'm going mad with this arrangement!"

And she was speaking a lot of French, a harbinger of trouble, to be sure.

The cook, a small man with kinky brown hair and a ridiculously small nose, threw up his hands. "This is my kitchen. And I'll thank you not to barge in here whenever you wish. And speak our language, for goodness sake! This isn't France, you know. My lord"—he turned to his employer—"I don't mean to be disrespectful, but this is most unusual. I realize this is her house—"

"Yes, it is." David knew exactly where to direct his loyalties. "And it is mine as well. Now this has gone on long enough, you two. All my wife asks is one burner and a large pot to make soup. Why do you have such difficulty with that?"

Camille turned on him. "*Nom d'un chien!* Just fire the man, *mon mari*! I'm going crazy! These English people!"

"Now, *chérie*, I know the life of a countess isn't all you thought it would be."

"Would you rather me be one of those women who keep getting their rooms repainted!" Camille spat. "If I could just bake a little bread, make a little soup, I'd feel so much better. And I wanted to try an old recipe of Mai-Ling's for a tea cake she used to make me in Paris. It would be perfect for the charity tea. But *monsieur* over here—"

"Come, Camille, let's try and work this out. Please. Mr. Joyce is a very good cook."

Joyce drew himself up proudly.

"I'm sure we can come to some sort of agreement," David continued.

"*Lavette!*" she spat at him.

Heavens, but this cheered him up immensely! Nothing like watching Camille get annoyed to get his blood flowing like a raging river. What a woman! "I am not a dishrag, *chérie*. It's simply that a good cook is very hard to find in London." He turned to Mr. Joyce. "One pot, one burner. And perhaps a corner of the oven."

"And one corner of the worktable!" Camille stomped.

"It's all I ask, Joyce," David said.

"All right," the cook conceded, clearly not happy. "But I won't have her telling me how to make my sauces!"

David turned to his wife. "Will you promise to keep that pretty mouth of yours quiet?"

Her eyes were still blazing when he reached forward and caressed her cheek with his fingers. She nodded with a grudging smile and leaned forward. "Why do you always do this to me? Why can I not control myself around you? You say 'Do this,

Camille' and I do this, you say 'Do that, Camille,' and I do that. *Juste ciel!*"

"Make me a nice pot of soup, *chérie*. Do you hear that, Joyce?" he yelled above her head. "I want my wife's soup for supper tonight. No arguments! But some of your chess pie would be a lovely dessert!"

"*Lavette*," Camille whispered.

"I am *not* a dishrag. I'm merely being diplomatic."

She put her hands against his chest and shoved lightly. "Then go be diplomatic at that boring club. You'll be late for your meeting with Cyprian Door."

He bowed, taking her hand and kissing its palm. "I hear and obey you, my lady."

Turning, he walked through the door.

"*Lavette*," she mumbled just loud enough for him to hear as he started up the steps.

"I heard that!" he yelled.

"Good!" she shot back.

"We'll take this up later, *chéri*!"

"I'm looking forward to it, *mon mari*."

He turned back around to look at her at the foot of the steps. One hand was placed provocatively on one hip, the other on her ribcage beneath her breast. "Perhaps I should forget Cyprian Door," he said softly.

"No, no. You are a man with a mission, remember?" She winked slowly. "I'll be here when you return, *chéri*."

"I'm counting on it, my love."

He hurried through the entry hall, grabbed his coat and hat, and climbed into the waiting coach. In a few days' time he should receive a letter from Elspeth, but until then, he had to go on as before. She would expect nothing less. But his heart ached inside, a pain he would carry with him wherever he went, one that wouldn't go away until Elspeth knew happiness once again.

But Camille surely was doing her best to tend the wound. Thanks be to God for that woman!

It didn't take long to get to Brooks's. The gentlemen's club, an apolitical haven where both sides of the aisle cast aside their differences, stood in St. James's Street. The lovely building was designed to look like a small country house in the city. "Like a duke's house—with the duke lying dead upstairs," David had heard a cynic say during a recess at the House of Lords.

Years before, the club had been split practically in two during the hurricane surrounding Gladstone's Home Rule Bill. Blackballing occurred with such frenzy the situation grew grave. Finally, Lord Granville pleaded with all the passion he could muster that one place in London should be reserved where men tethered their politics at the door and old friends could greet each other on benevolent ground.

David enjoyed the varied men that inhabited the club. Once a gambler's mecca, Brooks's now possessed a peaceful quiet. David had to admit he enjoyed the calm atmosphere and the smell of the oil lamps and beeswax candles that illumined the intimate gathering place.

Cyprian Door waited for him in the coffee room. The chamber doubled as the library, its walls lined with beautifully crafted shelves. He stood to his feet immediately as David entered, a genuine smile opening up his face. "What better place for friends to meet?" he said.

David walked over and shook his hand. "Indeed." He looked around him at the empty room. "A slow day today, hmm?"

"Yes. But that's good. We've much to discuss, and you know how garrulous some of the others can be." He indicated the leather chair next to his own, the two separated by a small round table. "Have a seat. They're threatening to serve lunch soon."

David sat down, settling into the chair more easily than he had since his return from French Guiana. Yes, all the walks he took with Camille, all the good food she and Joyce prepared, had done much to strengthen him. He felt like a new man these days.

A waiter cleared his throat from beside David. He ordered some tea and turned to Cyprian. "Did you get a chance to meet with Forester?"

He nodded with enthusiasm. "And Gladstone too. The Education Act will be going up for vote."

That children between the ages of five and thirteen would be getting an education was good on more than just the obvious front of enlightenment. Now they would be in school, unable to be abused by cruel taskmasters. "So the vote will be coming up shortly?"

"Yes. And the sooner the better, I say. As far as we know we've enough MPs committed to it, and more than enough votes in the Lords."

David had been enjoying this life so far. He found having little free time to be a boon. It kept him out of trouble. *And, believe me, I'm naturally prone to that!* he thought, looking over at Cyprian Door.

The two men had spent reams of time in one another's company since the Youngbloods returned from Christmas at Greywalls. Though now convinced that Cyprian Door didn't lay a finger on his parents, David still felt compelled to clear Becket's name. But as Cyprian's friend, he could no longer do anything but bring his past to light, to tell him of Becket's death, to divulge his mission.

No time like the present, David. It had been one of his mottoes during his wayward years, and he supposed that maxim applied to good as well as evil. Yet, could this be a foolhardy move?

Truth was never wrong. Trust in the truth was never wrong, he reasoned. And the truth was this, God had given him the same love for Cyprian Door he had felt those years on Devil's Island for Becket Door. The truth was, he felt ashamed he had been anything other than upfront with this man. He prayed for an opening, asking God to lead the way.

"Why do you do this, Door?" he asked the question he asked many of his newfound political cronies. "You have no children of your own, and yet something prods you forward?"

This type of discussion seemed more appropriate to a chilly day fishing on the Tyburn, but Cyprian didn't seem to mind. "I just believe it's the right thing to do."

"You're accused of being an ambitious so-and-so. You know that, don't you?"

He shrugged, picked up his teacup, and took a sip. "In that, I suppose, we're two of a kind."

David laughed. "Agreed. Why in heaven's name would that scalawag David Youngblood suddenly emerge on the scene if not for political power."

"Exactly. With me, it was forced upon me. And, to be truthful, David, my life has always seemed to fall into place. Through no great doing of my own. Through adverse happenings at times."

"The death of your parents?" Hopefully he would take the bait.

The waiter announced that luncheon was being served.

Cyprian stood up from his chair. "You've been wanting to ask this a long time, haven't you?"

"Truthfully? Yes." David arose as well.

"Why?"

He leaned forward and spoke as softly as he could. "I served time with your brother Becket on Devil's Island."

Cyprian Door turned a sickly shade of white, pushed past David, and rushed from the room. Without bothering to grab his hat and coat from the porter, he yanked open the front door and slid out onto the street.

CHAPTER ❖ THIRTY-ONE

Elspeth felt like a nosy-parker opening all the corridor doors, but setting her feet to the curved iron stairway to the cupola, she thrilled with a sense of adventure.

Lovely *and* exciting. How nice. Like an illustration in a childhood storybook, the light from the doorway shone in a thick, dusty beam, illuminating a trap door at the top of the steps. Her hand went flat against the wooden surface of the door, and she pushed against its rough, unpainted surface.

Again, the anticipation that perhaps an enchanted treasure box hid itself up there, or that mounds and mounds of pillows in shades of purple, gold, and silver lined the room, caused her heart to race. *Maybe there is even a genie living here!* she chuckled.

Her reaction to this sudden shift in her life surprised her. A fresh start had been afforded her. Clearly this wasn't just some interim of "different" bifurcating the same old existence she called her life. She could go anywhere from here. If she didn't choose to, she needn't look back.

Elspeth gave the door a mighty shove. It banged loudly against the floor of the cupola as it landed, the sound echoing against the rafters of the dome. And if the fanciful dome, each segment depicting a day of creation, was any indication, she had most likely just found her favored spot at blind Lord Hayden Walsh's St. Stephen's Hall.

As her head rose above the surface of the floor, she let out a small cry of delight. The octagonal room, made up entirely of windows, bore resemblance to a small chapter house. The sun shone through spotless glass, and no cobwebs, not even a speck of dust sullied the place. It was a daylight room, obviously, for no lamps, no candles hung from the woodwork. Other than a single, straightbacked chair near the window that faced the sea, the room boasted no other furnishing.

Elspeth completed the climb. And though beautiful and pristine, the room itself couldn't begin to compare to the view. The English Channel moved beneath her gaze, a fabulous play of blues and grays kissing each other in the shadow of the clouds passing overhead. Boats bobbed or sped upon its surface, and the sun sparked in quick, tiny flares on each wave. "Oh, my!" she breathed, laying a hand upon the surface of the cold glass. "I could stay here forever."

After several minutes she tore her gaze from the water and looked out over the grounds of St. Stephen's Hall. She'd seen her fair share of manor houses during her days at school, but none of their grounds could compare to this. A lawn, dormant now in winter, unfolded toward the sea, and Elspeth could imagine what it was like in spring, the verdant contrast it would make against the cool waters of the Channel. Border gardens guarded the other sides of the lawn. The plants were trimmed back now, and some had been wrapped in burlap to protect them from the chill, but Elspeth knew that in a few months St. Stephen's would be alive with color. And fragrance.

Ahh. Fragrance.

Yes, that made sense.

A stone pavilion overlooked the frigid surface of a small pond. Scalloped sheets of ice clung to the water's edge. A pebbled path meandered around the edges of the gardens leading finally toward the sea. It led to an observation platform just where the lawn dropped off.

That puzzled her. Why did a blind man care so much about views?

A man emerged just then, from somewhere near the house. He negotiated a wooden wheelbarrow over the pebbled path. And though a shovel and a hoe rattled in the bowl of the vehicle she could not hear them.

The gardener. One of the few servants.

He looked up. Spying her in the cupola, he waved, grinned, and kept walking.

Elspeth dragged the chair over more closely to the window and watched as his attention was suddenly stolen. He stopped, turned his head, and listened to somebody obviously yelling to him from the house.

He nodded, set down the handles of the wheelbarrow, and made for the observation deck, disappearing over the side. Elspeth hadn't noticed the steps that apparently led down to the water.

Two minutes later he emerged alone. Cupping his hands against the sides of his mouth he called, "He's fine!" toward the direction the voice had come. Elspeth couldn't hear the words, but they were plain to read upon his lips.

Might as well get this over with, she decided. She hurried down to her room to grab her coat and hat and a good dose of courage. Her stomach tied itself in knots, and she didn't really know why.

⌒

The tea was coming together nicely. First there would be a tour of the mission and clothing factory next door. The owner said he'd be more than willing to move his operation out to the country if the price was right. Of course, that would mean less jobs for the people of the East End, so housing would need to be provided as well for the workers. They'd keep their jobs, get out of the slums, and have a brand new life.

All that money needing to be raised, Camille thought. Well, the tea was just the beginning! The replies had come pouring in, mostly in the affirmative. Of course, the tea biddies would all be there, and Lord Campbell's wife, the opera singer Maria Rosetti, had agreed to sing. That had been a real draw.

Lady Daria had decided to turn the ballroom on the top floor of her spacious home into a winter garden. Camille, on the advice of almost every one around her, just let Daria have free rein. Meanwhile, she thought about what she would say, and invited Reverend Williams to give a speech.

"We have to line up some staff too," Williams told her at a Thursday night meeting. "These institutions don't run themselves!"

"Well, Reverend," Camille laughed. "You prayed a sinner like me into your mission. I'm sure God has someone in mind."

"Too bad Lady Daria doesn't need a job," he said, laughing.

Now Camille sat at the table in the dining room eating a piece of Mai-Ling's tea cake. The moist dainty melted on her tongue. Yes. This would surely do.

~

"Cyprian! Wait!" David called, running down St. James's Street.

Cyprian ran around the corner to the left, down Pall Mall toward Trafalgar Square.

"Please, have a little mercy!" David yelled, his back screaming above the jolts of his feet pounding the street.

Cyprian ran on, but he was slowing down. David stopped. He watched Door come to a halt and finally turn around. And he waited for the baron of Dividen to come to him. It had to be that way.

Cyprian's face shone wet with tears. He wiped them on his coat sleeve as he approached.

David held out his hands, palms up. "It appears we both have much to hide, Cyprian."

Cyprian looked to the side, unwilling to meet David's gaze. "Is he dead?"

"Yes."

"When?"

"About four years ago."

"He'd have to be." Door rubbed a hand down his face. "And you've come to seek his vengeance?"

"I don't think the middle of Pall Mall is the place to discuss this, Cyprian. Let's go back to Brooks's and get our things. We can go back to my home."

Cyprian nodded and they walked back to the warmth of the club in the midst of a stiff, belting silence. Hemmed in on all sides by their secrets, their regrets, the matters that would never cease to torture them in the night, they could say nothing just then.

Finally, an excruciating thirty minutes later, they sat in David's study.

He poured Cyprian a cup of tea, then one for himself, and sat down on one of the two leather chairs that faced the fire. "Who should go first?" David asked.

Cyprian shrugged, shook his head.

"You do realize," David said, "that I don't hold all the cards here, my friend. You do realize that I am as vulnerable to you as you are to me."

Cyprian sighed. Then he turned to David. "Do you know what it is like to live with a weight of guilt so great, you fear one day it will stop your very breath?"

Silence sat between them for a moment as David chose his words carefully. "I am the chief of sinners, Cyprian Door."

"No. I consigned my brother to Devil's Island. It is because of me he ended up there."

"It's true. You killed your parents, then?"

He shook his head and set his tea down, docking his vision into the blaze. "No. But neither did Becket. And I let him suffer the consequences."

"Why did he not go to the guillotine, then?"

"I did that. I couldn't see that happen to him."

"If he didn't do it? Then who did? Charlotte?"

"Yes." Cyprian dropped his head into his hands. "We were having an affair. Charlotte and myself. When Becket brought her back from India ... well ... the first time I saw her I wanted her. And she felt the same way, I soon found out. She made that very clear."

"She seems the type that gets what she wants."

He looked up. "It's never been boring with Charlotte, David."

Time to lay it all bare. "I promised your brother I would clear his name when and if I returned."

Cyprian turned his tortured features toward David. "He thought I did it. Didn't he?"

David nodded. "He had no clue it was Charlotte. So why did you allow Becket to take the blame?"

He looked up at the ceiling, trying to control himself. "Thing was, I believed he did it. For a year I believed he was the one that poisoned my parents. There was evidence, a great deal of evidence that he did it. Charlotte told me he wanted the power, that he said he would stop at nothing to gain the title sooner than he ought."

"He obviously knew nothing of your affair."

"No, he did not."

"He acted as if the memory of her was one of the only things that kept him going on Devil's Island." David was more than curious. "What is it about Charlotte that enslaved both you and your brother?" For himself, he just couldn't see it concerning that woman. She left him feeling like a spider had crawled down his shirt.

Cyprian thought for a moment. "A sense of protectiveness, I suppose. She's frightened, David. And her fears drive her. She gets what she wants in any way that she can. To feel safe. She wanted out of India so badly, and she used my brother to get away."

"So why did she kill your parents then?"

"My mother found out about our affair and was threatening to tell my father. Charlotte was crazily in love with me those days. Not like now." He shook his head. "Although she needs me more these days. Anyway, Mother told me if I didn't end things, she'd make sure Charlotte was sent back to India."

"Could she really do that?"

Cyprian pulled a handkerchief from his pocket and wiped his brow. "Becket never bucked her. So I broke things off, and Charlotte did what she felt she had to do in order for us to be together."

"So why did your father die, then?"

"It was a matter of chance. She ground up several castor beans and put them in my mother's brandy. Father never took brandy, but he came down with a severe chill after a rainy hunt and, well, Mother gave him the brandy and ... you know the rest."

"How did she implicate Becket?" David asked.

"An anonymous tip, obviously given by Charlotte. The police searched their home and discovered a suit of Becket's clothing, the pocket of which was dusted with the powder of ground castor beans."

"And so assumptions were made."

"Yes. Becket swore he was with Charlotte that night, and she played the dutiful wife. I told you she was shrewd. But in the end, the jury decided against him. He had motive merely being the eldest son. Even though I thought he was guilty, I paid his way out of the guillotine to a very dirty judge. I felt so guilty about the affair. If I had resisted the temptation ... Oh, God!" The emotion of the confession overwhelmed him. "That night, over a year later, when Charlotte told me what she had done, I could hardly believe it. I should have turned her in then." Tears filled his eyes and he banged a fist onto the arm of the chair. "But I didn't. If I hadn't committed adultery with her, hadn't seduced her in the first place, it would have never happened." He looked up at David. "I share the blame as well."

"And you've stayed with her all of these years?" David asked incredulously.

"I can't very well divorce her, David. Not in my station."

"But how can you trust her, Cyprian?"

"The truth is, I can't. But I can't very well put her onto anybody else or send her back to India. She won't tell a living soul about what it was like there. Not even Absinthe Pencraig knows about her childhood. And she's confided everything to that woman, much to my dismay."

"Women need confidantes," David said.

"I've got to keep her close, David. I've got to make sure she never does anything like this again. And if I put myself in danger, so be it. God be the judge."

David arose to put more wood on the fire.

Cyprian's voice was faint. "So what will you do with this information?"

David shook his head, threw on a log, and turned around. "I don't know. But I wanted you to know I knew Becket. And I wanted you to know I knew that he was innocent."

"I'm glad you do. It's a relief. And yet, I cannot let you turn us in." His voice held a necessary threat. "Nothing personal."

David handed him his tea and took a sip of his own as he sat down. "Turning you in is the last thing I want to do, Cyprian. Not when there's so much to be done. With the Education Act coming up . . ."

Cyprian put a hand on David's arm. "Tell me why you were on Devil's Island. In that way, you'll have to decide someday if turning me in would be worth it."

"You'd spill my secret?" He knew the answer to that one.

"If I had to. I have to protect her, David."

"Why?"

"My love compels me to do just that. I'm not asking you to understand our sordid affections. That would be impossible. Besides," Door continued, "the fact that you were on Devil's Island speaks to a great guilt. My knowledge of that fact alone should be enough to keep you silent."

"Conceded. Let me ask you something, though, Cyprian. Has Charlotte committed any more such acts?"

"Not a one."

"Are you certain?"

"I've made it my job to be certain. I told Charlotte on the day she confessed to me, that should she do anything else so horrible, so violent, I would leave her, and not only would I leave her,

I would send her packing off to India as well." He spread his fingers on the tops of his knees. "She's not as bad as she seems, David. She's been a good wife since then. She knows I'll protect her."

David's love for his friend overcame his revulsion just then. "I was sent to Devil's Island for the murders of Armand and Collette de Courcey."

As he uttered the words, it all came into a startling focus. As guilty as Charlotte Door, he'd killed for love, and he knew how good it had felt then. The clawing creature he once had been showed its face momentarily. *Who are you to judge?* it hissed. *Who were you to promise anything to the late Becket Door? Who, David Youngblood, do you think you are?*

"'Vengeance is mine. I will repay,' saith the Lord," David whispered to himself, his heart breaking with pity for Cyprian Door.

And so David related the entire black tale, leaving nothing out, filling in the valleys, leveling out the mountains that had briefly separated them.

God would take care of Charlotte Door. God would mete out his justice. The time had arrived to lay down the sword given to him by his friend Becket Door. It was time to leave Devil's Island behind him for good.

CHAPTER ✦ THIRTY-TWO

Elspeth didn't bother to make her descent of the steps quietly. In fact, she had enough sense to call out in advance. "Lord Hayden!" The wind pilfered her voice, but he turned his head in her direction.

"Miss Elspeth?"

Most of Elspeth's life she'd compared herself to others, and she'd become quite used to the fact that she never measured up. She believed this to be quite true. And yet, standing before her now, coming toward the steps to join her was quite possibly the most wonderful looking man she'd ever seen. So glorious. Yet so strange. So devoid of the normal trappings of society. Unadulterated. Unmasked.

His white shirt gleamed next to his wind-ruddied skin. Everything else he wore echoed the dark of the night before—except for his tie, a bold yellow silken knot tied carefully beneath his collar. The blond hair she had seen in the dim light of the candle the night before proved to be an ash shade painted with lighter yellow streaks by the brush of a frequently felt sun. Pulled back into a heavy ponytail, it reached between his shoulder blades, the ends ragged.

He reminded her of a lion. A great lion with a broad nose, a low forehead, small ears, and fleshless cheeks.

And when he smiled, he bared large beautiful teeth. Sharp canines, displayed easily by the wide, clear grin, lent him a feral air, feral yet tamed by his affliction. This man clearly had nothing to hide.

As a Youngblood, that fact alone meant the world to Elspeth.

"Yes, it is me, Elspeth," she answered.

His hand groped for the railing, finding it quickly and pulling himself up the first step to begin the descent. "And you had a good sleep?" His deep voice reverberated with warmth.

"Lovely. The best I've had in months."

"You've used the perfume."

He came closer, his hand touching the banister lightly as he ascended. Strong hands, scarred and nicked, their heavy nails sheltered the dirt of his gardens beneath them. Elspeth could see his eyes. Sightless yes, that much was evident by the way he looked past her, by the lack of true focus on any one thing. They were a beautiful shade of gold, ringed with green. To have such lovely eyes and not be able to use them—it wounded Elspeth's heart.

Next to her now, he extended a hand. "May I kiss your hand? Aunt Gwynneth always taught me to kiss the back of a lady's hand when meeting."

Could this really be the same man who guided them last night? "Of course."

She placed her hand in his, and he raised it to his beautiful mouth. Elspeth yearned at the feel of such lips on her hand.

"I'm sorry I was so abrupt last night. I knew you were tired and probably didn't wish to be bogged down by chitchat."

"You were right. Although now I'm in need of some. St. Stephen's is fascinating."

"It's almost time for dinner," he said. "We eat our large meal early in the day here after my constitutional. My father liked it that way and so we've kept to the tradition. Would you care to take your meal with me in the dining room and you can ask all the questions you want?"

Elspeth hesitated, imagining the scene. A warm fire, good food. The smell of gardenias.

Immediately, he said, "Of course, if you'd rather eat by yourself—"

"No, no, Lord Hayden. I was only thinking how wonderful it would be."

Almost to the top of the steps now, he turned. "This is a godsend, you know, you coming here," he said.

"How so? I rather think it's the opposite way around."

Again that smile. "I was beginning to think I had been forsaken by God. Silly, I suppose. I've got everything I need or want. But I'm so lonely."

His candor was uncanny. No one had taught him how to veil his thoughts, how to hide himself from those around him, how silence supposedly equals strength. "I've been feeling the same way." She followed suit.

"May I put my hand on your arm?" he asked. "I'm quite fine with my cane, but a warm arm is a much nicer guide. Tell me, Elspeth, if your voice is giving you away correctly. You seem as if you are happy to be here."

"Most happy, Lord Hayden. And there's no good and proper explanation for it. I should be miserable right now."

He stopped and turned to face her. "St. Stephen's Hall is a lovely place to grow a baby."

That bluntness again. "Yes. So Lady Daria told me."

"At the risk of being too open, I want you to know you may stay here as long as you need to. Even after the child is born. There's more than enough room."

Elspeth smiled and realized he couldn't see it, so she patted his hand. "It's a wonderful place to be. You must love it here."

"I do. Wonderful sounds, all around, Elspeth. God's sounds. It's why I cannot leave this place. It's why I've never been off my grounds. It would be too confusing."

"You've never been off of your land?"

"Ridiculous, isn't it?" He chuckled a singular, apologetic "Hnh."

Elspeth wanted to lay her head against his broad arm. A protective, almost motherly feeling came over her as they entered the house. It appeared she had been sent to St. Stephen's Hall to give as well as to receive.

One pot, one burner, one end of the worktable. *Juste ciel!*

Camille turned to Mrs. Wooten. "If I'd have known he was having all of these distinguished men to dine tonight, I'd have never given Joyce the night off! And now, nothing but stew!" To think she had only herself to blame for this predicament!

The sun had already set, Joyce was nowhere to be found, and five men had gathered in David's study awaiting supper.

"Ah, there now, love, women have been dealing with this for years. I say let's just feed 'em your stew! It's a lovely stew, all of that chicken and sausage. I even snuck a taste myself!" Mrs. Wooten whipped out a rag and began to dust the sideboard in the dining room. A young housemaid set the table, the soft clink of china and silverware hardly comforting. In thirty minutes they'd be in here eating nothing but stew and bread. Luckily, Camille had made enough to feed the entire House of Lords, and the Commons as well!

She frowned, listening to the hum of the men's voices. David's mingled with the voices of Cyprian Door, Aaron Campbell, and Gerald Raines. Her husband had definitely become the D'Artagnon of the group—the brash newcomer who believed himself ready for anything. Thank goodness they seemed to be accepting of his enthusiasm.

With a sigh heartier than her stew, she went to change for dinner. Well, if the meal wasn't spectacular, she would just have to make up for it with her appearance. And indeed, beyond cooking, beyond politics, *that* was definitely her specialty!

David felt immensely proud of his wife in that moment. She sat there at the foot of the table, sparkling in her jewels, profusely apologizing about the stew and looking more breathtaking than he had ever seen her looking before.

Good heavens, but the green of the dress exactly matched the color of her eyes, and the way she had pulled back her blond hair, well it made his fingers itch to pull out the pins, to see the curls spill around her lovely face. He promised himself he would do that later. And then he'd take her into his arms, and reach for the buttons on her gown . . . and . . .

"David? David? Are you with us?"

The laughter of the rest of the group pulled him back to the much less exciting prospects of supper with a roomful of men.

Aaron Campbell had spoken. And he continued. "Saw the way you were staring at that lovely wife of yours. And none of us can blame you. Lady Youngblood"—he turned to Camille—"you are a saint to have invited us to dine like you did, at the last minute. And so I propose a toast!" He raised his glass. "To the most intriguing woman in London and perhaps the most kind woman too." His aged face, still holding its own, creased further with a wide smile.

"Hear! Hear!" the others cried and raised their own goblets.

David watched her blush from the bottom of her chin to the tips of those delicious ears. His eyes met hers. "Hear, hear, *chérie*," he said softly, wondering how he had failed to love this woman all of those years.

Compliments about the stew and the bread bounced from one end of the table to the other, March declaring that such simple fare put heart into a man. They discussed Jules Verne's *Twenty Thousand Leagues Under the Sea*, the founding of Keble College in Oxford (they were all Oxford men), and the possibility of revolt in Paris. Couldn't these Frenchmen ever make up their minds as to what form of government they wanted?

David was glad to be out of that country for now. And judging by the look on Camille's face during that particular discussion, he knew she felt the same. The Grace Home was also discussed, all three guests declaring she could count on them for heavy financial support.

Finally, matters of the crown—inevitable, considering the crowd gathered around the Youngblood's table. They enjoyed the dessert Joyce had made before he left, a large plateful of orangeat petit fours as well as the requested chess pie, when the conversation began.

"Horrible about the queen falling so ill, isn't it?" Viscount March said, biting down into the dainty.

It was the first David had heard of it. Not surprising. "How so?"

"They're not sure. She's having tremors and even hallucinations at times," Campbell supplied. "They're very worried."

Camille said nothing, just looked down at her plate. David knew she was trying to hide a distinct lack of pity.

Cyprian Door nodded. "Charlotte's been telling me the same. Every time she comes back from attending the queen, she reports the queen's condition grows worse. Of course, they're doing their best to hide it from the people."

And the conversation meandered down many other paths, threatening to wind late into the night.

He'd shown her the entire house, touching frames and woodwork as he went. Elspeth had been astonished the way Lord Hayden could navigate St. Stephen's Hall.

Pleased she loved the cupola so much, he impulsively declared her the new owner of the room. "There's not much use I have for it," he said as they climbed the steps after their dinner that afternoon. "But I had it cleaned up and painted for you. My aunt always told me that every woman needs a retreat of her own."

"As if the bedroom wasn't enough," Elspeth laughed.

His face looked sheepish. "I had Lady Daria tell me how I could make your time here at St. Stephen's wonderful for you."

"Why?"

"A healthy, happy mother makes a healthy, happy baby."

"And that is important to you?"

He faced the window, unable to see the wonderful view before him, but still appearing to gather strength from it. "My mother was very sick, and she was very unhappy when she was expecting me. She took medicines, you know. And they think that . . . well, that's how they explain my blindness. Whether it's true or not, only God knows."

"I'm sorry, Lord Hayden. I'm sorry that you're blind."

"I've never known anything else."

"Is it something you don't wish to discuss?"

He smiled. "Oh dear, no. There isn't a subject out there I'm not willing to discuss. When you can't see, you have to take your stimulus where you can find it. Touching things only goes so far. And appearances, even felt ones, can be deceiving." He held out his hand, scarred many times over with tiny white lines. "I love to garden, you know. But I have a distinct disadvantage of having to feel for thorns rather than see them. The bloom feels so fine, and then my fingers travel down and—"

"Ouch!" Elspeth finished.

He nodded. "Precisely! It's a distinct disadvantage, I tell you."

"Why garden then?"

"Because I can, Elspeth."

"I see." She looked down at her own white, perfect hands.

"Yes, you do. And I don't. My point exactly." His laugh filled the room, as warm and large as himself. The beauty of his beauty, Elspeth realized, was that he had no idea he possessed such. His comeliness was on display for everyone else but himself.

They stood in silence for a moment. He cleared his throat. "Do you mind talking about your own physical thorn?"

"Aptly put," Elspeth said. "It's not something I'd discuss with just anybody, I suppose. It hasn't been easy to live with."

"You speak well enough despite it," he remarked.

"A lot of hard work, I assure you. I can remember standing in my room, looking in my mirror and working so hard to compensate. I must employ my mouth in ways other people aren't forced to do."

"You have a beautiful voice, though. Can you sing?" His expression was one of pure hope. "I love music."

"I'm sure you do. Yes, I suppose I sing well enough. Not like an opera singer or anything, but . . ." Hopefully, he wouldn't pull out his harp!

"I'll play for you on the piano and you can sing," he said, laying a hand on the windowsill. "Would that be agreeable to you?"

"You can play the piano?" she asked, unable to hide the surprise in her voice. "I thought you played the harp."

"Don't sound so shocked! Playing the piano requires touch more than anything else. The harp too. So why should I not?"

"No reason that I can see."

He assumed his version of a disapproving look. "There you go using that verb again. And we've got away from the topic at hand. Which was you."

Elspeth sat down in the chair with a sigh. Arranging her skirts she said, "It hasn't always been easy being me. In fact, I think that's why I'm so happy to be here at St. Stephen's."

"You like the seclusion as much as I do, then?"

"Oh, yes. But I'm more secluded than you are."

He nodded. "Even from my eyes are you hidden."

Elspeth folded her hands. "Yes. And I am free. For the first time in my life."

"Lady Daria tells me you have the most beautiful eyes she has ever seen. Is it true? Are your eyes beautiful?" His face bore such eagerness his innocence could not help but shine through his expression.

"That's what people say. I've done my best to avoid mirrors."

"And what color are they? Do they have long lashes?"

"They are gray, much like the channel on a cloudy day. And yes, the lashes are much too long. They're always getting stuck in my eyes when I blink."

He laughed with pleasure, clapping his hands together once. Then he sobered. "So you do have beautiful eyes." Holding out a hand, he reached for her. Elspeth took it in her own. And he pulled her to his feet. "Do you have any idea what that means to me?" he asked.

Looking at his perfect, firm mouth, Elspeth could truly say, "More than you could possibly believe, Lord Hayden."

He burst into a smile again. "I like you, Elspeth. I said I was glad you'd come before, and I'm still glad. Very glad, in fact."

Making for the steps, he turned back around quickly to face her. "One last thing for now. Do you believe in God?"

"Oh, yes."

"Wonderful. So you've worked things through with him, then?"

Elspeth wanted to laugh. He understood. This man understood everything important! "I'm still working on it. But it gets better day by day, I suppose."

"Still angry?"

"Yes. And you?"

He grabbed onto the railing and started down the steps. "Not since I woke up this morning. Shall I see you tomorrow morning, then?" His eyes looked just past her right side. "Breakfast is at seven-thirty."

"Lord Hayden, I'll be there with bells on!"

His face took on a look of mock horror. "Oh no, dear, the perfume will do the job just fine."

She laughed. And so did he, his bass voice echoing against the walls as he descended the staircase. He left her alone, but not really. Elspeth knew she'd never be alone at St. Stephen's Hall.

"By the way!" his voice called from downstairs. "Call me Hayden! I don't suppose being so formal is all that wonderful considering the circumstances!"

"Hayden it is!" she yelled back, hugging her arms around her body as the sunset warmed the frigid skies of winter. She was safe. Finally safe. The warm light caressed her there in the cupola, and as Lord Hayden slowly made his way down the corridor a cheerful whistle accompanied his steps.

CHAPTER ❖ THIRTY-THREE

Georginia expected Absinthe might pop an eyeball if she caught her snooping about in her study. But Absinthe wouldn't catch her because Absinthe wasn't home! The older woman rubbed her hands together and set about finding that journal in which Lady Pencraig penned all her thoughts and findings.

This alone would be worth the expense of having her entire downstairs repainted! The fumes hadn't abated yet, though it had been two days since the painters had finished. Perhaps tomorrow she'd go back home. The Pencraigs, such busy people and all, had little time left over to entertain their house guest.

Even now Absinthe and Charlotte were visiting the queen, and acting most officious about it, if Georginia did say so!

Sitting down in Absinthe's comfortable chair, she slid the tops of her palms against the polished, beveled edge of the desk. Everything in perfect order, a leather blotter with clean black paper lay at the ready. A capped, crystal inkwell stood beside an arrangement of ebony pens with fancifully carved silver nibs. The room glimmered with light from the gas lamps on the walls.

Easy reading, then, well?

Georginia reached out for the small leather volume that lay quietly at the upper lefthand corner of the desk. *Didn't have to look hard for this little thing!* She picked it up in her hands. A tickle of guilt turned her head sideways. Perhaps she shouldn't do this. Even a five-year-old knew it was beyond nosy to read another person's private thoughts. It was a moral offense, something that bad brothers did to their sisters.

But bad brothers were found out and, "Let's be honest, Georgie," the old woman whispered, "Abby will never know."

Might as well get it over with and have a cup of tea to drown out the guilt.

Well, on with it, then. One more time wouldn't make a difference.

The leather of the book, cool to the touch and softly slick beneath the surface of her knotted fingers, smelled earthy and new. Opening the volume she realized it had been begun only two months previous. And here it was, almost full! Georginia couldn't imagine where Absinthe kept her journals or how many completed the set.

She pulled up on the black, attached woven bookmark and thought she'd read only that day's entry. *That won't be so bad, will it?*

Her eyes navigated Absinthe Pencraig's stalwart penmanship, her brain barely understanding the garbled rantings . . . against who? All this about tonight being the night. About plans set in motion. About death. Whose death? And when?

Georginia felt her heart drum a turbulent beat. She put a fragile hand up to her flat chest, barely noticing the prickle of her scalp. Her brain took over the helm of even her conscious thought as she read the blur of angry words, their bitter meaning layered within. She felt as though she stared at the waves of a caustic sea over the edge of a swiftly moving ship, leaving them behind the moment she saw them. Their impression burned into her memory.

Faster she read. And the faster her brain conquered the words, the greater the speed of her heart, the heavier the dread grew down in the hold of her stomach.

⁓

"I fear we've started our own gentlemen's club right here in your home, David!" Merlin Pencraig raised his glass in a toast. "Blast it, but I'm almost glad Abby's away every night with the queen!"

"Almost?" David drawled.

"Hang it, then. I'm thrilled!" Merlin's laugh echoed, a singular boom.

David heard the doorbell ring and did a quick head count. Everyone accounted for. Pencraig, March, Door, and Campbell. True, Merlin didn't arrive until the leisure time began, but he provided a comic relief for the group of visionaries planning to change their world.

Camille stood at the door to the study, beckoning David. He stood quickly to his feet. "Excuse me, gentlemen," he said, crossing the room.

He pulled her gently into the reception area, eyes alighting on Georginia Stiles. "What is it?"

Georginia rushed forward. "It's a horrible thing! I didn't know what else to do! Where else to go! Monica is feeling ill, and my own dear hus—"

"What's wrong, Georgie?" Camille asked.

"Charlotte is with the queen, and according to Absinthe's diary she's in on it too!"

David felt the flesh thicken on the back of his neck. "In on what?"

"The assassination of the queen!"

Camille had already warned him of this woman's propensity for a stolen word or two. "Come into the drawing room. Camille? What do you know of this?"

"Nothing, *chéri*."

They all sat down on the sofa, Georginia in the middle, David holding her right hand, Camille her left.

"Now just speak slowly and clearly, Georginia," Camille said patiently. "You know how you can embellish. Tell us simply what has happened."

The older woman breathed in deeply. "Well. Charlotte and Abby went out for the evening, to Kensington, and left me all alone to my own devices."

"Georginia, you didn't!"

"I did!" she cried. "I went snooping!"

"Oh, dear!" Camille patted her hand sympathetically. David began to feel agitated. But he knew women. And they needed to go at their own pace for the most part.

She shook her head slowly. "I couldn't help it. I was lonely and there was nothing to do."

"You poor thing. Where were you snooping?"

"In Abby's study. I"—she looked down and took her hands back—"I looked at her diary!" she wailed.

"No!" Camille cried. "Oh, Georginia!" She reached forward and hugged her friend.

David stepped into the conversation gently. "Surely that's not all you've come to discuss, my dear? What's this about an assassination?" He doubted true cause for concern existed. Not if it concerned Absinthe Pencraig! Now there was a woman who wanted only the best for her country.

"No, no. You're quite right." She pulled open the satin purse hanging on her arm, drew out a handkerchief, and blew her small nose in a large way.

David's eyes met Camille's as they both stifled a laugh at the loud, unladylike honk.

Georginia, composed once again, reached yet another time into her bag and pulled out the diary. "Here, read for yourself. This part here."

Even though Camille's eyes rounded, David felt no compunction about taking the book.

"Read the last page," Georginia instructed.

And so he did, a mixture of fear, revulsion, pity, and dread mingling into a horrible brew inside of his heart as his eyes read the words of Absinthe Pencraig.

> *Tonight Victoria will die. Tonight she will finally pay for her murderous deeds of many years ago. And to think that Charlotte Door agreed to start administering the poison. Sleeping draught indeed! What a gullible, idiotic sovereign we have! Of course, Charlotte has everything to gain if Bertie becomes king.*
>
> *Enough.*
>
> *Sweet little castor bean. Ah, magic little castor bean.*

David ran out of the room toward the study. "Wooten!" he yelled as loud as he could. "Have the fastest carriage brought round, as well as Lord Campbell's."

The others were already on their feet, faces displaying their concern. "What's going on, Youngblood?" Merlin asked.

"I'll explain on the way," David said, then turned to Aaron Campbell and Gerald Raines. "March? Campbell?"

"What is it?" Campbell asked.

"The queen's life is in danger, and I may need you there."

The two men, knowing time was at a premium, needed no other explanation. "We'll take my coach," Campbell told March. Wooten brought their coats in immediately, and both carriages were pulled up to the curb.

"Merlin, Cyprian. You both should come with me," David said.

"Where to? Kensington?" Cyprian asked, fear nestled firmly in his eyes. "Is Charlotte all right?"

David committed to nothing. He merely took his coat and hat from Wooten and slid his arms through the satin lining of the sleeves.

"I'm going too!" Camille entered the room, already bundled up in a green woolen cape. "And don't try to talk me out of it."

With the women already involved in this situation, it might be wise to have Camille on hand. He couldn't imagine it would turn violent. "Go on down to the carriage," he said. "Who's taking care of Georginia?"

"Mrs. Wooten."

"All right then."

Once they were racing westward toward Kensington, David began the dreadful task of explaining. "There's a reason for the queen's sickness," he said. "She's being poisoned. Slowly. But tonight a final lethal dose will be given to her."

"A dose of what?" Merlin asked.

"Castor bean." David held up Absinthe Pencraig's diary, and even in the dim coach lights, it was easy to see both men pale.

"Oh, dear Lord," Cyprian mumbled, his exhaled breath staccatoed. "Oh, dear God. No."

Merlin held out his hand with a shake of his mammoth head. David placed the journal in his huge paw. "The last two pages say it all, friend."

The Welshman's eyes darted quickly back and forth over the damning words found in his wife's unmistakable handwriting. When he finished, he said, "Here," and handed the book to Cyprian.

With a look of regret, Cyprian took the book. Hands trembling, he read the final passages. He looked up, tears filling his eyes. "Castor beans."

"What will we do once we get there?" Merlin asked, breathing in deeply yet looking paler than Cyprian.

"I don't know," David said, used to maneuvering through life by the seat of his pants, but not liking it one bit. "I just hope we make it in time. According to Absinthe's diary, one ground-up castor bean is enough to kill someone. And it's a slow death at that. Innards shutting down."

Merlin made a disgusted noise. "Yes, it's just like Abby to be gleeful about the particulars."

"Does this not surprise you, Lord Pencraig?" Camille asked, her voice dropping in dismay.

"I didn't think she had the guts to do anything quite this extreme."

"Why, then?" David asked.

Merlin shook his head. "I suppose we'll have to read the rest of the diaries to find the answer to that question. Funny, I never cared enough to look in them. Perhaps I should have."

David placed a hand on Camille's arm. "Shh," he warned, knowing instinctively she wished to say something to Merlin. "Not now, *chérie*."

They pulled through the black filigreed gates and up to the beautiful south face of Kensington Palace. A guard stood at the doorway and asked their business.

"I'm here to see the queen on a most urgent matter," David said. "It's truly a matter of life and death."

"Now, look, your lordship," the guard said. "I can't be disturbin' the queen on any little thing. Especially with her not feelin' well."

"I tell you this is a matter of utmost importance!" David knew he raised his voice too loudly for such a late hour, but he didn't care. Maybe someone else would overhear and take him seriously. "And it isn't up to *you* whether or not the queen is disturbed. Let me speak to your captain."

Another voice jumped into the fray, coming from inside the dim palace. "What's all the puff an' bluster aboot here, men?"

The voice held a thick Highland accent, and a stocky, bearded man in a kilt appeared. The queen's closest companion, her servant Mr. John Brown, strode across the entry hall. The guard rolled his eyes. Mr. John Brown was clearly not a favorite with the young man.

David spoke up. "We believe the queen's life to be in danger, Mr. Brown."

"And what proof have you?"

"No real proof other than proof of intent. Here, in this diary." He held up the book.

"And whose diary is it?" Brown scratched the side of his beard, his hooded eyes boring into David.

"Lady Pencraig's."

"Ahhh, she's with the queen now. Tell me about it, then. Come inside. All of you."

Ushered into the palace and into a long corridor where royal portraits were on display, David held tightly onto Camille's hand and waited patiently while Brown read the diary's final entry. Several seconds later, the man ran toward the queen's private apartments, bellowing for several guards to follow.

~

The dim bedroom, barely lit by the single candle, stank with sickness.

"Are you ready for bed now then, your majesty?" Charlotte asked.

Absinthe Pencraig licked her lips as she watched the scene unfolding before her. It took all the self-control she possessed not to hop with glee right there at the foot of the bed. But she stayed sober and nodded with sympathy as Charlotte helped the obese old woman onto the mattress. The séance mood faded quickly with the reality of physical matters.

"I feel so dreadful these days," Queen Victoria said sadly. "These times with Albert are my only solace."

"And you've been sleeping well?" Charlotte asked, patting her hand, then bringing the heavy covers up over the queen's ample bosom.

"Yes, child. At least there is that." She looked up at Absinthe with a grateful expression, not quite a smile. "Your grandmother's remedy, Lady Pencraig, has at least provided me with the respite of sleep."

"Charlotte told you it was my family remedy?" She smiled, her heart suddenly beating wildly. But not to worry. Come morning, this conversation would be erased forever.

"I didn't want to take the credit for your kindness, my lady," Charlotte whispered. Absinthe still couldn't believe how differently Charlotte behaved in front of the queen. "Now, your majesty, here is your drink. Sleep well tonight."

Absinthe watched as the warm wine she herself had laced with sleeping herbs and a ground castor bean was held up to the lips of the queen of the realm. "Drink it all, your majesty," she said. "It will go far in taking away your ailments." Boy, would it!

"Yes," Charlotte cooed. "Take this now."

Slowly Charlotte Door lifted the cup to Victoria's lips. "There now," she said. "This will be so good for you."

Victoria nodded. "My physician would be most unhappy with me. But he's yet to do anything right on his part. I'll drink now." The queen freed an arm from the bed clothes, took the goblet, and rested it against her bottom lip.

Tilting it slowly, the scarlet liquid ebbed in the cup like an incoming tide, a thick bloody tide. Absinthe sucked in her breath, balling her hands into fists. *Yes. Yes. This was it. This was finally it. Her job was almost done.*

Go, Victoria. Just drink the blasted stuff!

The queen smiled briefly as the liquid began to flow between her lips.

The doors to her chamber crashed against the wall as they were pushed open from the other side with a mighty heave. "Your majesty!" a man shouted, running across the room.

Victoria was so startled, she spilled half of the contents down the front of her nightgown. "Mr. Brown!" she yelled most regally. "What mean you by barging into my chamber like this?"

Absinthe waited, still holding the breath she had taken earlier. *Caution, Abby. This could be about something else.*

"It's this wine. It's poisoned, your majesty." He took the cup from her hand and passed it to a waiting guard.

"What?" Victoria sputtered. "What are you talking about?"

Mr. John Brown motioned to two more guards and without warning, Absinthe felt a pair of iron arms circle her upper body even as she watched the same action taking place on Charlotte Door. "These women. These women have been poisoning you."

"No!" Charlotte screamed. "I've not been poisoning her!"

Just then another guard entered with "Prince Albert." Victoria gasped and pointed at him. "Who are you?" she screamed, fear and rage shaking her body.

"He's my gardener." Charlotte's eyes darted wildly from window to window. "Please, he was just a man for hire. And I didn't poison anybody. They were Absinthe's herbs."

Absinthe remembered all the money she had paid the man. Would he come through for her?

"I was only following orders, your majesty," he bowed. "I was only doing what that woman told me to do." His finger pointed in accusation against Charlotte Door.

"No!" Charlotte screamed again, struggling against the bonds of the guard. "I've not done this. Absinthe? Please, help me. This is some dreadful misunderstanding."

"I don't think so," John Brown said.

Absinthe struck like a coiled serpent. She would free herself from this no matter what. "They may have been my herbs, but there was nothing lethal in them. Just a sleeping potion! Why, see what kind of poison is inside that cup!"

"I already know," John Brown stated. "It was castor beans."

Charlotte closed her eyes.

"Oh, lovey," Absinthe said, her voice falling with a theatrical sympathy. "Castor beans? Why castor beans?"

"What are you talking about?" the queen asked, her face reddened with anger.

Absinthe struck again. "Find out how the late baron of Dividen and his wife were killed eight years ago. Find out what grows in Charlotte Door's drawing room."

"Abby, no!" Charlotte cried. "Don't do this to me. You know I didn't do this."

Victoria waved a hand over them all. She closed her eyes. "Take Lady Door away from my sight."

Absinthe sagged with relief as they were turned around to face the door.

Then John Brown spoke again. "Take them both!" And as he spoke he pulled a book from his inner coat pocket. It was a familiar book. A telling book. A damning book.

"You might wish to read this, your majesty," he said, handing Absinthe Pencraig's diary to the enemy.

Charlotte sobbed as the doors to the queen's bedchamber closed.

"Oh, shut up!" Absinthe hissed. "You idiotic little fool!"

"But why?" Charlotte asked, her wet face turned toward Absinthe's.

"I deserved revenge and you, Charlotte, deserved to pay for what you've done."

"But I didn't do it."

Absinthe laughed. "Neither did Becket Door."

As the guards led them outside, several bobbies waited to transport them to the London jailhouse. Paraded by a line of familiar faces, Absinthe screamed in rage and frustration as Charlotte cried, reaching out. David Youngblood remained stoic, as did Lord Aaron Campbell and Viscount March. Cyprian and Merlin turned away, refusing to meet their wives' eyes.

"Cyprian!" Charlotte screamed. "My love!"

But Cyprian said nothing as they pushed his wife through the door. Absinthe began to laugh, her voice echoing off of the high ceilings. They were locked inside the carriage. It started on a slow roll toward the city. Moving slowly and deliberately, Absinthe Pencraig reached down and pulled up her skirts. Strapped to her thigh was a small stiletto. Yes. Good. It was still there.

Good, then. Backup plans were always good, her Scotsman had told her long ago.

Time to go home. Time to see Ma and Da and, well, everyone, really.

CHAPTER ❖ THIRTY-FOUR

On the second day of her stay at St. Stephen's Hall, Elspeth Youngblood fell in love. She didn't expect this, didn't feel as though she even deserved it. Not that she assumed Lord Hayden would just up and fall in love with her. Heavens, no! But just to be able to feel like this, even once, seemed to be a privilege. These feelings he evoked in her were nothing like the ones Sir Keir had coerced to the surface. There was no desperation, no simpering gratitude. With Hayden there couldn't be. He saw her for who she really was, without her face getting in the way. He understood her.

She accompanied him on his walk that morning, by his request. Breakfast had been quite the spectacle. Surprisingly, for a man with such a simple lifestyle, his meals were elaborate blends of tastes: sweet, salty, sour, spicy. The sausages almost sent her out of her seat to jump into the cool waters of the Channel.

"Again," he explained, "it's a matter of employing the senses I do have to their utmost."

Now they stood together at the bottom of the cliff staircase. A light fog shrouded the waters in front of her.

"Describe it all to me, Elspeth."

"It's foggy today, Hayden."

"Yes, it breathes foggy."

"Just a swirl of gray mists out there."

"I can picture that perfectly."

"Do you have a bit of sight, then?"

"Yes. Lights and darks. But not much more."

"No color at all?"

"Unfortunately, no. I thought I saw red once, in a dream." He put an arm around her shoulders. "You're such a warm type of person."

"I've always been that way. Dad and I are both like that." She laughed. "And then Camille came into our lives, exactly the opposite, always snuggling up with a blanket. But she's a dear, really. Perhaps you'll meet her someday."

He turned his face toward her then, and she caught her breath again at the beauty of him. He bared his feral teeth in another smile, this gentle beast. "I plan to, Elspeth. And your father as well."

A bell sounded in the distance at three-second intervals. Very faint. "Where is that coming from?"

"It is the fog signal at the breakwater lighthouse."

"Where?"

"You should have seen it from the cupola. Just as you leave Plymouth Sound."

"I'll look for it on the next good day."

"Whenever that may be," he said. "But there's an even better lighthouse further out. Eddystone."

"How far out is it?" Elspeth asked.

"Fourteen miles, they say."

Elspeth frowned. "I doubt if I'll be able to see it from the cupola."

"I would assume you're right. It has a fascinating history, though."

A wave crashed on the rocks, spraying them with large droplets of water. Elspeth cried out in surprise while Lord

Hayden barely flinched. "I could hear that coming," he said. "Sorry I didn't think to warn you. Would you like to sit at the bench up top?"

Elspeth declared she would. "I hate to sound so prissy, but ..."

"I'd hate for the smell of that lovely perfume you're wearing to be spoiled. Go on ahead of me." He breathed in as she passed him. And he sighed, closing his sightless eyes. He trailed a hand along her arm.

They climbed up the steps and sat together. "So you've lived here by this lighthouse all of your life and have never taken a boat out there?" Elspeth asked.

"Oh, no! Not many people do. It takes several hours at least to get out there."

"Would you like to, though? Someday?"

He laid his right ankle atop his left knee. "I suppose so. I don't know how happy the keepers would be to see us pull up unannounced, though."

"I should think they'd be quite happy to have a bit of company," she said brightly.

He placed a hand over hers, then twined her fingers among his own. "I've never really considered an actual visit, but I'm sure I could hire a fishing boat to go out that far and—"

"Of course you could! It would be a lovely outing, wouldn't it?"

He sat back against the bench. "It would. Would you go with me?"

"Oh, yes! I'd love that. I've never been to sea before."

"Then we've got that in common too."

The wind off of the Channel began to chill her. "I'm ready to go back, but tell me about Eddystone along the way."

He stood to his feet, never letting go of her hand. Their steps were measured and slow. "The light that stands there now is the fourth to do so," he said.

"When did the first one go up?" Elspeth asked, waving to the gardener who busied himself by digging up a new border garden. She knew Hayden had plans to put in various kinds of daylilies because he'd told her at supper the night before.

"Late 1600s. The tower there now was built by some fellow named Smeaton. Sturdy job he did of it too, I hear."

"Is it on an island?" She hoped so. Those kind that just sat on rocks with the sea pummeling at them day and night like some belligerent pugilist daunted her. Perhaps she should have waited to find this out before glibly pronouncing she'd accompany him on the journey.

"Not really. It sits directly on the Eddystone rocks."

Elspeth rolled her eyes and said sweetly, "Well you just say the word, Hayden, and we'll do the trip. You and I, together."

His grip on her hand tightened, and she felt his warmth and prayed he'd just forget about the entire idea!

⌒

The scandal surrounding Absinthe Pencraig and Charlotte Door set London ablaze with conversation. Everyone had a theory, but Camille refused to get involved, staying true to her purpose. Two weeks after Absinthe's death, Camille arrived home from Daria's. Lily waited in the study, as did David, and they played Chinese checkers for real. David was getting, as he would say, "the pants beat off of him."

He looked up, saw Camille, and stood to his feet. "How was the charity tea?" he asked, walking over to pull her into his arms.

"Delightful." Camille hugged him back. "Nothing about the scandal was mentioned. I know that Daria had connections, but *juste ciel*, David, that woman can get blood out of an onion!"

"That's turnip, *chérie*."

"Those too." She unpinned her hat and set it on the side table. "Some of the women promised to talk to their husbands about ongoing patronages!"

"Congratulations! It seems the Grace Home is on its way."

"It will probably be a while before we have enough money to buy the property next door. But we're off to a good start, I'd say."

"What do you mean 'we,' my love? This has been your project from the very beginning. I'm proud of you."

"Me too, *Maman*. Me too!" Lily shouted, dancing her jig and raising her arms to be picked up.

David reached down, settled his hands beneath her arms, and lifted her onto his shoulders. He winced at the strain on his back, but a smile soon replaced the grimace. "We held supper for you."

"You did?"

"Yes, although, it isn't much," he said. "Joyce finally had enough."

Camille threw up her hands. "At last!"

"I'm afraid all we've got for tonight is a good cheddar and some of Mrs. Wooten's clootie dumplings."

"Lead the way, *mon mari*!" She pushed the twosome forward. "I was so busy at the tea that I forgot to eat."

They wound their way into the dining room.

Camille stopped still. *Forgot to eat?* Well, it really was a good day! *Perhaps there is hope for me yet!* Her laughter filled the hall.

CHAPTER ❖ THIRTY-FIVE

The fire burned low in the small room off of the main hall of Lord Hayden's home. A small lamp sputtered on the table beside the soft, red sofa, its pops and hisses drowned out by the sweet tone of Elspeth's voice. She ran her fingers through Hayden's thick mane. His head lay upon a thick pillow on her lap.

"I fall through the universe, dancing in the Father's light," she said, reading from her own journal. "This minute roars for but a whisper of time. Celebrate it. Relent not."

"You wrote that?" he said.

"Yes."

"When?"

"Two days ago."

"Really? You wrote that here?"

"I did."

He closed his sightless eyes. "I'm glad."

She shut the journal and laid it beside her. "You bring out good things in me, Hayden."

He smiled. "It seems now that I can't remember a time when you weren't here."

Elspeth stared down at him, loving him so greatly. The past two months had been idyllic. Long walks in the morning, lounging contentedly in the cupola in the afternoons. Her eyes kept wandering to the breakwater lighthouse, and Hayden, much to her chagrin, continued to talk about the trip to Eddystone light. The Channel had been rough for weeks, though, making such a journey impossible.

"I think we'll go out to Eddystone next week, if the sea calms," he said as she blew out the lamp. Only the warm light of the fire illumined them now. "Even if I do get seasick."

She laughed nervously. Going out to a lighthouse on the rocks. *Juste ciel!* as Camille would say. "A big man like you?"

"Well, I don't know what size has to do with it. From my understanding, mal de mer cares little about gender or physique."

Oh, well, a promise was a promise. "But it will just be me going with you. I won't think any less of you. Besides, you've seen me sick enough times."

It was true. She'd only just overcome her nausea.

"And I don't think any less of you," he said reassuringly.

"And believe me, Hayden, you know loads about me that could only lead to a lesser opinion of me."

He sat up. "Don't say a thing like that, Elspeth. Please."

"But I don't deserve you. We both know that. And you are so able to overlook the obvious. I don't understand it."

He reached out, searching for her face, finding the curve of a cheek he would never see. Both hands cradled her face. "And you overlook the obvious too."

"How so? You're so pure and undefiled, sequestered here at St. Stephen's."

"Exactly. I've done nothing with my life."

"But—"

"And even though I can't see, that's never been an excuse not to engage myself in the affairs of those who need a hand."

"You can't honestly think that."

"I do. But, I'll tell you this, Elspeth. You've given me courage." He caressed her jaw with his thumb.

"You have no idea what you've done by your presence."

"I feel the same. But doesn't it bother you, the baby and all?"

He pulled her close, her cheek against his chest. "Of course it does. I can't imagine you with another man." His lips rested briefly on the top of her head.

"But it's what brought you here to me, isn't it?"

"Yes." How she enjoyed this closeness. This true intimacy.

"And I'll treat the child as if she were my own."

Elspeth pulled back her head to stare into his eyes. And though he couldn't see back into hers, the connection was somehow there. It went beyond the sight of the eyes directly to the sight of the soul. "What do you mean?" she asked.

"I'm asking you to love me, Elspeth. I'm asking you to stay on here after the baby is born. I love you."

He took her hands, and kissed her palms. The feel of his touch sent a jolt of warmth through her.

"Will you, Elspeth?" he asked. "Can you love someone like me?"

Elspeth was on his lap the next second. "I already do."

"And not just because you're feeling sorry for me?" he asked.

"Oh, no! It is you who should be feeling sorry for me!"

"Then, I suppose, we must be the perfect match," he laughed.

The perfect match. Perfect. Not an adjective anyone had ever used before in connection with anything to do with Elspeth Youngblood.

"May I kiss you now?" he asked.

She felt the familiar shame flare within. "But my mouth is. . ."

"Mine," he said.

And so Elspeth pulled his face toward hers. It was her first kiss. Her very first kiss.

Many more kisses followed, that evening, and in the days and weeks to come. Their souls fed upon each other for two months, their feelings echoing the blooming of the gardens on Hayden's estate.

"Promise me you'll tell me as soon as you feel the baby kick," Hayden said one morning after breakfast. Elspeth had come to enjoy this new form of stability she had found in Hayden and his ways. After a hearty breakfast they'd repair to the library for prayer, had been doing so for two weeks now.

"I didn't ask this of you at first," he explained, "because, well, it just seemed to be asking too much. But now that you love me and all . . ."

She'd kissed him soundly and led him into the large room. And she listened to him pray, not joining in, but holding his hands in hers, letting his deep, scratchy voice escort her soul with his on the heights of communion with God. The Holy Spirit visited Hayden quite frequently in a powerful way when he prayed. Elspeth knew this, because when the Spirit descended, it moved her to tears.

But today she finally felt comfortable enough to pray as well. Hayden's arms circled her as she thanked God for all the goodness he'd brought into her life. For Hayden. For her parents. And for the baby. She prayed that God would use them, the three of them, in a perfect way.

She said, "Amen."

His lips brushed her temple, and they sat in silence for several minutes. The windows had been opened wide, and the April air slid across their faces, freshening their clothing. "I've arranged for a boat, sweet Elspeth," Hayden suddenly said.

"Really?"

"We're going to the lighthouse."

Oh, dear. "When?" she asked, her voice much too high.

"May eleventh."

"Well, what if the sea is rough?"

He took her hands. "Let's just have faith."

"Why the eleventh?"

"It's my birthday. I'll be twenty-five years old. I'd say twenty-five years is long enough to live like this."

Elspeth had to agree.

⌒

On the eighth day of May the contents of Lady Absinthe Pencraig's diaries were disclosed to the public. No one really knew how the *Times* spirited the damning entries from the slick, sturdy pages of the leather volumes onto their flimsy ragged newsprint. Who deciphered Absinthe's handwriting and typeset her letters for the world to see? The *Times* certainly wasn't going to let go of that kind of information.

Absinthe had known everything. Cyprian had spilled it to Charlotte, and Charlotte had passed it onto her best friend. David shook his head. He had expected as much, really. It came as no surprise that the public bought up all copies of the paper in almost record time. Scandal at its finest never remained on the shelf for very long. He, of all people, knew that.

In her own words: "I found out today that David Youngblood, earl of Cannock, is the true murderer if the de Courceys and a Devil's Island convict, no less! Quite a piece of intrigue, that! You have to admire the man's tenacity! I'd love to thumb my nose at the entire court the way he's done."

"Well." David shrugged, tossed the paper into the bin, and winked at Camille who sat across his desk from him. "At least she was looking on the bright side! So the world knows it all now."

Camille nodded. "I feel relieved, truth be told."

He should have been more upset, really. Blast it, this news should be devastating, but it was not.

"There's only one honorable thing to do, *chérie*."

"You must give up your title." She sounded just a bit too eager.

"Yes. Tobin will be furious with me, but I never deserved it anyway."

She got up from her chair and came around to sit in his lap. "We all get what we deserve in the end."

He kissed her cheek. "So you're saying we deserve each other?"

She wrapped her arms around his neck. "*Bien entendu!* Was there ever a doubt? Besides, I'm not a lady. I never was, and I never will be. The title meant nothing to me. Ever."

"Truly?" He wanted to lose himself in her green eyes just then. The woman could be so distracting!

In answer she placed her lips on his, her hand cradling his cheek. "*Je t'adore*, David."

"You do adore me, don't you?"

"Yes. You are all things to me, *chéri*."

David knew she accepted him. Totally and completely. No title soon, very little money of his own soon, as well. But he had this woman. "Well, *chérie*, we soon shall have very little else."

Camille smiled. "I'm selling my town house in Paris so I'll have a little money of my own, enough to really get us started."

Intriguing. "Started doing what?"

"Isn't it obvious?"

"One never knows with you, Camille. So, what have you cooked up for the Youngbloods?" he asked.

"Well, it is like this, *chéri*. You're basically a man who does whatever it is he sets his mind to do."

The excitement in her eyes warmed him. "Some people would say that I am bullheaded."

"Well, yes. And that's true. But I want to move to the East End."

"To the Grace Home."

"We've been trying to find someone to oversee the project, and then run it, and well, *zut alors*, *chéri*, the answer is obvious! You and I are the perfect people to take on the task. And"—she stood to her feet, shaking a pointing finger at her husband— "I've got another idea as well."

"I'm sure you do," he chuckled, unable to take his eyes off of her. Praise God for this woman!

"I want to start another kind of mission too, David. A special kind of mission for a special kind of people."

"Who, Camille?"

"People like us. The prostitutes, the prisoners."

She grabbed his hands. "Don't you see, *chéri*? We cannot escape our past, we cannot forget about it, so we might as well use it for the only thing it's good for."

"To serve God."

She nodded. "To glorify him. And to show the extent of his grace."

He hugged her tightly. "That, my dear, is the best idea I've heard in a very long time. I'll start on it right away. Reverend Williams will help us plan."

"And don't forget Daria. She's so much as told me she feels as though God has finally given her a job to do. And I've never heard her speak of God like that before." Her voice held an excited edge.

"Yes, well God has that way about him, turning people's hearts and all." He touched her chin.

Camille kissed him soundly. "You're such an exciting man. Has anyone ever told you that before?"

"In different terms, but yes, they have," he drawled.

"Tonight, I have plans for us, but for now"—she hurried toward the door—"I'll go tell Lily!" She turned at the doorway. "Do you realize what's happening here, David? The world is ours! God is giving us a fresh start."

She spun around, a whirl of ruby skirt, and was gone. Not knowing what else to do, feeling nothing to be of greater import, David Youngblood pushed out his chair and fell to his knees. He remembered the man he had once been, he pondered the man he was now, and he prayed that God would use him mightily, that he would use this broken human being to take the love of the Savior to the world-weary, the hardened, the fragment of society most despised.

Such a task belonged to him. He saw that now and thanked God for it.

He arose from his knees a man with a charted course, ready to do the will of the Father in a world shaded by sin, sins he had committed, sins from which he had been delivered, was being delivered.

So be it, then, David.

So be it.

CHAPTER ✦ THIRTY-SIX

He sought an audience the next day with the queen whose life he had saved. A summons to appear was directly extended. Victoria listened closely to David's speech, nodding every so often, almost imperceptibly, but her appreciation could not be mistaken. Neither could her relief. "You are a good man, David Youngblood, much to our surprise. I would bid you remain as you are, but I cannot. Were I not the queen and responsible for the moral fiber of this nation, I would simply wave my hand and declare your misdeeds forgotten." Her dark eyes lifted at the corners. "So you are beginning a mission?"

"Yes, your majesty," David said.

"With what funds, may I ask?"

"Heavenly ones, I suppose," he chuckled softly, not wishing to appear disrespectful. "With my estates gone, there's not much more to go on but faith. Camille has a few pounds."

"We've heard about your wife's work down in the East End so far. This is good."

He bowed. "Yes, your majesty, I believe so."

"You would have made your parents proud had they been that type," she said with a quick smile. Her eyes glimmered and she reached out with her fan and popped him on the arm. "Go on, Lord Youngblood. Go do all those good things you've been called to do."

"With pleasure, your majesty." One more bow and David Youngblood took his leave from the royal court forever. *Sometimes*, he thought, *what one is supposedly born to be, isn't what one was born to be at all!*

The day after David's audience with the queen, Mr. Brown came by with a signed bank note for a thousand pounds. "She truly believes you're doing the right thing," were his only words as he handed David the slip of paper.

That evening, on a walk with David and Lily, Camille took the last of her Claude Mirreault money, money not touched since she had married David, and threw it in the Thames. "And that's that!" she said, wiping her hands on her skirt. "Gone forever. *Au revoir.*"

"A clean start," David agreed. "You'll have to find other women to have tea with, *chérie.*"

Camille rolled her eyes. "I don't know why I thought I'd ever fit in with such a lofty crowd … what do you call them, hoity …"

"Hoity-toity."

"*Oui.* Well, I'm not that type at all."

He put his arms around her. "Neither am I, my love. Never have been. Never will be."

"We'll fit in well down at the East End," she chuckled.

"Much too well, *chérie.*" His laughter joined with hers.

"What's so funny?" Lily asked, tugging on her mother's skirt.

David hoisted her up on his shoulders. "Let's hope you, my sweet little daughter, never have to find out!"

Camille slid an arm around his waist and they walked home, ready to begin packing. "And I won't have to worry about some hoity-toity cook down there either!" she exclaimed, laying her head against her husband's strong shoulder.

CHAPTER ❖ THIRTY-SEVEN

Are you sure you don't mind this?" Lord Hayden asked, his hands holding onto the side of the fishing boat. "You're not getting sick, are you?"

Thanks be to God, May eleventh had turned out to be a calm day with just enough of a breeze to fill the sails. "Not at all. You?"

"I'm fine."

They sat near the bow of the boat, the air rushing past them. Hayden looked more like a lion than ever, his broad smile baring those sharp canines, an almost uncivilized happiness painted across his features in a masterpiece of human well-being. "Isn't this wonderful? If I had known the feeling of the sea beneath oneself, I would have done this years ago!"

"I suppose there has to be a first time for everything." Good grief, Elspeth thought, could I not come up with something more compelling than that? It seemed as if the lighthouse would never come into view, but finally it did. She clapped her hands automatically with excitement. They'd talked about this structure, this trip, for weeks now.

"Do you see it?" he asked.

"Just barely. It's striped, just as you said. And it looks like it's coming directly up out of the sea."

"Yes, yes. That's right. Tell me more, my love."

So she described what she could see as they ventured closer, the darling little domed lantern, the way the water lapped gently against the rock on which the lighthouse had been so firmly planted. "It does look sturdy," she remarked.

"Oh, yes. From what I've heard, the stones of the foundation were dovetailed."

"Meaning?"

He put an arm around her. "Like a jigsaw puzzle. For strength."

"Oh, look!" she cried with delight. "The keepers are waving out of the window!"

Hayden immediately began waving. Elspeth's heart suddenly filled. Today was such a turning point for this man. A lighthouse. People. The sea. A boat. So many new things. And he could only move forward from here. She knew that after this taste, he wouldn't be satisfied to remain in his enchanted garden forever.

And, in all honesty, she wouldn't be either. Yes, it was tempting, in regards to her deformity, to stay behind the walls of the Walsh home for the rest of her life. But, heavens, with a man that looked like Hayden by her side, she'd only be envied. And only she would know him utterly for he would love only her.

The skipper helped them into a row boat that had trailed the fishing boat. "Here you go!" he cried in a cheerful, loud voice, his bright green eyes reflecting the sunlight. He held Hayden's arm and guided him over the side and then lifted Elspeth down.

Hopping easily into the boat, he took to the oars. "There's a ring out there in the rock that we can tie up to. I'll just wait in the boat."

"I can't believe we're actually doing this," Hayden whispered to her, his hand comfortably on her shoulder.

"Me either." Elspeth felt a giggle in her chest. And, well, why not just let it out? She hadn't giggled in years!

The keepers waited at the door in the base now, waving and shouting hello. They all yelled back in return. The sun shone brightly into Elspeth's eyes. How wonderful.

"Just get the boat right over there by that ring!" the man yelled. "Do you see those steps there? Careful, they're a mite slippery."

Elspeth wondered what kind of mites they had out there at Eddystone, because her mites had always been small and these steps were more slippery than a bucket full of eels.

One of the keepers realized the situation was made more difficult by Hayden's blindness. He nudged one of the other keepers and hollered, "We'll help you up!"

There were three keepers altogether. A large, blond, Norman-looking fellow. A man with brown eyes and a Scottish accent. And a skinny lad with red hair who appeared to be no older than Angus. Matt, James, and Bradley, they proclaimed themselves during a brief introduction. "And don't you know this is a fine treat for us!" Matt said.

Soon they all stood in the tower, in the main room of the living quarters. They were offered tea, which they accepted gladly.

"While you're waiting for the tea to boil," James said, "why don't you go out onto the balcony?"

"Will you light the light?" Elspeth asked.

Bradley piped up with a hearty, "Aye, then. I'd be happy to do that." He disappeared up the winding staircase, then reappeared moments later. "Not much room up there," he said. "You will want to go up on your own. Watch your step."

"They're so eager to please," Elsepth whispered as they climbed the final stretch to the lantern, Hayden following behind her, his hand firmly on the rail.

"You would be too if you were stuck out here. Believe me, I have an idea of what they're feeling."

Elspeth pulled herself up the final step, then turned to help Hayden. And finally, there they stood, at the top of the lighthouse. The English Channel stretched out below them, blue and gleaming. In the center of the lighthouse, the Fresnel lens soaked up the sunlight, its concentric rings casting a glimmer on their faces.

"It looks like a big beehive," she told Hayden. "Do you know what they're shaped like?"

"Unfortunately, yes," he muttered.

She laughed. "It's lit!" Elspeth cried, shielding her eyes against the blaring light as it slowly turned.

Hayden turned toward the lantern. His smiled broadened. "I see it, my love. I can see the flash from the bull's-eye."

She felt tears fill her eyes, tasted salt in her mouth. And she pulled him to her, loving him more in that moment than she had ever loved before. She reached up on tiptoes and kissed his chin. "I love you, Hayden."

"I love you, Elspeth."

The sea air rushed about them. "We only have a little while before the tide starts to come in," he said. "And I have something I need to ask you." His voice was serious suddenly, deep and firm.

Elspeth knew he was going to ask her to marry him. What other matter would be so grave? She was right. Yes, she knew his soul so intimately.

He took her hand and said, "Will you stay with me forever, Elspeth? Will you be my wife?"

Tightening her arms around his waist she replied, "I'd like nothing better."

Just then, an errant wave crashed against the structure, sending up a heavy spray.

"Let's go back, then," he said, urgency filling his voice. "There's a lot to do."

Elspeth laughed at his impulsiveness, but wouldn't dampen his excitement for the world. "I'll have to tell my parents about it. Hopefully they'll be able to come down."

"Oh no!" Hayden cried. "It's only fitting and proper that we get married at your home."

"London?"

"My dear, we must go to Scotland." He broke the embrace, then reached into his pocket. "I almost forgot. Give me your hand, Elspeth," he commanded.

When she did so, he lifted her third finger to his mouth. Elspeth felt the coolness of gold slide down the column of flesh and bone she'd thought destined never to be adorned. A pearl.

She gasped at the ring, its smooth centerpiece glowing in the sunlight, moving with a soft radiance.

He kissed her finger. "Remember the story of the pearl of great price?" he said. "How the man sold all that he had to buy it?"

"Yes, I do."

"I would give up everything I have for you, Elspeth. You've given me my life."

She threw her arms around him. "I love you so much, Hayden. I never thought anyone would ever love me like this."

"How much I love you."

He kissed her there at the top of the lighthouse, and Elspeth realized how gracious God had been, always there, a beacon in the darkness in which she'd found herself, leading her to safety, leading her to this very moment.

"Do you like it?" he asked several minutes later.

"It's lovely, Hayden. I shall never take it off." He kissed her sweetly in the flash of light, both of them aware they'd finally found a safe harbor.

They took their tea with the keepers, chatting politely. But she could hardly take her eyes off of her newly intended. She loved the fact that she could stare at him as hard as she liked for as long as she liked. The fact that he was always grabbing her hand, or laying his own hand upon her arm, back, or shoulder, was a small price to pay. She rather enjoyed it.

The boat rocked homeward on a calm channel. The sun set over their faces as they sailed back to St. Stephen's Hall. The warmth of crimson skies soaked their skin, and as the darkness finally fell upon the land, Elspeth snuggled into the arms of Hayden. Her Hayden. The man she was going to marry.

CHAPTER ✦ THIRTY-EIGHT

David, happy to see his daughter elated and loved and glowing, felt that it really didn't matter they couldn't throw a large, fanciful wedding in some large, sturdy church. Oh, Lady Daria had tried to get in on the act to be sure, suggesting at least ten different venues ranging from a Roman dig or a smuggler's cave to an open field with pony rides for all! But propriety dictated otherwise.

Elspeth herself, now sporting an obvious belly and eagerly looking forward to the birth of the baby in three months, had her own ideas. "I wish to be married at St. Ninians."

"The abbey ruins?" David said, mouth dropping. "Good heavens, Bethie, why?"

"That's where things truly began to change for me."

David remembered those desolate nights alone in the crypt of the crumbling structure where God had got hold of him and given him a good shaking. Where God had shown him how much he loved him. The girl, as usual, was right.

Presents had arrived, though there were only a few. Lord Aaron Campbell sent round a silver tea set. Pencraig gave an ancient suit of armor. They had all laughed at that when it arrived during dinner one night. And Cyprian Door, gone now to America after the execution of his wife, had a Chinese vase delivered. He sent along a note as well saying he was getting by, was relieved in a small way that it was over, but still, one couldn't be married for so long without grieving the loss of one's wife. He promised to return to England one day, but until then, "God go with you, David. Would that I could give up my life for others the way you have done." There was no return address.

At the end of June a small group gathered on the lush green grass that had grown over the floor of the nave. Elspeth wore a plain yellow gown and carried white roses. Lord Hayden, naturally, dressed himself in a black suit with a white shirt and a red tie. Red was Elspeth's new favorite color, for perhaps Hayden really did know what it looked like, she'd confided to her father the night before as *Tom Jones* was finally, completely laid to rest.

Hayden's touch never left her. And, she'd told her father, she'd be lying if she said she didn't love the feel of him, didn't relish in how good-looking everyone said he was. Oh, she knew that they all said, "Imagine a girl like her getting a handsome man like him," but it just didn't matter anymore. The fact was, he loved her for the Elspeth not many people had really bothered to know.

David, gazing at his beautiful wife, knew exactly how she felt.

Matthew Wallace officiated at the short ceremony. Tobin sang while Angus harmonized. Wooten and James MacDowell cleared their throats a bit too often, and the women? Well, they all cried tears of joy. Sylvie, Miranda, Camille, Daria, Mrs. Wooten, and Pamela MacDowell. And David, blast it all, joined right in!

Dear Reader:

Most books in Christian fiction written in the Victorian era tend to look upon Queen Victoria with kindness. You will find *Crimson Skies* to be quite another matter. Victoria, like the rest of humanity, had a side that was less than favorable. And although my research exposed that side to me, even providing one of the plotlines for this book, I have done my best to retain her dignity while showing that even queens are human and in need of God's grace.

The quote on women's rights by Queen Victoria was actually made in March of 1870 and not in 1869 as written in this book. My portrayal of early feminism was as fair as I could make it. Most likely I will have made those on both sides of the issue unhappy, so please, read this in the context of the social and political landscape of the time period in which this novel takes place. Many rights Christian women take for granted today—voting, running for the school board or even higher political office—were made possible by the feminists of yore, regardless of their motive or their spiritual state.

The Ceremony of Introduction into the House of Lords was actually done for new peerages, not as I have used for the beginning of David Youngblood's career in the House of Lords. I did this because I thought such a ceremony would be of some interest to the reader and for the sake of the story itself. I love a little grandeur now and then!

There were five assassination attempts during the life of Queen Victoria. The attempt described herein is completely fictitious, but, as there were so many other attempts, it is not a historical stretch to make up a plotline regarding such. Please extend a little mercy to this yarn spinner.

I do hope you've enjoyed this series. As it comes to a close I feel a little sad at leaving these characters behind, but none more than David Youngblood. Out of all the characters I've created in the ten books I've written, he is my favorite. But all authors must say good-bye to their creations at some point, and so to David and Camille Youngblood, Miranda Wallace, Tobin Youngblood, Matthew, Sylvie and Elspeth and even dear Angus, I bid a fond good-bye. Thank you for taking the time to get to know them, and getting to know me, a little bit better.

God bless you.

Fondly,

Lisa Samson